D0605435

RECEIVED

MAY 03 2017

BROADVIEW LIBRARY

NO LONGER PROPERTY OF
SEATTLE PUBLIC LIBRARY

EAT DELICIOUS

Eat Delicious

125 RECIPES FOR YOUR DAILY DOSE OF AWESOME

DENNIS THE PRESCOTT

WILLIAM MORROW

An Imprint of HarperCollinsPublishers

EAT DELICIOUS. Copyright © 2017 by Dennis Prescott. All rights reserved. Printed in the United States of America. No part of this book may be used or reproduced in any manner whatsoever without written permission except in the case of brief quotations embodied in critical articles and reviews. For information address HarperCollins Publishers, 195 Broadway, New York, NY 10007.

HarperCollins books may be purchased for educational, business, or sales promotional use. For information please e-mail the Special Markets Department at SPsales@harpercollins.com.

FIRST EDITION

DESIGNED BY RENATA DE OLIVEIRA

PHOTOGRAPHY BY DENNIS PRESCOTT

HAND-LETTERING BY JOEL HOLLAND

Library of Congress Cataloging-in-Publication Data has been applied for.

ISBN 978-0-06-245603-8

17 18 19 20 21   QDG   10 9 8 7 6 5 4 3 2 1

For Leanne

Contents

Introduction

HI. MY NAME IS DENNIS.

First off, you are all awesome. I want to thank each and every one of you for the massive gift of being a small part of your lives. There is an enormous responsibility that comes with the knowledge that families will join around the dinner table with recipes that I've created and with inspiration taken from my photographs. I do not take that lightly, and I want to thank you from the bottom of my Canadian heart for allowing me the privilege of joining you and your family at mealtime.

My journey in the food world has been a somewhat recent, entirely unexpected, and altogether wonderful adventure. I grew up eating for necessity, like many folks I know. We ate between activities and often as quickly as possible, to get back to whatever was on tap for that day (basketball/baseball/sports games/mischief). I had zero interest in the gastro world, had never heard the phrases "locally sourced" or "organically grown," and was perfectly content to eat boxed macaroni or bad takeout for the rest of my life. I was blessed with an incredibly loving family and wonderful friends, but completely unaware that I existed in an extremely underseasoned and un-delicious bubble.

After attending college for one year, I was asked to go on the road, traveling through the southern United States and Canada as the electric guitar player in a band. I had no love at all for the business degree that I was "studying" for, so after about half a minute of careful consideration, it was settled. And there began a ten-year, perfectly random journey throughout Canada and the United States in various bands, basically living out of a fifteen-passenger van. Touring life is awesome, but most certainly not the glamorous vision of rock stardom most people have in their heads. No room service, no home in the Hollywood Hills.

Over the years I landed in countless cities, restaurants, and homes, experiencing local culture and local cuisines and savoring every last bite. It was my culinary awakening, my baptism into the world of the delicious. But it's a very slippery slope, friends. Once you slide, prepare to land facefirst in a massive pool. I experienced Indian food for the first time in Montreal, sushi in Vancouver, BBQ in North Carolina, and pizza (errr, *proper* pizza) in New York City. And I wanted more. The floodgates were blown wide open, and I had zero interest in returning to the same old, same old meat and potatoes diet I'd grown up on. My palate was expanding and my taste buds were exploding. But every tour has a start date and an end date, and while these breaks were a welcome respite from the road, when I returned home, I was back to eating my childhood staples. I had no idea how to cook and, if I'm honest, no interest in learning.

My band members and I had reached a critical stage in our career and felt it was time to set up shop in a major metropolis. After much planning, debate, and maybe a few tears, we—and our eternally supportive families—landed in Music City: Nashville, Tennessee. Nashville, and the South in general, affected me in a way for which I'll be forever grateful. I forged lifelong friendships with incredible like-minded musicians from all over America, and I woke up every day with access to bona fide Southern cuisine, aka the Food of the Gods—fried chicken, pulled pork, biscuits, and sausage gravy. Oh my! It was an unending treasure trove of tasty eats. But there was only one problem: I had no money.

I wouldn't trade my time as a touring musician for anything, but let's just say that the benefits package leaves something to be desired. We were rich in access but poor in cash. Working on a record meant the band wasn't touring. No tour = no money. No money = the cheapest food possible, which typically translated to the dollar menu at a fast-food chain (read: gross).

We arrived at financial ground zero, and my wife, Leanne, graciously decided to travel home to Canada to work and help support our situation. This resulted in us living apart for several months.

Alone, broke, and questioning why I would choose to live this way, I wanted to feel as if I had control of something, as if I wasn't in a total downward spiral. Meanwhile, I couldn't bear the idea of even one more bowl of cereal for supper. So, for the first time since college, I got my hands on a library card. I strolled into the food section of the Nashville Public Library, full of hope, head held high. I borrowed three cookbooks that day, all of them written by a charismatic, inspiring English bloke who wrote recipes that I could relate to, that looked incredible, and that I felt, with a little practice, I could pull off.

One by one, I started cooking through the books, and with each passing recipe, I grew more and more addicted to cooking, tasting, and trying new foods. Jamie Oliver taught a Canadian musician living in Nashville to cook—and literally saved me from a life of un-deliciousness.

When I wasn't at the studio, I was cooking several recipes a day. Stir-fries, curries, steak, eggs. I was cooking so much, in fact, that I decided to start taking photos of the dishes with my phone, to remember what I'd cooked the week before and avoid repeat dishes.

Shortly thereafter, I moved home to Canada and brought my passion for the kitchen (and a budding passion for photography) along with me. I decided to open an Instagram account, because all the cool kids were into it, and started posting (really poorly shot) images of food. Copying my quickly named Gmail account handle, I landed on Dennis The Prescott, entirely unaware that the DtheP moniker would stick in such a significant way. It was completely for fun; I assumed that nobody would look at my account. I plugged along, posting photos almost every day, and picked up new followers here and there. Then, one glorious day over Easter vacation, Nigella Lawson and the folks at Instagram gave me a shout-out on a list of her favorite accounts, and within twenty-four hours I gained ten thousand followers. I.N.S.A.N.E. My phone battery was working overtime, and I knew that this thing—whatever it was, exactly—had just gotten serious. I will be forever grateful to have connected with a wonderful community of food-loving, passionate folks from all over the world via social media.

Whether it's working in the kitchen, creating videos, photographing dishes, or writing this book, I still pinch myself almost every day. It's still hard to believe that a Canadian musician with zero backup plan has ended up where I am, and I remain more in love than ever with food and food culture. My hope is that my journey, these recipes, and these images inspire you to create delicious meals for your friends and family. To help you fall deeper in love with food, to share your journey with others, and ultimately to help in growing a culture of people who are passionate about taking back mealtime. My story is proof positive that truly anyone can create impressive and approachable meals at home for a fraction of the cost of eating out. You can step away from the same old, same old. And you can ultimately inspire others to join you on the brightly lit path toward culinary nirvana.

If we're blessed enough to be able to enjoy three meals a day, let's make them as freakin' delicious as possible.

From the bottom of my heart, thank you.

—DtheP

Photography Saved My Creative Life

For real. Second only to my love of food, my unexpected love of photography saved me from a life of creative confusion. Music may no longer have been a viable full-time career option, but a creative must create. Artists, painters, dancers, chefs, musicians, writers, thinkers, dreamers—we're born with an inherent need to exercise our creative muscle and tend to go a little cabin-fever crazy when restricted. Not fun. Photography pulled me from my funk and helped cure a stale, confused, and depressed Dennis, sparking a passionate creative fire.

I'm often asked photography questions by other food-obsessed folks. Many of the lessons I've learned, and the tips and tricks I've collected along the way, have been hard-fought, failing forward toward technical and creative breakthrough. I've become an everything-photography junkie, collecting photog magazines, reading how-to web articles, and, most important, studying the work of inspiring photographers. Here are a few practical tips on creating delicious, mouthwatering, "I want to eat you right now" food photos.

RUN TOWARD YOUR PASSION

If you're not passionate about your work, it will show 100 percent of the time. Guaranteed. If a band was onstage kind of phoning it in, or a comedian wasn't really feeling his jokes, the audience would see straight through that inauthenticity. If you don't believe in your work as creatives, your viewers won't believe in you, either. If you're adapting someone else's style, you're not selling your best self. And your best self is awesome. If you run toward current trends only because they're current, you'll never do your best work. Passion drives creativity, and people flock toward passion. Passion is inspiring and exciting. Embrace the things that get you creatively excited. Never sacrifice authenticity to a culture of cool.

RUN TOWARD YOUR PERSONALITY

I'm a very happy person, I think. Most of the time, anyway. But I've never been a bright bubbly super-duper over-the-top gleeful shout-from-the-rooftops kind of dude. I sometimes wish I were. Like the person who just dances like no one is watching. Or sings while walking to work. I'm envious of that

all-out explosion of joy. Me? I love bands like Radiohead and Sigur Ros, I dig thoughtful indie movies that are slightly melancholy and force you to consider your life choices after watching them. I dress like Johnny Cash. I love dark shadowy bars and smoky New York City–style jazz bands.

In photography, that means that I'm probably not going to shoot my best work if I'm photographing bright, backlit, white background happiness. I love that style of photography, but it would be a totally inauthentic shooting style for me, and my images would certainly suffer because of it. I'm so much more on point when shooting darker, moodier images that have a raw and rustic aesthetic. I connect with it, it makes sense to me, and it just feels right.

If you're a bright, bubbly person, I've no doubt that you'd shine at photographing bright and bubbly images. If you're more like me, embrace the dark side. Your personality will absolutely shine through your work—so capitalize on it, harness it, and use it to your creative advantage!

PHOTOGRAPH SOMETHING OTHER THAN FOOD

Possibly the greatest inspirational boost in my photography is shooting something other than food. I love waking up at four A.M. and shooting the sunrise. I love street photography, landscape photography, and taking portraits of my friends. These images rarely find themselves on my social accounts, my website, or as part of a commercial shoot. It's not about growing my platform. It's about constantly forcing myself to see new and exciting subjects through my lens. This will help you better understand light and composition, and result in your becoming a much more versatile photographer. Like tools in your tool box. If we spend all of our time studying food images, and photographing food, it tends to become increasingly difficult to create unique photographs in this oversaturated, visually driven world. Shoot something other than food that may or may not see the light of day. Different is good. Run toward different.

CAMERA GEAR

This is by no means the most important element (possibly the least important, in fact), but it's by far the topic I'm asked about the most. Your camera doesn't matter. My camera doesn't matter. You just need to own a camera. Purchasing an expensive camera with a suitcase full of professional-quality lenses will no more help you take professional food photos than buying a basketball will make you Michael Jordan. Sir Michael is the best because he practiced. Every single day. For hours and hours and hours. There's no secret key. No magic wand. And most certainly no quick and easy crash course. It takes years of practice. But take heart! It's a delicious, inspiring, life-altering practice.

BECOME A STORYTELLER

Become a great storyteller, friends. We all have a unique self, a unique style, and a unique story—the key is learning to tell that story well. If you photograph creative images that you're passionate about, that inspire and excite you, that are authentic to your personality, and that speak to the micro-niche that has connected with you and your work—it's a total game changer.

I love comfort food, classic home-style dishes. They sing a special song to my soul. Mac and cheese, pulled pork, chicken wings, cheeseburgers, I love it all! And that, paired with my passion for folks to celebrate food, celebrate food access, and to get back to spending quality time around the community table is what has inspired and driven me in my personal photography work. I love telling the story of food and community, a story we all share. For me, food *is* community.

THE STORY

What story are you trying to tell through the image that you're shooting? Is it a date night? Game day? A dinner party? A family-style feast? These are all very different events that require scene-appropriate lighting, composition, and focus. The stronger the story, the stronger the photograph. Determining the story and processing how best to sell the scene are the first steps in a great food image.

THE HERO

Like Superman, or Bono, or Marilyn Monroe, there is an element in every dish that seems to have a special sprinkling of fairy dust on it. It could be the fresh basil leaves carefully styled on top of a beautiful pasta dish, or an especially mouthwatering piece of fried chicken in a basket full of heaven, or the thick-cut bacon on a burger. It's the place that you, the photographer, want to draw the viewer's eye. Deciding on your hero element is essential in determining the styling and layout of the composition of your image.

COMPOSITION, VISUAL INTEREST, AND MY ODD NUMBER RULE

Odd numbers have always made sense to me. Three just feels better than two. Well, in photography, that is. (Let's just stop with any innuendo right here.) In the photographic world, where composition is king, styling in odd numbers can help to create lasting visual interest.

This is applicable in any number of different scenarios, but here are a few to wet your whistle:

1. Try garnishing that dish of pasta, that lovely roasted chicken, or those killer tacos with three (or five) fresh herb sprigs.

2. Rather than plating two dishes and photographing them, plate three. Even

if this means running one dish off the page, that's perfectly okay, and kind of the point. You'll draw the viewer's eye to your determined hero and create visual interest throughout the entire image.

3. Arrange three filled drinking glasses around that family-style dish of goodness, helping to give extra visual interest to the image and fill in any potential blank spaces. Helpful tip: If beer is your delicious liquid of choice, be sure to pour it just before taking the final shot. This will ensure that you capture all of that glorious collar.

COLOR SEPARATION, WHEN TO SHOUT, AND WHEN TO WHISPER

When you're photographing an image, be very aware of similar colors that are touching within the frame. Try to avoid this, or break it up as much as possible. Best case scenario, you divide the colors into odd-numbered groups. This will result in visually interesting repetition throughout the frame, and your image will be much more well defined.

When we view a photograph, or a painting, we subconsciously examine it from the top left corner to the bottom right corner. Knowing and considering this when styling your images, you can maximize on creating visual interest throughout the entire frame.

And interest can be filled space or empty space. One of the greatest lessons I learned as a guitar player was when to play and when to shut up. I had an incredible mentor teach me that my job wasn't to play fifteen notes as quickly as possible; it was to play three and really make them count. Create a melody that folks would be singing in their car hours after hearing it on the radio. Similarly, knowing when to speak and when to be quiet while styling an image is vitally important. Learn to be comfortable in the silence.

If you study the images in this book, and in the majority of my Instagram and client work, patterns will no doubt emerge. This is because, though every dish is different and should be styled accordingly, there are simple, subtle touches that help refine an image composition and a personal style. The stronger the composition, the stronger the image.

Always.

THE MOVEMENT

For me, movement is the fun in photography and honestly, the cherry on top of every image. Whether it's capturing wine being poured into a glass, maple syrup being drizzled over waffles, or a chef slightly out of focus while working hard in a restaurant kitchen, movement adds an important human element to the image and helps us to become more invested in the scene. Investment will always create the strongest photograph and help in telling an unforgettable story. Art is connection.

THE HUMAN ELEMENT

Hypothetical situation. You scratch-make this killer batch of homemade ice cream. It looks incredible, like Martha herself prepared it for a dinner party. You scoop it out into cones, then quickly transfer them into the freezer to harden up the ice cream again. Then you set up your camera and style the scene. The lighting is on point, and you shoot as quickly as possible before the ice cream melts. Will that image look great? Probably. Will it relate? Maybe. Maybe not. What is the connection, the human element that every single person can relate to when it comes to ice cream? The drip. The almighty drip. We can all relate to eating an ice cream cone on a hot July day, then looking down to see a drip working its way down the cone. And we quickly lick the drip. The human element. The connection. When you look at your image, find the drip, photograph the drip, and sell the drip.

CONTROLLED CHAOS

Avoid perfection. I know, the idea of intentional (minor) chaos can be a near impossible concept for the perfection-loving creative. This is a lesson I still have to learn and relearn on an almost daily basis, but it's vital in creating images that transport the viewer to a feeling, a space, a moment. Images that are overly staged, with every element placed just so, have a tendency to look a tad fake. If a few flecks of sea salt, a droplet or two of sauce, or a couple of lettuce leaves fall onto the surface, fear not! Run after the real. It's all going to be okay. Trust me. This rustic, raw styling approach will give authenticity, drama, and texture to the final image. Run toward perfect imperfection.

SHOOT WITH A STAND-IN

Every single time I photograph food, I shoot with a stand-in. Here's my daily workflow:

BEFORE turning on the oven, boiling a pot of water, or getting my *mise en place* on, I style my scene. I choose my backdrop, dishware, silverware, glasses, and any fun extras, and stage the image. My tripod is set, the camera is ready, and the exposure is dialed in.

WITH everything primed, I choose a few raw fruits or veggies, then place them throughout the scene and shoot a few test images. As food cools, it tends to lose its freshness, crispiness, and warmth. Being photo-ready helps to ensure that when the final dish is in place, you're well ahead of the clock and your image will look stellar.

WHEN the food is cooked and ready to go, it's time to plate up. Always style to camera, paying close attention to each detail and consistently scanning

the camera's viewfinder to ensure that you're pleased with the composition and food styling choices. Build the dish(es), taking the time to consider height, color variation and separation, and intentional rustic imperfection. Beautiful but raw, staged but real. Fill the frame while taking care to not overfill the plate itself. Be sure to add any garnish or raw greens at the very last minute, just before pressing the shutter, to keep them from wilting.

THE ONLY WORK required after styling the final image is to make any minor exposure adjustments to compensate for potential changes in the sun or clouds. Way less stress, and dinner is still warm(ish). Perfect.

LIGHTING, SHADOW, AND MOOD

Lighting is vitally important in all photography, and especially in food images. How the light touches the dish and the resulting shadow will ultimately decide whether the colors pop to create a jaw-dropping image. The best composition in the world, and the most beautifully prepared dish in the world, will live and die by the lighting (or lack thereof). A simple onion peel can transform into a thing of beauty thanks to heavenly light.

Soft, diffused, natural sunlight reigns supreme. Find a space in your home where natural light is available (a north-facing window, if available, lets in superhero-quality sunlight. Find it. Become best friends. Hang out often. Live happily ever after). Invest time studying how the light hits the subject. Walk around the dish, noticing the subtleties in how the light changes as your position shifts. What do you notice? What do you like? What don't you like? Why? A quick and easy way to test the light characteristics in your home is to grab a stand-in (like an apple) and place it near each window in the house. Then shoot like crazy! Photograph your fruit model in every which way possible, in every room possible, then upload those images to your editing software. (Lightroom is my editing software of choice.) You'll instantly notice

backlighting subjects, chasing that romantic warmth kissing the subject. Some prefer side-lighting, playing with the dramatic light and the resulting dark and moody shadow fall. The key is to research lighting and its point of origin, then practice and work toward creating your own unique style by harnessing that light.

My ultimate desire is for these images to inspire you to find your own creative eye. This takes time. Real, legit, down-in-the-trenches kinda time. It's a marathon. You will fail. You will have off days when nothing seems to go quite the way it was planned, and you will want to scream at your camera to just cooperate. You may set up the perfect scene with the ideal light and the perfect artistic vision, only to have an epic food fail. But take heart! Fight through all of it. Trudge forward. Study the work of other photographers who especially inspire you—the images that make you smile and feed your creative soul. Study not just what food is in the scene, but how it's cooked and the stylistic choices that were made. Never accept the status quo. Shoot *everything*. Shoot something new every day. Find that voice. Fail forward. Fall in love with food and food photography. The journey is one of artistic fulfillment that is second to none. We all love delicious and have a special connection to the story of food. It's our job as photographers to capture those moments, capture that nostalgia, and tell unforgettable stories.

massive variances in the light quality and contrast of the images. Some you'll love, some . . . not so much. Problem solved, window light preference determined.

After choosing your window weapon of choice, you may need to soften that light to help take your photographs to the next level. If the window light is a tad on the harsh side, a store-bought diffuser (or even a white bedsheet) can help create a soft, gorgeous glow of sunlight.

Every photographer has his or her own lighting preferences. Some love

1

Breakfast Food,

YOU'RE A ROCK STAR

BREAKFAST IS THE MOST IMPORTANT MEAL OF THE DAY.

You've heard it like a million and one times in your life. From your parents, television, the Internet, and that annoying Facebook friend with the emotional range of a watercress sandwich who relentlessly spams your newsfeed with uppity article reposts. But it's true.

In my previous life as a touring musician, I rarely ate anything before noon. And if I happened to eat something, it was more than likely a bad gas station doughnut with an extra-large coffee on the side, or a piece of cold, leftover pizza. Shortly after moving to Nashville, I decided that it was high time I take my health back. I was sick of feeling like trash every morning when I woke up. So for the first time in my life, I reluctantly started running every morning, followed by

eating a balanced wholesome breakfast. Green smoothies, egg white omelets, Greek yogurt, and whole-grain everything. I quit fast food cold turkey and tossed any boxed product that had unpronounceable ingredients. In nine months I lost eighty-seven pounds. Seriously.

Now, I'm no scientist, but I truly believe that eating breakfast (with a little exercise on the side) will vastly improve the quality of life for you and your family. Kick-starting your day with a bite will not only make you feel so much better, but will increase concentration and performance and problem-solving skills, and it helps with weight control to boot. Wowza! Get your breakfast food in, friends. Your health and your taste buds will thank you.

THE PERFECT EGG

EGGS are so amazing. In a world where #putaneggonit exists and entire cookbooks are dedicated to the humblest (and arguably most important) of ingredients, learning the basics of cooking an egg is essential.

FOR THE MOST INCREDIBLE, addictively delicious eggs, head to the local farmers' market or find a farmer in your town where you can buy top-quality farm-fresh eggs. They taste heaps better than store-bought, have that glorious sunset-colored yolk, and, because they're much fresher, will hold up properly when cooked.

EGGS FOR BREAKFAST? Here are my top three favorite basic egg-cooking methods. Give it a little time, patience, and practice, and you'll be an egg master in no time flat.

THE PERFECT SUNNY-SIDE UP

MAKES AS MANY AS YOU LIKE! • The perfect sunny-side-up egg is all about time, love, and tenderness. Eggs are delicate, and to achieve the perfect sunshine of deliciousness, they should be cooked slowly and gently. Delicious served with a pinch of salt and pepper and your favorite hot sauce.

Cooking fat (butter, olive oil, bacon fat)

Egg(s)

GRAB a cast-iron or nonstick skillet and set it over medium-low heat (see Note). Melt 1 teaspoon of fat (butter, olive oil, bacon fat) per egg in the pan. Carefully crack in the egg(s), being careful to not crowd the pan and leaving room between each for the whites to run. Fry until the whites are cooked through but the yolks are still nice and runny, about 5 minutes. If you're unsure, give the egg whites a touch. If they're slimy (no one likes undercooked egg whites), keep on frying away. Transfer to a plate and dab any excess grease with a paper towel.

FOR OVER-EASY EGGS: When the whites are just about cooked through, carefully flip each egg and fry for 15 to 20 seconds on the other side. Done and done.

NOTE: *Skillets of different sizes and materials tend to carry heat differently, so become best friends with your pan, watching, timing, and learning how eggs react to the heat source. If the fat begins to spit or the eggs start to dance, take the pan off the heat for a minute or so and turn down the heat. It's all about slowly heating the eggs until the whites are cooked through.*

THE PERFECT POACHED EGG

MAKES AS MANY AS YOU LIKE! • Poaching eggs can be a bit tricky (it took me a few dozen eggs before I got the knack). Practice. Practice. Practice. It makes perfect.

Two things to remember: First, for the finest poached eggs, become best friends with a farmer and get the freshest farm eggs you can. The fresher, the better. Eggs purchased at a major grocery store are typically older, and won't hold together as well when poached. Second, keep the water temperature just below a boil. Minutely controlled water temperature is key.

1. Fill a wide 3-quart saucepan with water and heat over medium-low heat until bubbles form in the water at the base of the pan, but the water is not simmering. You want to avoid boiling water. If the water gets too hot and steamy, remove the pan from the heat for a minute to let it cool down.

2. Crack each egg into a separate small dish. Add a splash of white wine vinegar to the water (this will help the egg white hold together). Using a spoon, swirl the water in a clockwise motion and carefully drop in one egg, sliding it out of the bowl in a fluid motion.

3. To check for doneness, remove the egg with a slotted spoon and gently give the yolk a poke. It's all down to instinct and preference at this point. You'll know right away how soft the yolk is. If you prefer your eggs a little firmer, carefully drop the egg back into the water and continue poaching until they've reached your desired doneness. A very soft poached egg will take around 2 minutes and a medium to hard poached egg will take 3 to 4 minutes, depending on the pan you're using.

4. Use a slotted spoon to transfer the poached eggs to a plate lined with paper towels to absorb excess water, then serve immediately.

THE PERFECT SOFT-BOILED EGG

MAKES AS MANY AS YOU LIKE! • This method is all about timing that egg like it's a science experiment. For me, the perfect soft-boiled egg has a cooked white with a creamy, soft yolk. Perfect for dipping toast, veggies, or just enjoying with a spoon. Delicious with a pinch of salt, pepper, and ground cayenne. For next-level soft-boiled action, serve with grilled asparagus for dipping and a little prosciutto for good measure.

1. First, prepare an ice bath (see Note). Fill a large bowl with ice and cover with cold water. Set aside.

2. Bring a saucepan of water to a rapid boil and get a timer ready (smartphone, it's your time to shine).

3. Carefully drop the eggs into the water and set the timer for 6½ minutes. This is the perfect time to enjoy your morning cup of joe. When the timer goes off, remove the eggs and immediately transfer them to the ice bath. (If you prefer your egg yolks a little more cooked through, continue cooking for another minute, then transfer to the ice bath.) Let the eggs hang out in the ice bath for 5 minutes to cool.

4. Carefully crack and remove the shells.

NOTE: *Ice baths work wonders in shocking everything from eggs to asparagus, stopping the cooking process quickly.*

BREAKFAST SANDWICHES WITH CHILE-FENNEL SAUSAGE PATTIES

MAKES 4 SANDWICHES • The first moment you dive into a homemade breakfast sandwich marks the last time you'll crave a McAnything. The sense of accomplishment in making something so quick and delicious will have you loving on scratch-made everything.

This sandwich combines the classic combo of pork and fennel, some heat from the red pepper flakes, and a gorgeous golden sunny-side-up egg. Perfect with Homemade English Muffins (page 22) and a giant cup of joe.

SAUSAGE PATTIES

1½ teaspoons fennel seeds

1 teaspoon dried oregano

1 teaspoon red pepper flakes

1 pound best-quality ground pork

½ teaspoon sea salt

½ teaspoon freshly cracked black pepper

1 tablespoon olive oil

4 slices Swiss cheese

SANDWICHES

1 tablespoon butter

4 large free-range eggs

4 English muffins, store-bought or homemade, split and toasted (page 22)

¼ cup Spicy Herb Homemade Mayo (page 74)

1 large heirloom tomato, thinly sliced

4 sandwich-size lettuce leaves

1. Make the sausage patties: Using a mortar and pestle, smash together the fennel seeds, oregano, and red pepper flakes. In a large bowl, combine the ground pork with the spice mixture, salt, and black pepper. Give the sausage a good mix, separate it into four equal portions, and shape them into patties. The patties should be just larger than the width of the English muffins, as they will shrink when cooked.

2. Heat two large skillets, one over medium heat and the other over medium-low heat. Pour the olive oil into the first pan and, working in batches if necessary, fry the sausage patties for 5 minutes per side, or until crispy and cooked through. When you flip the patties, top each with cheese.

3. Melt the butter in the second pan. Crack in the eggs, taking care to not break the yolks. Gently fry the eggs until the whites have set but the yolks are still nice and runny (see page 4).

4. While the eggs and sausage are cooking, spoon a heaping spoonful of the mayo onto each muffin half.

5. To build each breakfast sandwich, lay a sausage patty, tomato slice, and fried egg on each English muffin bottom. Sprinkle each egg with a pinch of salt and black pepper, then top with a lettuce leaf and the other muffin half. Serve immediately.

FRENCH TOAST WITH GRILLED PEACHES AND SPICED RUM–BROWN SUGAR SAUCE

MAKES 4 SERVINGS • A classic diner dish, French toast is beloved by millions across the globe with good reason: it's delicious, it's quick to prepare, and it's the perfect way to use up that slightly stale day-old bread in the cupboard. One of the greatest experiences of my life as a cook was making French toast in the Kenyan Highlands, cooked over an open flame, with my friend Joyce. After she taught me how to make green gram stew (a fantastic local Kenyan dish), I showed Joyce how to make French toast using affordable local Kenyan ingredients. Many of the ingredients were picked from the trees on her family's land. Incredible! Food is the common thread that runs through us all. No matter the language you speak or where you live in this world, everyone has a favorite dish to eat. We all love delicious.

This is French toast, all grown up. Perfect for the spiced rum fans in your life. This dish is a slightly indulgent caramel twist on a breakfast staple, and possibly the best way to drink guilt-free before noon.

If serving for the entire family, kiddos included, substitute the caramel for a booze-free alternative by topping with maple syrup, some Greek yogurt, honey, and fresh fruit.

SPICED RUM–BROWN SUGAR SAUCE

- ¼ cup packed brown sugar
- 1½ tablespoons pure maple syrup
- ½ cup (1 stick) butter
- ¼ cup spiced rum
- 1 teaspoon pure vanilla extract

(Ingredients continue on the next page.)

1. Get the spiced rum–brown sugar sauce ready to go: In a small saucepan, combine all the sauce ingredients and bring to a simmer over medium heat. Let it simmer away until the sugar has dissolved and the sauce has thickened slightly, about 5 minutes. Remove from the heat and set aside. (To save a few minutes and make breakfast time extra chill, this sauce can be prepared the night before, then warmed in a saucepan while you're cooking the French toast. Awesome.)

2. Preheat the oven to 225°F.

3. Make the French toast: Grab a large high-sided baking dish and crack the eggs into it. Pour in the milk and give the

FRENCH TOAST

4 large free-range eggs

½ cup whole milk

2 teaspoons orange zest

¼ teaspoon ground cinnamon

Pinch of salt

2 tablespoons butter

8 slices thick-cut white bread

3 large peaches, halved, pitted, and sliced into ½-inch wedges

1 cup Greek yogurt, for serving

whole thing a good whisk until well combined. Add the orange zest, cinnamon, and salt and whisk again.

4. Heat a large skillet over medium heat and drop in the butter to melt. Working in batches, dunk the bread in the egg mixture, flip, and coat the other side. Fry the toast for about 3 minutes per side, until nice and golden brown. Transfer to a rimmed baking sheet and place in the oven to keep warm. Carry on making the rest of the French toast.

5. While the toast is doing its thing, heat a grill pan over medium heat (if you don't have a grill pan, a regular grill or very hot pan will work fine). When the pan is hot, place the peaches on the grill pan. When the peaches have developed nice grill marks, about 1½ minutes, turn them over and baste them with the rum–brown sugar sauce, reserving some sauce for drizzling over the final dish. As it cooks, it will begin to caramelize around the fruit and turn deep golden brown. Deep caramelization equals maximum deliciousness, but there's a thin line between caramelized and blackened. Be sure to keep a watchful eye so the fruit doesn't burn. Remove from the heat and set aside.

6. Serve 2 slices of French toast per person and top with 5 or 6 peach slices. Drizzle the remaining sauce over the toast and serve with ¼ cup of the Greek yogurt.

Joyce at her home near Iten, Kenya, with the banana French toast we made together.

MAPLE SPICED RUM BACON

MAKES 1 POUND SPICED BACON • Bacon. The holy grail of deliciousness for meat lovers. Obviously incredible on its own, the bacon in this recipe is kissed with sweet maple syrup, gorgeous spiced rum, and fragrant lime zest, which candy their way around the bacon as it cooks. Morning perfection!

1 pound smoked bacon, best quality you can get your hands on

¼ cup pure maple syrup

2 tablespoons spiced rum

Zest of 1 lime

¼ teaspoon cayenne pepper

½ teaspoon sea salt

1. Preheat the oven to 350°F. Line a large rimmed baking sheet with parchment paper.

2. Arrange the bacon on the parchment paper in a single layer. In a bowl, whisk together the maple syrup, spiced rum, lime zest, cayenne, and salt. Baste the top of each slice of bacon liberally with the maple-rum mixture, reserving about 2 tablespoons of the mixture. Bake for 15 minutes, flip, and baste the bacon again with the remaining maple mixture.

3. Cook for 10 to 15 minutes more, until dark brown and crispy. Transfer the cooked bacon to a wire rack to cool for about 5 minutes. Take care not to leave the bacon on the rack for too long, or it may stick. As the bacon cools, the maple-rum mixture will harden and candy. So awesome.

RED SUITCASE FILLED DOUGHNUTS, THREE WAYS

MAKES 14 TO 16 FILLED DOUGHNUTS • A few years ago, my brother and I ran a coffee and doughnut pop-up at a weekly market in Fredericton, New Brunswick. Red Suitcase Coffee & Doughnuts was both one of the most difficult and rewarding things I've done in my life. I hated my alarm and its four A.M. wakeup call, but I loved baking hundreds of doughnuts with my brother. I loved spending every Saturday working with family. And most of all, I loved the expression of absolute joy on our customers' faces when they dove into that doughy piece of heaven.

Doughnuts are universally smile-inducing and a guaranteed hit in your home, with your friends, and with your colleagues. Pure happiness.

These little doughy bundles of joy require a little lead time, so it's best to think ahead.

1 tablespoon active dry yeast

¼ cup lukewarm water (see page 18)

2¾ cups plus 1 teaspoon sugar

1 cup whole milk

2 large free-range eggs

1 teaspoon pure vanilla extract

5½ cups all-purpose flour, plus more for dusting

1 teaspoon table salt

½ cup (1 stick) butter, at room temperature

Canola oil, for greasing the bowl and frying

2 cups filling of choice (recipes follow)

1. In the bowl of a stand mixer fitted with the dough hook, combine the yeast, water, and 1 teaspoon of the sugar. Stir well. Let the yeast come to life, about 10 minutes.

2. While the yeast is activating, in a small saucepan, combine ¾ cup of the sugar and the milk and warm it over medium-low heat. Stir the milk every minute until all the sugar has dissolved, 5 to 6 minutes. Do not let the milk scorch. Remove from the heat.

3. When the yeast is ready to go, add the eggs, vanilla, and warm milk to the mixer. Add 4 cups of the flour and the salt, then turn the mixer to low speed. Knead the dough for 5 to 6 minutes, scraping down the sides of the bowl as needed, until it starts to come together. Cut the butter into 1-inch cubes and add them to the flour, one at a time, until incorporated. The dough will be very wet at this point, but don't be scared—everything's going to be okay.

Lukewarm. Baking recipes often call for lukewarm water. But what does it mean?! Lukewarm water is typically around 95°F. Think baby bottle here: not hot, not cold, just right.

4. Add the remaining 1½ cups flour to the dough. When all the flour has worked its way into the dough, increase the mixer speed to high and knead the dough for 5 minutes. It will become buttery, soft, dough ball perfection.

5. Transfer the dough to a lightly oiled bowl, turn to coat, and cover with plastic wrap. Find the dough a warm temporary home in the kitchen. After 1½ hours, the dough will have doubled in size and is ready to go.

6. Punch down the dough and turn it out onto a lightly floured surface. Roll out the dough into a large, ½-inch-thick rectangle. Cut out rounds with a 3½-inch biscuit cutter. (Because we'll be filling these little dudes, you don't want a cutter that will make a doughnut hole. The rim of a large glass can work in a pinch.) Try to avoid pressing and turning too much, as this compresses the edges and prevents the doughnut from rising. Knead the dough scraps and repeat the process. You'll end up with 14 to 16 large doughnut rounds.

7. Transfer the rounds to a lightly floured surface and cover with a damp tea towel. Leave to rise a second time, about 30 minutes, or until doubled in size.

8. In a large Dutch oven or deep-fryer, heat 3 inches of canola oil to 350°F. Set up a wire rack and put the remaining 2 cups sugar in a bowl.

9. Working in batches, fry the doughnuts for 1½ to 2 minutes per side, until golden brown. Keep a watchful eye on the oil temperature, as it may decrease between batches.

10. Immediately toss the cooked doughnuts in the sugar, coating all sides. Set the doughnuts on the rack to cool for at least 30 minutes.

11. Fill a piping bag with your chosen filling and pipe 1½ to 2 tablespoons into each doughnut.

12. These doughnuts are best eaten within a few hours, as they don't store well. So overindulge as necessary, or gift any leftovers to someone who needs a ray of sunshine in their life.

DOUGHNUT FILLINGS

CHOCOLATE GANACHE

MAKES 2 CUPS • This is just about the easiest chocolate ganache recipe on the planet. While operating our doughnut shop, my brother and I never had enough time and would rely heavily on recipes that were quick and easy to bang together but still tasted incredible. This was one of our go-to recipes.

2 cups semi-sweet chocolate chips
1 cup heavy cream
½ teaspoon pure vanilla extract
Pinch of salt

POUR the chocolate chips into a large bowl. In a medium saucepan over low heat, bring the cream and salt to a boil. Pour the cream over the chocolate and let it melt, about 5 minutes. Add the vanilla and stir until the chocolate is silky smooth. This ganache will harden as it cools, so it's best to use it within a few minutes of preparing.

MAPLE CUSTARD

MAKES 2 CUPS • Custard in any form is the height of food luxury. It's perfection. This custard requires an overnight fridge rest but it will keep for 2 to 3 days, so make it ahead of time and you'll be ready for your doughnuts (unless you eat all the custard first).

1½ cups whole milk
4 large free-range egg yolks
½ cup sugar
¼ cup all-purpose flour
¼ teaspoon sea salt
1 teaspoon pure maple extract

1. In a medium saucepan, warm the milk over medium heat until bubbles form around the edges of the pan, just before it begins to simmer. Remove from the heat.

2. In a large bowl, whisk together the egg yolks, sugar, flour, and salt. Slowly pour the milk into the yolk mixture, whisking continuously. Transfer the egg-milk mixture back to the saucepan over medium heat. Whisk continuously until the mixture comes to a boil and thickens, about 5 minutes. Pour the mixture through a fine-mesh sieve set over a bowl and stir in the maple extract. Cover with plastic wrap, pressing it directly against the maple custard to prevent a skin from forming, and refrigerate overnight.

FRUIT JELLY

MAKES 2 CUPS • Choose your fave! What's important is using a jelly that's smooth, with very few large fruit pieces, so the filling easily moves through the piping bag.

2 cups strawberry, raspberry, or blueberry jelly
1 to 2 tablespoons fresh lemon juice

IN a large bowl, stir the jelly, breaking up or removing any large lumps that may catch in the piping bag. Add lemon juice as needed to loosen the jelly to the consistency of a doughnut filling.

CURED SALMON WITH AVOCADO AND HOMEMADE ENGLISH MUFFINS

MAKES 8 TO 10 SERVINGS, WITH LEFTOVER SALMON • The Maritimes, my home on Canada's east coast, are all about amazing seafood, with a special love for our Miramichi River salmon. When salt cured with beets, the color of this fish is gorgeous and the taste is outstanding. Served with Homemade English Muffins, this salmon is seriously impressive weekend brunch business. Curing fish may sound like it requires a culinary degree, but it really couldn't be simpler. It's all about a fantastic piece of fresh fish, enough time, and a comfy home in your fridge. This recipe makes a lot of cured fish, but it can be kept in an airtight container in the fridge for 4 to 5 days. If you can get your hands on rainbow beets, the color is full of sunshine and rainbows. If not, regular beets will work perfectly fine.

SALMON AND CURE

3 pounds fresh salmon fillet

1 cup grated peeled rainbow beets (use the large holes on a box grater)

1 tablespoon whole white peppercorns

1½ cups kosher salt

¼ cup sugar

1 bunch dill

3 tablespoons lemon zest

TO SERVE

Homemade English Muffins (page 22)

3 large ripe avocados, pitted, peeled, and smashed

½ cup cream cheese

2 large shallots, very thinly sliced

½ English cucumber, sliced

Capers

Lemon wedges

Fresh parsley

1. Cure the salmon: Remove the skin from the salmon (or ask your fishmonger to do this). Pat the fish dry with a paper towel.

2. In a food processor, combine the beets, peppercorns, salt, and sugar and pulse until blended, about 2 minutes. The rub should have the texture of sea salt. Line a deep baking sheet with a piece of plastic wrap that's larger than the length of the salmon and place the fish on it. Pick the leaves from half the dill and place them on top of the salmon, along with 2 tablespoons of the lemon zest. Pour the flavored salt on top of the fish and pack it down with a spoon.

3. Tightly wrap the top and sides of the fish with the plastic wrap, covering it entirely, and transfer the pan to the fridge. Place something heavy (like cookbooks, a cast-iron pan, or a bunch of condiment jars) on top of the fish to weight it down. Leave it in the fridge for 48 hours to let the cure work its magic.

4. After 2 days, take the salmon out of the fridge, unwrap it, and wash off the salt cure, dill, and lemon zest. Pick the

leaves from the remaining dill and sprinkle them over the fish with the remaining 1 tablespoon lemon zest.

5. Transfer the fish to a serving board and slice on an angle into very thin strips. Serve on top of your delicious home-made English muffins, with the smashed avocado, cream cheese, shallots, cucumber, capers, lemon wedges, and parsley.

HOMEMADE ENGLISH MUFFINS

MAKES 12 MUFFINS • English muffins have long been a staple grab-and-go breakfast option in my house. A light toasting, a little peanut butter, and we're out the door and off like the wind. But I spent many a year taking this little gem completely for granted. Homemade English muffins are truly a next-level thing of beauty, and the perfect crevice-laden vehicle for butter, jams, and all manner of delicious. Well, well worth the effort.

2 teaspoons active dry yeast

1 teaspoon sugar

3 tablespoons lukewarm water

1¾ cups whole milk, at room temperature

3 tablespoons butter

1 tablespoon pure maple syrup

1½ teaspoons table salt

4½ cups all-purpose flour

Olive oil, for the bowl

5 tablespoons yellow stone-ground cornmeal

1. In a small bowl, stir together the yeast, sugar, and water. Set aside to let the yeast activate, about 10 minutes.

2. In a small saucepan, combine the milk, butter, and maple syrup and warm it over medium-low heat. As soon as the butter has melted, remove the pan from the heat.

3. In the bowl of a stand mixer fitted with the dough hook, combine the salt and 2½ cups of the flour. With the mixer running on low, pour in the yeast mixture and slowly drizzle in the milk mixture. When the dough starts to come together, add the remaining 2 cups flour and knead for 2 minutes. When all the flour has been incorporated, turn the mixer to high and knead the dough for 5 minutes. The dough will be quite wet—that's totally cool. Transfer the dough to a lightly oiled bowl, cover the bowl with plastic wrap, and place in a warm spot in the kitchen.

4. Let the dough get nice and comfortable until it's doubled in size, 1½ to 2 hours. If planning ahead, the dough can be covered with plastic wrap and chilled in the fridge for up to 24 hours at this point; warm the dough for 30 minutes on the counter before moving on to step 5.

5. When the dough is ready to rock, punch it down and turn it out onto a lightly floured surface. Divide the dough into twelve equal portions (see Note). Shape the portions into

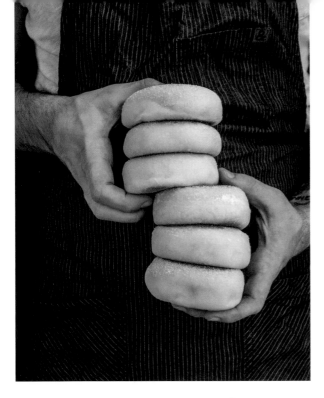

small balls and roll each dough ball on your work surface with your palm to close off any openings. Using your palms, press the dough into flat ½-inch-thick circles.

6. Sprinkle a large rimmed baking sheet with 3 tablespoons of the cornmeal. Place the dough circles on the baking sheet, leaving at least 1 inch of space between them, and cover with plastic wrap. Let the muffins rise until doubled in size, about 45 minutes.

7. Heat the largest skillet you have over medium-low heat. If you own a large electric griddle, even better. Sprinkle the remaining 2 tablespoons cornmeal in the pan or over the griddle.

8. Working in batches, carefully transfer the dough circles to the pan (I'm able to cook four muffins at a time in my pan) and cook the muffins until they turn a deep golden brown, 9 to 11 minutes per side. To check for doneness, split a muffin open to ensure it's cooked through, or if you have an instant-read thermometer, check the internal temperature: It should be 200°F. Carry on to cook the rest of the muffins.

9. Let the muffins cool on a wire rack for a few minutes before serving. They will keep in an airtight container at room temperature for several days.

NOTE: *Weighing the dough will ensure that each muffin is the same size; they should weigh about 80 g/2.8 ounces each. A kitchen scale will seriously up your baking game and is well worth the investment.*

CHRISTMAS MORNING STICKY BUNS

MAKES 9 LARGE BUNS • In our house, sticky buns are packed with yuletide nostalgia. They're the perfect holiday morning indulgence, and an annual tradition for our family. And the best thing about this recipe—you get them ready to rock the night before, then wake and bake. More time with family, less time in the kitchen, and no compromise on deliciousness. Caramel sticky-bun heaven.

DOUGH

1 cup whole milk

½ cup (1 stick) salted butter, cut into ½-inch cubes

½ cup sugar

1 tablespoon active dry yeast

4 cups all-purpose flour, plus more for dusting

1 teaspoon salt

2 large free-range eggs

2 teaspoons pure vanilla extract

1 to 2 teaspoons vegetable oil, for the bowl

CARAMEL HEAVEN

½ cup (1 stick) butter

1 cup packed dark brown sugar

1 cup heavy cream

⅓ cup pure maple syrup

¼ teaspoon sea salt

FILLING

½ cup packed dark brown sugar

1 teaspoon ground cinnamon

2 tablespoons butter, melted

1½ cups pecan halves, chopped

1. The night before, get the dough ready: In a small saucepan, combine the milk, butter, and sugar and heat the mixture over medium-low heat, giving it a stir every minute or so. When the butter has melted and the sugar has dissolved entirely, remove the pan from the heat. Be careful not to let the milk boil. If it gets too close, remove the pan from the heat and let it chill out for a few minutes.

2. Sprinkle the yeast over the milk mixture and let it sit and bubble and do what it does best. After about 15 minutes, it'll be good to go.

3. While the yeast is coming to life, in the bowl of a stand mixer fitted with the dough hook, combine 2 cups of the flour and the salt. With the mixer running on low, crack in the eggs and pour in the vanilla. Slowly stream the yeast mixture into the flour. Turn off the mixer, add the remaining 2 cups flour, and crank the mixer back on medium speed. Let the dough knead away for about 5 minutes, until all the flour is combined. Turn the mixer speed to high and let it go to town, kneading that dough for another 5 minutes.

4. Transfer the dough to a large, lightly oiled bowl, cover with plastic wrap, and give it a home somewhere warm for about 1½ hours, or until doubled in size.

5. While the dough is rising, make the caramel heaven: In a small saucepan, combine the butter, brown sugar, cream, maple syrup, and salt. Bring the mixture to a boil over me-

dium heat, then reduce the heat to medium-low and let the sauce simmer away for 5 minutes, or until the caramel is deep golden brown and has reduced slightly. Set the pan aside off the heat. Be very careful not to touch the sauce. Caramel is crazy hot and can easily make for a bad day. Please keep your day awesome. (Time bonus! This saucy business can be prepared several days in advance and kept in an airtight container in the fridge.)

6. Transfer the dough to a lightly floured surface. Roll out the dough into a 12 x 24-inch rectangle that's about ½ inch thick.

7. Make the filling: In a small bowl, combine the brown sugar and cinnamon. Brush the dough with the melted butter and sprinkle the brown sugar mixture on top, leaving just under an inch of space around the edges. Working on a long side, roll the dough up into a long, jelly roll–style situation. Cut the roll crosswise into nine large buns.

8. Pour the caramel sauce evenly over the bottom of a 9 x 13-inch baking pan and sprinkle the pecans on top. Add the buns to the pan, cut-side up. Cover with plastic wrap and refrigerate overnight or for at least 8 hours.

9. The next day, preheat the oven to 350°F. Let the buns sit on the counter for 10 minutes to lose their chill. Bake for 35 to 40 minutes, or until cooked through, golden brown on top, and entirely delicious. Let them hang out in the pan for 10 minutes, then run a knife around the edges of the pan in case any caramel decided to stick. Turn the buns out onto a serving board so that the gorgeous caramel is on top.

10. These are best eaten while still warm and fresh, but will be delicious for a couple of days, stored in an airtight container at room temperature. Just pop them into a 350°F oven for a few minutes to warm up before serving if you by some crazy chance have any left the next day.

BREAKFAST PIZZA

MAKES TWO 12-INCH PIES • Pizza for breakfast isn't just for college kids anymore. It's a real pleasure in the morning, and perfect for brunch at home. The secret to great, restaurant-style pizza at home is preheating an oven fitted with a baking stone to 550°F for at least 30 minutes before baking. Perfectly crispy on the outside, amazingly soft on the inside.

If your home oven doesn't go as high as 550°F, fear not! Just set the oven as hot as it will allow, and add a minute or two to the baking time, keeping a watchful eye on your pizza so it doesn't burn.

DOUGH

2 teaspoons active dry yeast

1 tablespoon honey

1 cup plus 5 tablespoons lukewarm water

1½ cups all-purpose flour, plus more for dusting

1½ cups "00" flour (see opposite)

2 tablespoons olive oil

1 teaspoon sea salt

PIZZA

10 pancetta slices

2 tablespoons olive oil

1 cup cherry tomatoes, halved

1 (8-ounce) ball fresh mozzarella cheese, cut into thin slices

1 tablespoon red pepper flakes, plus more as needed

1 teaspoon freshly cracked black pepper

6 large free-range eggs

6 prosciutto slices

½ cup baby arugula leaves

¼ cup fresh basil leaves

1. Make the dough: In a large bowl, combine the yeast, honey, and water and stir well. Let the yeast activate, bubble, and come to life, about 10 minutes.

2. Add the flours, olive oil, and salt and stir with a wooden spoon until a dough begins to form. Turn the dough out onto a floured surface and get those arm muscles ready. Knead away until a soft dough ball forms (see page 31), about 10 minutes. (Alternatively, you could use a stand mixer fitted with the dough hook on medium speed and drink a coffee while it's doing the work for you.)

3. Transfer the dough to a lightly oiled bowl and cover with plastic wrap. Give the bowl a temporary home in a warm spot in the kitchen and let the dough double in size, about 1½ hours. (If you're a planner, this can also be done the night before. Just cover and chill in the fridge overnight. The dough will slowly rise there, making tomorrow's work that much easier.)

4. Make the pizza: Set a baking stone in the oven and preheat the oven to 550°F, letting it heat for at least 30 minutes prior to baking.

"00" flour (also called doppio zero or tipo 00 flour) is an Italian-style flour with a fine grind, perfect for creating a super-smooth, elastic texture with a light and crispy finish in fresh pasta or pizza dough. It's genius, and well worth sourcing at your local Italian deli or specialty grocer. If you can't find "00" flour, fear not! Just be sure to substitute with a strong flour that is high in gluten. The higher the gluten, the better the dough.

5. Heat a skillet over medium heat. Fry the pancetta for 2 to 3 minutes per side, until crispy. Blot it on a paper towel to remove extra grease and set aside.

6. Divide the dough into two equal portions and flour a work surface. Roll each portion into a 12-inch round and brush each with 1 tablespoon of the olive oil. Scatter the cooked pancetta and cherry tomatoes over the dough. Divide the cheese between the pies. Sprinkle 1½ teaspoons of the red pepper flakes and ½ teaspoon of the black pepper on each pizza.

7. Carefully crack 3 eggs onto one pizza, leaving room between the eggs, and transfer to the oven (see tips for easy transferring on page 110). Bake for 7 to 8 minutes, until the egg whites have set and the crust has turned a deep golden brown. Repeat to make the second pizza.

8. Top each pizza with 3 slices of the prosciutto and half the arugula. Sprinkle with the basil and, if you're a fan of spicy, more red pepper flakes.

Kneading by hand is all about getting properly stuck in and working the dough like you're at the gym. On a floured surface, press and stretch the dough with the heel of your hand, fold over, rotate 90 degrees, and repeat for 8 to 10 minutes, until a soft, smooth, and elastic-feeling dough ball forms.

MAPLE-BACON SCONES

• There are flavor combos that were just meant to live together: pizza and beer, peanut butter and jelly, and maple and bacon. On their own they taste great, but together they're magic. This recipe is a spin-off of a doughnut we served at Red Suitcase (see page 17). They flew off the shelves. Every week we made more, and every week we sold out in minutes. This scone version is just as delicious and ready in less than half the time. Awesome.

SCONES

8 smoked bacon slices

½ cup plus 2 tablespoons pure maple syrup

3 cups all-purpose flour, plus more for dusting

1½ teaspoons baking powder

¼ teaspoon baking soda

½ teaspoon kosher salt

½ cup (1 stick) cold butter, cut into ½-inch cubes

½ cup walnut halves, chopped (or substitute pecans)

2 teaspoons lemon zest

½ cup heavy cream

1 large free-range egg

MAPLE GLAZE

1 cup confectioners' sugar

3 tablespoons pure maple syrup

3 tablespoons butter, melted

½ teaspoon pure vanilla extract

1. Make the scones: Preheat the oven to 350°F. Line two rimmed baking sheets with parchment paper.

2. Lay the bacon on one of the baking sheets and baste with 2 tablespoons of the maple syrup. Bake for 25 to 30 minutes, turning halfway through, until nice and crispy. Transfer the bacon to a wire rack to cool for 20 minutes, flipping halfway through so it doesn't stick. The maple syrup will candy around the bacon while it cools.

3. Into the bowl of a stand mixer fitted with the paddle attachment, sift the flour, baking powder, baking soda, and salt. Add the cold butter, turn the mixer to low, and beat for 20 seconds.

4. Crumble 4 strips of the bacon into the bowl, add the walnuts and lemon zest, and mix together.

5. In a medium bowl, whisk the cream, egg, and remaining ½ cup maple syrup. Pour this mixture into the dry mixture and beat on medium speed until the dough just comes together, about 1 minute. Do not overwork the dough.

6. Transfer the dough to a floured surface. Dust the top of the dough with flour and shape it into a 1-inch-thick circle with a 12-inch diameter (again, avoid kneading or overworking the dough). Slice it like a pizza into 8 triangular pieces.

7. Transfer the scones to the second prepared baking sheet and bake for 25 to 30 minutes, until they turn golden brown and the kitchen smells like baked maple syrup heaven. Transfer the scones to a wire rack to cool for 30 minutes.

8. Meanwhile, make the glaze: In the bowl of a stand mixer fitted with the paddle attachment, beat the confectioners' sugar, maple syrup, butter, vanilla, and 1 tablespoon water until smooth.

9. Crumble the rest of the bacon into small bits. Top each baked scone with 2 tablespoons of the maple glaze and sprinkle the candied bacon on top.

10. These scones are best served immediately, but will taste delicious for up to 2 days if kept in an airtight container at room temperature.

MANGO-LIME DUTCH BABY PANCAKE

MAKES 4 SERVINGS • While living in Nashville and teaching myself the basics of cooking, I came across a recipe for a Dutch baby pancake. The first pancake I made completely blew my mind. I topped that insanely puffed, crispy, buttery goodness with a little powdered sugar and lemon and never looked back.

Dutch babies are a weekly breakfast staple in our home, really quick to assemble and perfect for eating around a communal table. This recipe features a combination of mango, lime, and a delicious blueberry sauce, but Dutch babies will work smashingly with almost any combo of citrus and other fruit.

1 cup plus 2 tablespoons all-purpose flour

2 teaspoons lime zest

¼ teaspoon sea salt

1 cup whole milk

2 tablespoons pure maple syrup

3 large free-range eggs

1 teaspoon pure vanilla extract

3 tablespoons butter

2 cups blueberries

2 tablespoons pure maple syrup

1 tablespoon fresh lime juice, plus more for serving

1 tablespoon confectioners' sugar

½ cup plain Greek yogurt

2 large ripe mangoes, cubed

Fresh mint leaves

1. Preheat the oven to 425°F with a rack in the middle position. Place a 10-inch cast-iron (or other oven-safe) skillet in the oven to get nice and toasty.

2. Combine the flour, lime zest, salt, milk, maple syrup, eggs, and vanilla in a blender and blend on medium speed until the batter is smooth and foamy.

3. Carefully add the butter to the hot pan in the oven to melt. When the butter is good to go, remove the pan from the oven, quickly pour in the batter, and immediately return the pan to the oven. Bake for 20 to 25 minutes, until the pancake is puffed like crazy and browned on top.

4. Meanwhile, in a medium saucepan, combine the blueberries, maple syrup, and lime juice. Cook over medium-low heat for 8 to 10 minutes, until the blueberries are jamming. When most of the berries are cooked down but some remain whole, you're golden. Perfect texture. Set aside.

5. Dust the cooked Dutch baby with the confectioners' sugar and squeeze over some fresh lime juice. Top the pancake with the yogurt, blueberry sauce, cubed mangoes, and a few fresh mint leaves.

EGGS BENEDICT, THREE WAYS

AS CLASSIC AS brunch itself, eggs Benedict may be the quintessential weekend breakfast dish. Homemade, a solid Benny is an over-the-top treat for your family and friends.

HERE are three eggs Benedict recipes for you. The eggs, the sauce, and the muffin stay the same, and you choose which filling will guide you to delicious-land.

KNOW the three key elements to great poached eggs: the freshest farm eggs you can find, controlled water temperature, and a little practice. You're not boiling the eggs, just slowly poaching them, so the water should be softly and gently bubbling away (see my tips on page 7).

EGGS BENEDICT WITH MUSHROOMS AND GRUYÈRE

MAKES 4 SERVINGS

3 smoked bacon slices, diced

1 tablespoon butter

1 tablespoon minced garlic

3 cups cremini mushrooms, cleaned and cut into ¼-inch-thick slices

1 teaspoon fresh thyme leaves

¼ teaspoon sea salt, plus more as needed

¼ teaspoon freshly cracked black pepper, plus more as needed

8 large farm-fresh eggs

Splash of white wine vinegar

4 English muffins, store-bought or homemade (page 22), split and toasted

½ cup grated Gruyère cheese (about 4½ ounces)

Blender Hollandaise Sauce (page 44)

2 tablespoons finely diced chives, for serving

1. Preheat the oven to 350°F.

2. In a skillet, fry the bacon over medium heat until crispy, about 5 minutes. Transfer to a dish with a slotted spoon and set aside, leaving the bacon grease in the pan.

3. Melt the butter with the bacon grease. Add the garlic and sauté for 30 seconds. Add the mushrooms, thyme, salt, and pepper and toss to combine. Cook the mushrooms, stirring often, until softened, 6 to 7 minutes. Crumble the bacon into the mushrooms and set aside, off the heat.

4. Heat a wide 3-quart saucepan of water over medium heat and add a pinch of salt. The water temperature you're looking for should be just before a simmer, when bubbles begin to form on the base of the pan. Carefully crack each egg into its own small dish (like a ramekin). Add the vinegar to the saucepan, give the water a swirl with a spoon, and transfer the eggs to the pan (two or three at a time) in one fluid motion. Poach for 2 to 3 minutes, until the whites are cooked through but the center is still nice and runny (see page 7 for more on poaching). Transfer the poached eggs to a plate lined with paper towels. Repeat with the remaining eggs.

5. Place the English muffins on a baking sheet lined with parchment paper. Top each muffin with about 2 tablespoons of the mushroom mixture and cover with the cheese. Bake for 5 minutes, or until the cheese is melted and bubbling.

6. Top each muffin half with a poached egg and 1 tablespoon of hollandaise sauce and season with a pinch each of salt and pepper. Sprinkle with the chives and serve immediately.

EGGS BENEDICT WITH ASPARAGUS AND BRIE

MAKES 4 SERVINGS

24 medium-thick asparagus spears

2 teaspoons fresh lemon juice

Salt

8 large farm-fresh eggs

Splash of white wine vinegar

4 English muffins, store-bought or homemade (page 22), split and toasted

4½ ounces Brie cheese, cut into thin strips

Blender Hollandaise Sauce (page 44)

Freshly cracked black pepper

1. Preheat the oven to 350°F.

2. Bring a large saucepan of water to a boil. Cut off and discard the woody ends from the asparagus and boil the spears for 5 minutes, or until fork-tender but still firm. Drain, transfer to a dish, and sprinkle the lemon juice on top.

3. Heat a wide 3-quart saucepan of water over medium heat and add a pinch of salt. Poach the eggs as directed in step 4 on page 38.

4. Place the English muffins on a baking sheet lined with parchment paper. Top each muffin half with 3 asparagus spears and 2 slices of Brie. Bake for 5 minutes, or until the cheese is melted and bubbling.

5. Top each muffin half with a poached egg and 1 tablespoon of the hollandaise sauce and season with a pinch each of salt and pepper. Serve immediately.

EGGS BENEDICT WITH FRIED CHICKEN AND AVOCADO

MAKES 4 SERVINGS • Quite possibly the ultimate eggs Benedict. This recipe requires overnight marinating in the fridge, but believe me, there's a whole lotta deliciousness on the way.

CHICKEN

Two 6-ounce chicken breast halves, cut into angled 1-inch strips

1 cup buttermilk

1 tablespoon pure maple syrup

½ teaspoon cayenne pepper

Canola oil, for frying

1¼ cups all-purpose flour

½ teaspoon sea salt

¼ teaspoon garlic powder

¼ teaspoon onion powder

2 teaspoons lemon zest

EGGS BENEDICT

Salt

8 large farm-fresh eggs

Splash of white wine vinegar

2 large ripe avocados, pitted and peeled

1 tablespoon fresh lime juice

Freshly cracked black pepper

4 English muffins, store-bought or homemade (page 22), split and toasted

Blender Hollandaise Sauce (page 44)

1. Make the chicken: Place the chicken in a freezer bag with the buttermilk, maple syrup, and ¼ teaspoon of the cayenne and toss to mix. Give the chicken a home in the fridge overnight.

2. In a high-sided Dutch oven or deep fryer, heat 3 inches of canola oil to 350°F.

3. In a large bowl, combine the flour, salt, garlic and onion powders, remaining ¼ teaspoon cayenne, and the lemon zest and whisk to combine. Working in batches, dredge the chicken in the flour mixture, shaking off any excess flour, and fry it for 5 to 6 minutes, until cooked through and golden brown.

4. Make the eggs benedict: Heat a wide 3-quart saucepan of water over medium heat and add a pinch of salt. Poach the eggs as directed in step 4 on page 38.

5. Mash the avocados in a bowl, squeeze in the lime juice, and season with a pinch of salt and pepper. Set aside.

6. Top each English muffin half with 2 tablespoons of the mashed avocado, 1 or 2 chicken strips, a poached egg, and 1 tablespoon of the hollandaise sauce. Crack over some black pepper and serve immediately.

BLENDER HOLLANDAISE SAUCE

MAKES ¾ CUP • When I started cooking, nothing scared me more than making hollandaise. I was completely (unnecessarily) freaked out.

The secret to hollandaise, along with so many of the best things to come out of the kitchen, is time. It's all about patience, perseverance, and being willing to learn from a few mistakes along the way.

Sometimes, though, you want a delicious sauce stat. Right now, no waiting required. Enter the Blender Hollandaise. This little banger of a sauce is so crazy easy that all you need is a blender, a few ingredients, and a strong desire for brunching.

½ cup (1 stick) unsalted butter, cut into ½-inch cubes

4 large free-range egg yolks

2 tablespoons fresh lemon juice

⅛ teaspoon ground cayenne

¼ teaspoon sea salt

1. Melt the butter in a small saucepan over medium-low heat. Set aside.

2. Crack and separate the eggs, placing the yolks in a blender (save the whites for another recipe, such as the Smashed Pavlova on page 305). Add the lemon juice, cayenne, and salt and turn the blender on low speed. With the machine running, slowing drizzle in the melted butter, adding about 1 tablespoon every 30 seconds, until it has completely emulsified with the egg yolks and the sauce is thick and glossy.

3. Transfer the Hollandaise to a dish. If it's too thick, add 1 to 2 teaspoons of water to thin it to your liking. Serve warm.

CHEESY SHAKSHUKA WITH FRIED HALLOUMI

MAKES 4 TO 6 SERVINGS • This recipe is my ultimate morning-after dish. When you've stayed out late, gotten into a little trouble, and need that extra kick to jump-start your day, this is it: eggs poached in a spicy tomato sauce and topped with melty cheese. Slightly indulgent and jam-packed with flavor, it's the height of delicious and, for me, the perfect breakfast comfort food.

1 teaspoon fennel seeds

1 teaspoon red pepper flakes, plus more as needed

1 tablespoon butter

2 tablespoons olive oil

1 cup finely diced red onion

¾ teaspoon sea salt

1 cup chopped red bell pepper

1 tablespoon minced garlic

1½ teaspoons smoked paprika

½ teaspoon ground cumin

1 (28-ounce) can diced tomatoes

1 tablespoon lemon zest

½ cup vegetable stock

1½ tablespoons fresh lemon juice

1 teaspoon freshly cracked black pepper

6 large free-range eggs

1 cup grated mozzarella cheese (about 4½ ounces)

7 ounces halloumi cheese, cut into ½-inch slabs (about 1½ cups)

4 or 5 fresh parsley sprigs

Lots of crusty bread

1. Preheat the oven to 350°F.

2. Using a mortar and pestle, bash the fennel seeds and red pepper flakes together.

3. Heat a 10-inch oven-safe pan over medium heat. Melt the butter with 1 tablespoon of the olive oil, then add the onion and ¼ teaspoon of the salt and sauté for 5 minutes, or until the onion is softened and translucent, stirring often.

4. Add the bell pepper, garlic, paprika, cumin, and fennel–red pepper flake mixture, stir, and cook for 2 minutes, or until the spices are fragrant and the bell pepper has started to soften.

5. Add the tomatoes, lemon zest, and stock and bring to a simmer. Let the sauce bubble and simmer away for 6 to 8 minutes, until slightly thickened and reduced. Remove the pan from the heat and add the lemon juice, ½ teaspoon of the black pepper, and the remaining ½ teaspoon salt.

6. Transfer the sauce to a blender and puree (or puree directly in the pot using an immersion blender). Pour the pureed sauce back into the pan.

7. Use a spoon to make six wells in the sauce, then crack an egg into each well. Be careful to not break the yolks. (If you do, it's cool—your breakfast will still taste delicious.) Sprinkle the mozzarella over the sauce, avoiding the egg yolks. Bake for 9 to 11 minutes, or until the egg whites are cooked but the yolks are still a little runny.

8. Meanwhile, get the halloumi ready. In a skillet, heat the remaining 1 tablespoon olive oil over medium heat. Add the halloumi and fry for 1½ to 2 minutes on each side, or until the cheese is crispy and golden brown.

9. To serve, garnish the shakshuka with the fresh parsley, then top with the remaining ½ teaspoon black pepper, and if you're feeling extra spicy, add some more red pepper flakes. Serve with crusty bread and the fried halloumi.

CAESAR COCKTAILS WITH BACON AND SNOW CRAB LEGS

MAKES 8 COCKTAILS • All hail Caesar, king of the Canadian brunch. The cocktail with as many ingredients as a traditional curry. Or just call it a Canadian Bloody Mary. Whatever the name, this spicy, full-flavored cocktail will take you from zero to hero in no time flat. Perfect for a boozy brunch at home.

BACON

8 thick-cut smoked bacon slices

2 tablespoons pure maple syrup

2 tablespoons vodka

1 tablespoon lime zest

COCKTAILS

1 (8-ounce) bottle clam juice

4½ cups tomato juice

1 cup vodka

3 tablespoons fresh lime juice

1 tablespoon prepared horseradish

1 tablespoon Worcestershire sauce

1 teaspoon hot sauce

½ teaspoon smoked paprika

¼ teaspoon cracked black peppercorns

GARNISHES

1 lime

¼ cup BBQ spice rub, such as My Favorite Spice Rub (page 168)

8 long pickle slices

4 celery stalks, halved

8 snow crab legs

1. Preheat the oven to 350°F.

2. Cook the bacon: Line a baking sheet with parchment paper and lay out the bacon in a single layer. Combine the maple syrup, vodka, and lime zest in a dish and use a brush to baste the bacon with it on both sides. Bake for 25 to 30 minutes, until crispy and golden brown. Transfer to a rack to cool completely.

3. Make the cocktails: Combine the cocktail ingredients in a large pitcher along with 2 to 3 cups of ice. Stir several times to chill and combine.

4. Prepare the garnishes: Halve the lime and run it over the lip of eight glasses. Place the BBQ spice rub in a shallow dish and rim each glass with the rub while it's still wet with lime juice.

5. Portion the Caesar into the prepared glasses and add 1 slice of bacon, 1 pickle, ½ celery stalk, and 1 snow crab leg to each cocktail. Serve immediately.

2

Burgers,

SANDWICHES, AND HANDHELD DELICIOUSNESS

DO YOU REMEMBER THE FIRST TIME YOU ATE A BURGER?

No? It's cool, I don't remember either, but I'm quite confident that it was handed to my parents through a window at a drive-through. But do you remember the first time you ate a proper burger? The kind of burger that makes the heavens open wide with cherubim's song resounding, mountains moving, oceans roaring, and your taste buds forever altered from the deliciousness? I most definitely do.

My father and I were road-tripping, making our way down I-95, and decided to stop at a local diner for lunch. I ordered a cheeseburger and fries with a chocolate shake on the side. Classic. I took my first epic bite into that flattop-cooked cheeseburger and time stood still as I thought, *Wait now, don't rush this. Really taste every single mouthful. Savor each bite.*

After all the burgers that came before it, what made this specific burger so memorable? Top-quality ingredients that were cooked simply and perfectly, seasoned with love, and given the respect they deserve.

The honest truth is that burgers, sandwiches, and all the delicious handheld foods we love have become such staple grab-and-go choices in our culture that often they're diminished by too-fast service, slapdash seasoning, and a general lack of care. This leads to lowered expectations when we sit down to an average burger, BLT, or plate of French fries. But a properly made, well-seasoned handheld meal, using the best-quality ingredients you can find, is one of the greatest things on the planet.

There are few joys in life like diving into a juicy brioche-wrapped cheeseburger, face-planting into a steak taco, or crunching away on crispy twice-fried French fries. If there's a happy food, if comfort food has a face, it's handheld. Burgers and sandwiches are the height of accessibility. Fun, approachable, and so very delicious.

Let's up our game here. Forget the takeout menu and start to scratch-make everything at home. You're well on your way to making your home kitchen the local burger joint, sandwich shack, taco truck, and comfort-food-loving locale in your neighborhood. Homemade is always better. You got this!

CLASSIC CHEESEBURGERS

MAKES 4 DOUBLE OR 8 SINGLE BURGERS • Growing up I had one food love that, no matter the situation, style of restaurant, or time of day, completely stole my heart: the Almighty Cheeseburger. There's just something magical about that handheld goodness that makes us instantly happier. When I started cooking, a juicy, cooked-to-perfection burger was on my top-ten list of things to master.

This recipe is for a classic, diner-style burger with all my favorite toppings. Adding a mustard layer to the beef before frying creates the most insanely delicious crust—you'll be an immediate convert.

1 pound ground chuck (80% lean)

1 pound ground sirloin

Sea salt and freshly cracked black pepper

4 or 8 Homemade Brioche Burger Buns (page 76)

⅓ cup yellow mustard

1 tablespoon butter

8 slices American cheese

4 to 8 (¼-inch-thick) tomato slices

4 to 8 (¼-inch-thick) red onion slices

8 pickle slices

8 burger-size lettuce leaves

Maple Curry Ketchup, for serving (page 73)

Spicy Herb Homemade Mayo, for serving (page 74)

1. In a large bowl, combine the ground chuck and sirloin and mix gently but thoroughly. Divide into eight equal portions and shape them into burger patties (see opposite for tips). Season both sides with salt and pepper and refrigerate for 30 minutes.

2. Preheat the oven to 350°F.

3. Heat a large skillet over medium heat. Split and toast the buns in the pan until toasty and golden brown. Set aside.

4. Remove the burgers from the fridge and place a thumbprint in the center of each patty. Smear 1 teaspoon of the mustard on both sides of each patty (*best burger crust ever*). Melt the butter in the preheated pan and, working in batches, fry the burgers for 3 to 4 minutes on each side, until a dark brown crust begins to form. The result: perfectly juicy medium-cooked burgers. For folks who prefer their burgers a little more well done, fry for 5 to 6 minutes per side.

5. Transfer the patties to a baking sheet as they're done. Top each with cheese and place in the oven to melt, 2 to 3 minutes.

6. Build the burgers on the toasted buns with 1 or 2 burger patties, a slice of tomato, pickles, a slice of red onion, and lettuce. Top each with ketchup or mayo. Or both. Serve immediately.

TIPS FOR MAKING THE BEST BURGER PATTIES

BUY the best-quality ground beef you can get your hands on, or better still, grind the meat at home from scratch. It's well worth paying a little bit more and going the extra mile here. Your taste buds will thank you.

MAKE the patties slightly larger than the width of the burger buns. As the beef cooks, it will shrink, and you don't want to be left with a mouthful of bread.

PLACING a thumbprint in the center of each patty halfway through the meat will help keep the beef from shrinking into a baseball.

FRIED FETA BLT SANDWICHES

MAKES 4 SANDWICHES • It doesn't get much more classic than a BLT.

I was born and raised on a steady diet of classic toasted tomato sandwiches, my father's specialty. Years later, bacon in all its glory entered the equation, dressed to the nines in crispy deliciousness and smelling like a million bucks. Sandwich heaven. It's simple, it's timeless, and it's near perfect. But even the classics need a little upgrade sometimes.

This recipe is a fantastic way to bring that magical sandwich into the modern age, with crispy feta cheese, sweet-and-savory maple bacon, and olive oil–grilled bread.

8 thick-cut smoked bacon slices

2 tablespoons pure maple syrup

8 slices sourdough bread

1½ tablespoons olive oil

Sunflower (or vegetable) oil, for frying

1 (14-ounce) block feta cheese

½ cup all-purpose flour

2 large free-range eggs

1 cup panko bread crumbs

½ teaspoon dried oregano

1 teaspoon lemon zest

¼ cup **Spicy Herb Homemade Mayo (page 74)** or prepared mayo

8 burger-size lettuce leaves

1 large tomato, cut into 4 thin rounds

1. Preheat the oven to 350°F. Line a baking sheet with parchment paper.

2. Lay out the bacon on the prepared baking sheet. Baste the bacon with the maple syrup and bake for 25 to 30 minutes, turning the bacon over halfway through, until crispy. Transfer to a wire rack to cool and candy.

3. Brush the bread slices on both sides with the olive oil and toast in a large skillet over medium heat until browned, about 2 minutes per side. Set aside.

4. In a deep saucepan, heat 1 inch of sunflower oil over medium heat to 350°F.

5. Slice the feta lengthwise into 4 long slabs. Prepare three bowls: one with the flour, one with the eggs (whisk them lightly with a fork), and one with a mixture of the panko, oregano, and lemon zest. Coat each feta piece completely by dredging it in the flour, then the eggs, then the panko mixture. Fry the cheese, in batches if necessary, until golden brown, 1½ minutes per side.

6. Build each sandwich on the sourdough bread with 1 tablespoon of the mayo, 2 lettuce leaves, a slice of tomato, 2 slices of bacon, and a piece of fried feta.

BUTTERMILK FRIED CHICKEN BURGERS

MAKES 6 SANDWICHES • I love the southern United States.

Living in Nashville changed me forever. I fell in love with the people, the land, the music, the pace of life, and, most important, the food. Before moving south of the Mason-Dixon Line, I thought I had tried fried chicken. Nope. Not even close. The fried chicken I experienced while living in Tennessee was something otherworldly—complete happiness in a dish.

This chicken sandwich is tribute to that Southern perfection with influence from my home and native land: sweet-and-savory maple bacon, fried chicken, avocado, and homemade mayo. Live long and prosper, fried chicken.

As with many of our favorite dishes, this chicken requires overnight marinating in the fridge. Buttermilk is a mildly acidic natural tenderizer that penetrates all the way through the meat, resulting in the juiciest, most incredible fried chicken imaginable. Once you go buttermilk, you never go back.

BUTTERMILK FRIED CHICKEN

3 (6-ounce) boneless chicken breasts

2 cups buttermilk

2 tablespoons pure maple syrup

¾ teaspoon cayenne pepper

Canola oil, for frying

1½ cups all-purpose flour

½ teaspoon garlic powder

¼ teaspoon dried oregano

¼ teaspoon onion powder

1 teaspoon kosher salt

½ teaspoon freshly cracked black pepper

1. Make the chicken: Butterfly the chicken breasts (see opposite) but cut them all the way through so that you have 6 thin breast slices. Place the chicken in a freezer bag and add the buttermilk, maple syrup, and ½ teaspoon of the cayenne. Seal the bag and give it a good shake. Chill in the fridge for at least 6 hours (overnight is best).

2. Prepare the sandwiches: preheat the oven to 350°F. Line a rimmed baking sheet with parchment paper.

3. Lay the bacon on the prepared baking sheet, leaving room between each slice. Baste the tops of the bacon with the maple syrup and bake for 25 to 30 minutes, flipping halfway through, until crispy. Transfer to a wire rack to cool. As the bacon cools, the maple syrup will candy around it.

4. In a deep Dutch oven or stockpot, heat 3 inches of canola oil over medium heat to 350°F.

**12 thick-cut smoked bacon
slices**

**2 tablespoons pure maple
syrup**

**1 ripe avocado, pitted, peeled,
and cut into 18 thin slices**

**1 large tomato, cut into
6 slices**

12 burger-size lettuce leaves

**6 tablespoons Spicy Herb
Homemade Mayo
(page 74)**

**6 Homemade Brioche Burger
Buns (page 76)**

5. In a large bowl, combine the flour, garlic powder, oregano, onion powder, salt, pepper, and remaining ¼ teaspoon cayenne and stir well. Dredge the chicken in the flour mixture, coating it on all sides. Working in batches as needed, fry the chicken for 6 to 7 minutes, or until the crust is golden brown and the juices run clear.

6. Build the sandwiches by topping each bun with 3 avocado slices, a piece of fried chicken, a tomato slice, 2 bacon slices, 2 lettuce leaves, and 1 tablespoon mayo. Serve immediately.

BUTTERFLYING

PLACE the chicken breast on a cutting board. Using a sharp knife, slice the chicken in the center of the breast, parallel to the board. Cut the chicken almost all the way through the meat, leaving a small hinge on one side. You'll then be able to open it up like a book. Or a butterfly.

SALMON BANH MI SANDWICHES

MAKES 6 SANDWICHES • I very clearly remember my first trip down banh mi lane. I was in New York City and stumbled into an unassuming, nondescript corner market, complete with a deli counter, that sold everything under the sun. Hungry and a little overstimulated (thanks, Times Square), I picked up a 99-cent sandwich. A dollar literally changed my food life. I had never tasted something quite like this. Incredible!

These Salmon Banh Mi sandwiches are easy to throw together and perfect when you need to feed a hungry crowd. The key is in marinating the salmon overnight, letting it soak in that flavor bomb of a marinade.

SALMON

¼ cup sugar

2 garlic cloves

1 (2-inch) knob fresh ginger, peeled

¼ cup fresh lime juice

2 tablespoons sriracha

1½ tablespoons rice vinegar

2 tablespoons pure maple syrup

¼ cup fish sauce

1 (1½ to 2-pound) skin-on side of salmon

SRIRACHA MAYO

½ cup prepared mayo

2 tablespoons sriracha

1 tablespoon fresh lime juice

QUICK PICKLED VEGETABLES

½ cup rice vinegar

2 tablespoons sugar

Pinch of sea salt

1 English cucumber, peeled and julienned (see opposite)

1. Make the salmon: Combine the sugar and 3 tablespoons water in a small saucepan. Heat over medium heat, stirring often, until the sugar has dissolved. Set the simple syrup aside to cool to room temperature.

2. Using a Microplane (or box grater), grate the garlic and ginger into a small bowl. Add the lime juice, sriracha, vinegar, maple syrup, fish sauce, and simple syrup and stir to combine. Place the salmon in a large freezer bag, cover with the marinade, and refrigerate overnight.

3. The next day, make the sriracha mayo: Stir together the mayo, sriracha, and lime juice. (This can be made ahead and kept in the fridge.)

4. Make the pickled vegetables: Combine the vinegar, sugar, and salt in a large bowl. Add the veggies and toss to coat them well. Cover, transfer to the fridge, and let them pickle away for 30 minutes.

5. Preheat the oven to broil. Line a large baking sheet with parchment paper. Place the salmon skin-side down on the prepared baking sheet and broil for 8 to 10 minutes, until golden, crispy, juicy, and all kinds of delicious. You'll know

2 large carrots, julienned

1 medium daikon radish, peeled and julienned

SANDWICHES

6 French-style baguette rolls

½ cup fresh cilantro

2 scallions, white and green parts finely sliced

2 to 3 jalapeños, sliced into thin rounds

the salmon is done when it easily separates with a fork and there's just a hint of pink remaining on the inside of the fish. Break the salmon into small sandwich-friendly chunks.

6. Build the sandwiches on the baguettes with 1 tablespoon of the sriracha mayo, about ¾ cup of the salmon, and ½ cup of the pickled vegetables. Top with the fresh cilantro, the scallions, and a few slices of jalapeño.

Julienne. A fancy term that basically means to cut whatever suits your fancy into equal-size matchsticks. The best way to accomplish this is to first create a flat surface: Cut the vegetable in half, place the flat side on a board, and slice away, then cut those slices into thin matchsticks.

GOAT CHEESE–STUFFED LAMB BURGERS WITH CARAMELIZED RED ONIONS

MAKES 4 BURGERS • Lamb burgers are a great way to switch up burger night at home. Change is good, y'all! Lamb has more of an earthy, gamey flavor than beef, and it's completely delicious paired with creamy goat cheese and deeply caramelized onions. If your burger night needs a little relief from the same old same old, give these a go.

CARAMELIZED ONIONS

1 tablespoon butter

1 large red onion, thinly sliced (about 2 cups)

¼ teaspoon kosher salt

¼ cup dark beer

LAMB BURGERS

1½ pounds ground lamb

1 garlic clove, minced

½ teaspoon smoked paprika

¼ teaspoon cayenne pepper

1 tablespoon chopped fresh mint

⅓ cup goat cheese

Kosher salt and freshly cracked black pepper

1 tablespoon butter

1 tablespoon olive oil

4 burger buns (such as Homemade Brioche Burger Buns, page 76)

4 tablespoons Spicy Herb Homemade Mayo (page 74)

4 slices cooked bacon (such as Maple Spiced Rum Bacon [page 15])

1 cup baby arugula

1. Make the onions: In a 3-quart saucepan, melt the butter over medium heat. Add the onion and salt, toss to combine, and cover. Cook for 20 minutes, stirring several times to ensure that the onion does not stick to the pan. Add the beer, stir, cover, and cook for 10 minutes. If the onion is deeply caramelized and the liquid has mostly evaporated, it's perfection. If not, cook for a few minutes more. Set aside.

2. Make the burgers: In a large bowl, combine the lamb, garlic, smoked paprika, cayenne, and mint. Mix well. Set aside 4 tablespoons of the lamb mixture and divide the remaining lamb into four equal portions. Shape them into patties slightly larger than the width of the burger bun. Using your thumb, make a well in the center of each patty, going halfway through the lamb.

3. Divide the goat cheese into four portions and place them in the thumb divots. Flatten each tablespoon of reserved burger mixture into a disc and place on top of the goat cheese. Pinch the edges to encase the cheese in the lamb. Season both sides of each patty with salt and pepper.

4. In a large skillet, melt the butter with the olive oil over medium heat. Fry the burgers for 4 to 5 minutes per side for medium doneness.

5. Place the burgers on the buns and top each with 1 tablespoon mayo, some caramelized onions, bacon, and ¼ cup arugula.

SAUCY SLOW-ROASTED PULLED PORK BURGERS WITH CREAMY COLESLAW

MAKES 10 TO 12 SERVINGS • When I left Nashville, of course I was obsessed with re-creating its fried chicken, but the other thing that kept me busy was mastering perfect pulled pork. The studio where my band spent our days and nights recording was just down the road from a local BBQ joint, the site of my baptism into all things Southern BBQ. We spent almost every lunch loving on their daily special, and three days a week it was an intoxicating variation of pulled pork.

On nachos, on a potato roll, in a taco, or by itself, pulled pork = heaven. This recipe is my version of a classic. The combo of fall-off-the-bone pork and slaw is seriously out-of-this-world, next-level sandwiching.

As with anything slow roasted to perfection, this recipe takes a little extra time to prepare, so it's best to plan ahead.

PULLED PORK

1 tablespoon chili powder

2 tablespoons brown sugar

1½ teaspoons smoked paprika

1½ teaspoons garlic powder

1½ teaspoons onion powder

1 tablespoon kosher salt

1½ teaspoons freshly cracked black pepper

1 (5-pound) bone-in pork shoulder

3 tablespoons olive oil

1 cup cola

1 recipe Spicy-and-Sweet BBQ Sauce (page 75)

1. Make the pulled pork: In a small bowl, combine the chili powder, brown sugar, smoked paprika, garlic powder, onion powder, salt, and pepper. Massage the pork shoulder with half of the olive oil, then coat it all over with the spice rub. Cover and refrigerate overnight.

2. Preheat the oven to 425°F. Let the pork come to room temperature on the counter for 30 minutes prior to cooking.

3. Heat a large Dutch oven over medium-high heat and add the remaining olive oil. Sear the pork on all sides until golden brown, 2 to 3 minutes per side. Pour in the cola and transfer the pork to the oven. Immediately decrease the oven temperature to 325°F and cook for 6½ to 7½ hours, or until the pork is basically falling apart and easily shreddable and the kitchen smells like heaven.

4. Rest the cooked pork on a board for 10 minutes.

COLESLAW

1 cup prepared mayo

1 tablespoon Dijon mustard

1 tablespoon apple cider vinegar

2 tablespoons fresh lemon juice

1 teaspoon sugar

½ teaspoon celery seed

½ teaspoon sea salt

½ teaspoon freshly cracked black pepper

4 cups shredded red cabbage

2 cups shredded green cabbage

2 carrots, grated on a box grater

FOR SERVING

10 to 12 burger buns

2 cups of your favorite sliced pickles

Your favorite hot sauce

5. While the pork is resting, make the coleslaw: In a large bowl, combine all the ingredients except the cabbages and carrots and mix until smooth. Add the cabbages and carrots and mix until the vegetables are coated and the coleslaw is creamy and delicious. Set aside.

6. Shred the pork with two forks, discarding any bones or excess fat. Toss the pulled pork in the pan juices, then pour over as much BBQ sauce as your heart desires and toss.

7. Serve on a bun with the coleslaw, the pickles, and some hot sauce. Delicious.

ANCHO-RUBBED STEAK TACOS WITH PINEAPPLE-AVOCADO SALSA

MAKES 4 TO 6 SERVINGS • Taco night, I love you. This little handheld delight has gone seriously gangbusters over the past few years, with folks from Toronto to Tokyo celebrating Taco Tuesday and all things deliciously wrapped in a tortilla. Long gone are the days when tacos were confined to seasoned ground beef, diced tomatoes, and iceberg lettuce. Nowadays, everything from steak to pulled pork to fried fish and even tofu are perfectly acceptable for taco action. They're easily customizable, so much fun, and wonderful served as a family-style meal, letting everyone build their own handheld masterpiece.

For maximum awesomeness and the best steak tacos ever, be sure to prepare the beef one day in advance, letting it soak in that flavor bomb of a spice rub overnight in the fridge.

STEAK

2 tablespoons ancho chile powder

1 tablespoon brown sugar

½ teaspoon ground cumin

½ teaspoon paprika

1 tablespoon sea salt

1½ teaspoons freshly cracked black pepper

1½ pounds flank steak

3 tablespoons olive oil

2 tablespoons butter

SPIKED SOUR CREAM

½ cup sour cream

1 tablespoon fresh lime juice

1 teaspoon chili powder

¼ teaspoon ground cayenne

Sea salt and freshly cracked black pepper

1. Make the steak: In a small bowl, combine the chili powder, brown sugar, cumin, paprika, salt, and pepper.

2. Pat the steak dry, then massage it with the olive oil and cover the entire surface with the spice rub. Transfer to a plate, cover with plastic wrap, and refrigerate overnight.

3. Let the steak come to room temperature for at least 1 hour before cooking.

4. Meanwhile, make the spiked sour cream: Combine the sour cream, lime juice, chili powder, and cayenne in a small dish and stir well. Season with a small pinch each of salt and pepper and refrigerate until it's taco time.

5. Make the salsa: In a medium bowl, gently mix the pineapple, avocado, onion, cilantro, lime juice, and vinegar. Season with the salt, mix, and cover with plastic wrap. Refrigerate while you crack on with the tacos.

SALSA

2 cups ½-inch-diced pineapple

1 large ripe avocado, pitted, peeled, and cut into ½-inch dice

½ cup finely diced red onion

¼ cup finely chopped fresh cilantro leaves

2 tablespoons fresh lime juice

1 tablespoon apple cider vinegar

¼ teaspoon kosher salt

TACOS

16 (6-inch) flour tortillas

2 limes

Fresh cilantro

6. Heat a grill pan (or cast-iron pan) over medium heat. Working in batches, lightly char both sides of each tortilla and shape them into half-moon shells. This will make the tortillas nice and crispy and give them a little extra flavor shot from the nice char. Life hack! Place a lime at each end of the tortillas, holding them in place until they harden up nicely.

7. Increase the temperature of the grill pan to medium-high. When the pan is smoking hot, grill the steak for 4 to 5 minutes per side for medium-rare. With 2 minutes of cooking time remaining, melt the butter in the pan and use it to baste the steak. Transfer the beef to a plate and pour the pan juices on top. Let rest for at least 10 minutes. Carve the steak into very thin strips, about ¼-inch thick. Pour the juices from the plate over the sliced steak.

8. Portion the steak into the tortillas. Serve up the tacos with the salsa and sour cream and garnish with cilantro and lime.

FRIED SHOESTRING ONION CHEESEBURGERS

MAKES 4 DOUBLE CHEESEBURGERS OR 8 SINGLE CHEESEBURGERS • When I was a nineteen-year-old budding guitar player, the incomparable Andrew Wigston invited me to join him and his band of gypsies on a six-week stint of shows in America. It was my first time traveling with a band, and among a million milestones and memories, I distinctly remember eating at a burger joint in Shelby, North Carolina, where they topped that perfectly cooked masterpiece with crispy onion rings. Mind. Blown! Fantastic crunch factor and flavor for days. And sporting a T-shirt in April was the icing on the cake for this Canadian.

Here's my version of that world-changing burger. Topped with ancho-lime-spiked fried onion shoestrings, candied maple bacon, and creamy avocado, this burger is a serious showstopper.

CANDIED MAPLE BACON

- 8 thick-cut smoked bacon slices
- 2 tablespoons pure maple syrup

BURGER PATTIES

- 1 pound ground chuck (80% lean)
- 1 pound ground sirloin
- 1 tablespoon BBQ sauce, store-bought or homemade (page 75)
- 1 teaspoon smoked paprika
- 2 garlic cloves, grated on a Microplane
- Sea salt and freshly cracked black pepper

1. Make the bacon: Preheat the oven to 350°F. Line a large rimmed baking sheet with parchment paper.

2. Lay the bacon in a single layer on the prepared baking sheet. Baste all over with the maple syrup and bake, turning halfway through, for 25 to 30 minutes, until crispy. Transfer the bacon to a wire rack to cool. As the bacon cools, the maple syrup will candy around it.

3. Make the burger patties: In a large bowl, combine the ground chuck, ground sirloin, BBQ sauce, paprika, and garlic and mix well. Divide the beef into eight equal portions and shape into patties that are slightly larger than the width of the buns. Season both sides of each burger with salt and pepper. Place a thumbprint in the center of each patty to help stop it from shrinking (see the patty-making tips on page 55). Chill in the fridge for 30 minutes.

4. Next, make the fried onions: In a high-sided Dutch oven or stockpot, heat 3 inches of canola oil over medium heat to 350°F. (If you have a deep fryer, even better.)

FRIED ONIONS

Canola oil, for frying

1½ cups all-purpose flour

½ teaspoon ancho chile powder

1 teaspoon lime zest

½ teaspoon sea salt

½ teaspoon freshly cracked black pepper

1 cup buttermilk

2 sweet (Vidalia) onions, halved and thinly sliced into half-moons

BURGERS

4 (or 8) brioche buns, store-bought or homemade (page 76)

1 tablespoon butter

8 slices sharp cheddar cheese

1 large ripe avocado, pitted, peeled, and mashed

1 tablespoon fresh lime juice

Pinch of sea salt

¼ cup Spicy Herb Homemade Mayo (page 74)

5. In a medium bowl, combine the flour, ancho chile powder, lime zest, salt, and pepper. Pour the buttermilk into a separate medium bowl. Working in batches (about ½ onion at a time), dunk the onion slices in the buttermilk, then toss them in the flour mixture, coating them well. Fry for 1½ to 2 minutes, or until golden brown and crispy. Transfer the fried onions to a baking sheet lined with paper towels to absorb any excess oil. Carry on cooking the remaining onions.

6. Burger time. Heat a large skillet over medium heat. Split and toast the brioche buns, then set aside. Melt the butter in the hot skillet. Add the burger patties and cook for 3 to 4 minutes per side, until a crispy crust forms and the inside is cooked through to the desired doneness. Top each patty with cheese. Combine the mashed avocado and lime juice, season with the salt, and give it a good stir.

7. Build the burgers on the brioche buns with a heaping tablespoon of mashed avocado, 2 slices of bacon, a handful of fried onions, and 1 tablespoon of the mayo.

JERK CHICKEN BURGERS WITH GRILLED PINEAPPLE

MAKES 4 CHICKEN BURGERS • Summertime grilling is a Zen-like culinary experience. We patiently wait through snow, sleet, rain, and gloom until that glorious moment when the summer sun strolls in like a total boss. We almost instantly move our nightly dining experience outside, opting for a backyard grill and patio lanterns. A hot flame, a cold beer, good friends, and the summer sun. Perfection.

This recipe is chock-full of summertime deliciousness. The marriage of spicy and sweet is seriously outta sight. My fellow spicy lovers, this one's for you.

4 (6-ounce) chicken breasts

1½ teaspoons kosher salt

2 teaspoons cayenne pepper

2 teaspoons dark brown sugar

1 teaspoon dried oregano

1 teaspoon chili powder

1 teaspoon smoked paprika

1 teaspoon freshly cracked black pepper

2 tablespoons olive oil

4 burger buns, store-bought or homemade (page 76)

1 small pineapple, peeled, cored, and sliced into ½-inch-thick rings

¼ cup Spicy Herb Homemade Mayo (page 74) or prepared mayo

2 tablespoons fresh lime juice

1 large tomato, sliced

4 burger-sized lettuce leaves

1. Place the chicken breasts between two pieces of plastic wrap and lightly bash them with a rolling pin or wine bottle to flatten them (this will help them cook evenly). Combine the salt, cayenne, brown sugar, oregano, chili powder, paprika, and black pepper in a shallow dish. Massage the chicken breasts with the olive oil, then coat them with the spice rub.

2. Heat a grill (or grill pan) over medium-high heat. Split the buns and toast them until lightly charred, 2 to 3 minutes. Set aside.

3. Grill the chicken until cooked through and nicely charred with those awesome grill marks, 7 to 8 minutes per side. Insert an instant-read thermometer into one piece. If it registers 165°F, you're golden. Set aside to rest a moment.

4. Pop the pineapple rings on the hot grill and cook until charred, 1 minute per side.

5. Stir the mayo and lime juice together in a small dish.

6. Build the chicken burgers on the toasted buns with 1 tablespoon of the lime mayo, a pineapple ring, a grilled chicken breast, a slice of tomato, and a lettuce leaf.

KETCHUP, MAYO, AND BBQ: SANDWICH SAUCE PERFECTION

KITCHEN cupboard staples might be my favorite DIY adventure. They're easy and cheap, so we almost never think about making them ourselves. But from scratch has become a no-brainer for me. They're easy, crazy delicious, and versatile, and most important, you'll know exactly what ingredients are in your food. No preservatives, no ingredients you can't pronounce, only goodness. Give these a go.

MAPLE CURRY KETCHUP

MAKES 3½ CUPS • Homemade ketchup truly is a thing of beauty. Chock-full of incredible, exciting flavors that partner with recipes to create unforgettable, showstopping dishes. It's well worth the time to make and miles better than the name brands. A jar of the stuff is always in my fridge. Always.

2 tablespoons vegetable oil
1 cup finely diced red onion
2 garlic cloves, minced
1 tablespoon tomato paste
1 teaspoon curry powder
½ teaspoon smoked paprika
¼ teaspoon cayenne pepper
¼ teaspoon ground cinnamon
¼ teaspoon ground allspice
1 (28-ounce) can diced
   tomatoes
½ cup pure maple syrup
½ cup apple cider vinegar
1 teaspoon kosher salt
½ teaspoon freshly cracked
   black pepper

1. In a large saucepan, heat the vegetable oil over medium heat. When it's warm, add the onion and garlic and sauté, stirring often, for 5 minutes. When the onion starts to become translucent, add the tomato paste, curry powder, paprika, cayenne, cinnamon, and allspice. Stir to combine and cook for 1 minute.

2. Add the diced tomatoes, maple syrup, and vinegar and season with the salt and black pepper. Bring the sauce to a simmer, then reduce the heat to medium-low and cook, un-covered, for 30 to 35 minutes, until reduced and thickened. Give the ketchup a stir every few minutes so it doesn't catch.

3. Remove from the heat and pulse in a blender until smooth (or puree directly in the pot using an immersion blender). Let cool completely, transfer to a jar, and refrigerate overnight so all those flavors can really get to know each other. The ketchup will keep in an airtight container in the fridge for up to 1 month.

SPICY HERB HOMEMADE MAYO

MAKES 2 CUPS • Homemade mayo, much like hollandaise sauce, takes a little practice to get the knack. It's like learning to ride a bicycle—once you've mastered the technique, it'll be with you for life. Be sure to come prepared, armed with a whisk and some extra patience. It's really all about whisking continuously as you slowly stream the oil into the egg yolks, little by little, letting the yolks take in every drop of oil. Slow and steady wins the race—this exquisite, delectable, over-the-top-awesome race.

2 large free-range egg yolks

1 teaspoon Dijon mustard

1¾ cups sunflower oil

1 tablespoon fresh lemon juice

1 tablespoon white wine vinegar

2 teaspoons hot sauce

1 garlic clove, grated

1 tablespoon thinly sliced fresh chives

1 tablespoon finely chopped fresh parsley leaves

¼ teaspoon sea salt

1. In a large bowl, whisk together the egg yolks and the mustard (see Tip). While whisking continuously, slowly stream the oil into the egg yolks a little at a time until completely emulsified. This will take 8 to 10 minutes. A little patience, strength, and ambition are required, friends.

2. When the mayonnaise has come together and is nice and thick, add the lemon juice, vinegar, and hot sauce and whisk for 30 seconds. Fold in the grated garlic and herbs and season with the salt. Taste and adjust the seasonings if necessary.

3. Check you out! You just made mayo!! It'll keep in an airtight container in the fridge for about 1 week. If it separates, add 1 to 2 teaspoons water to the mayo and whisk until smooth and combined.

TIP: *Set the bowl on a damp cloth for your whisking session. This will help the bowl stay put and make your whisking life much, much easier.*

Bonus! You can also make mayo in a food processor. Process the egg and mustard for about a minute, then slowly stream in the oil through the feed tube with the processor running until the mayo emulsifies and thickens beautifully. (If using a Mini-Prep, you can use the two little holes in the top of the lid to drip in the oil.) Add the lemon juice, vinegar, and hot sauce and pulse a few times until combined. Fold in the garlic and fresh herbs, and season with the salt. Sweet!

SPICY-AND-SWEET BBQ SAUCE

MAKES ABOUT 2 CUPS • My education into all things Southern cuisine went something like this: fried chicken, pulled pork, BBQ sauce. Oh, and sausage gravy, biscuits, grits, sweet tea—honestly, it doesn't get much better! God bless the South. Go visit immediately.

For me, a great sauce should be like the icing on the cake. It's there to propel your meal to the next level, elevating an already delicious dish into something remarkable. This BBQ is guaranteed to do just that. A little spicy, a little sweet, and completely legit.

1 tablespoon butter

1 cup finely diced red onion

½ cup dark beer

¼ teaspoon kosher salt

3 garlic cloves, minced

1 jalapeño, seeded and finely diced

1 teaspoon smoked paprika

¼ teaspoon cayenne pepper

2 cups store-bought organic ketchup

3 tablespoons dark brown sugar

2 tablespoons soy sauce

2 tablespoons Worcestershire sauce

1 tablespoon apple cider vinegar

2 tablespoons fresh lemon juice

1. In a medium saucepan, melt the butter over medium-low heat. Add the onion, beer, and salt, stir, cover, and cook gently for 15 minutes, watching carefully and stirring every few minutes so the onion doesn't stick to the pan. Add the remaining ingredients, stir, and bring to a simmer. Let the sauce simmer away for 30 minutes, stirring every so often.

2. Using an immersion blender, puree the sauce directly in the pot until smooth. (Alternatively, carefully transfer the sauce to a regular blender and puree until smooth. Be careful when blending hot liquids.)

3. Transfer to a jar, let cool completely, and store in the fridge overnight to allow the flavors to develop. The BBQ sauce will keep in an airtight container in the fridge for about 2 weeks.

HOMEMADE BRIOCHE BURGER BUNS

MAKES 16 BURGER BUNS • The ultimate handheld burger requires the best bun possible, and in my opinion, it doesn't get any better than a brioche bun. Sweet, buttery heaven!

In my part of Canada, the Maritimes, we don't have access to some of the food and grocery staples available in other, more populated regions. When I was first learning to cook, this meant either adapting recipes to incorporate locally available products or learning to make them from scratch. This guerrilla-style learning process most definitely helped in making me a better cook, a better taster, and ultimately more versatile in the kitchen.

My first big flour-based challenge: brioche rolls. Any time I had a burger that "changed my life" in a city far, far away, it was wrapped in a brioche bun. They're perfect in every single way.

Brioche takes a little time, a little patience, and a little practice, but the results are absolutely incredible.

5 cups all-purpose flour, plus more for dusting

1 tablespoon active dry yeast

3 tablespoons sugar

1 tablespoon kosher salt

½ cup cold water

6 large free-range eggs

1½ cups (3 sticks) butter, at room temperature

Olive oil, for the bowl

Sesame seeds, for topping (optional)

1. In the bowl of a stand mixer fitted with the dough hook, combine the flour, yeast, sugar, salt, and water. Crack in 5 of the eggs and beat on low speed for 3 to 4 minutes, until all the ingredients are combined, scraping down the sides of the bowl as needed. Knead the dough for 3 minutes more to make sure those ingredients are getting extra cozy.

2. Cut the butter into ½-inch cubes. With the mixer running on low, add the butter one piece at a time, until it works itself into the dough. This will take a few minutes. Perfect time to grab a coffee, check your e-mail, or stage a sweet Instagram snap. The dough will be quite wet at this stage, but fear not!

3. When all the butter has worked itself into the dough, turn the mixer to high and let it go to town, kneading the dough for 10 minutes. The side of the bowl should be clean, and the dough ball should be making a slapping sound against it.

4. Transfer the dough to a lightly oiled large bowl, cover, and let rise slowly in the fridge overnight.

5. The next day, let the dough sit out for 30 minutes or so to come to room temperature. Line two baking sheets with parchment paper.

6. Lightly dust a work surface with flour and place the dough on it. Using a kitchen scale, divide the dough into sixteen equal 3.15-ounce pieces (if need be, make 14 or 15 balls instead to get them to the right size). Using the palm of your hand, roll a piece of dough on the floured surface in a clockwise motion for about 1 minute. A perfect little dough ball will naturally form as it rolls on the counter. Pinch off the bottom of the dough ball to close it if necessary. As you finish each ball, place it on one of the prepared baking sheets, leaving at least 1½ inches between each ball.

Once you've got the brioche knack, the possibilities are endless! I use this dough recipe often to make a basic brioche loaf. It's sliced bread heaven and the building block of sandwich perfection. But don't stop there! This dough can be used for everything from cinnamon rolls to doughnuts, brioche au chocolat, or even Nutella-topped dessert pizza. Buttery bliss.

7. Cover the baking sheets with plastic wrap and let the dough rise until doubled in size, about 1 hour.

8. Preheat the oven to 350°F.

9. Crack and beat the remaining egg in a small dish. Brush the top of each dough ball with the egg, covering all sides. Repeat with a second coat of egg. You can either top each bun with 1 teaspoon sesame seeds or leave them plain. Choose your own adventure.

10. Bake for 30 to 35 minutes, until deeply golden brown. Let cool on a wire rack for a few minutes before serving. These brioche buns are best eaten the same day, but will keep in an airtight container at room temperature for 2 to 3 days.

THE PERFECT FRENCH FRY

MAKES 8 SIDE SERVINGS • French fries are absolutely next-level comfort food, and done right, they might just steal the show altogether. Once you've mastered a few simple techniques, you'll be guaranteed delicious and consistent fries at home every single time, just the way you like 'em. Never again risk the soggy, undercooked disappointment that so often plagues takeout orders. Crisped-to-perfection fries, in the comfort of your home kitchen. It doesn't get any better than that.

Here are two simple tricks to help you make perfect fries at home:

THE PRE-SOAK. After you cut your potatoes into strips, soak them in a large bowl of cold water. This will help to remove the starch.

THE DOUBLE-FRY. Frying your potatoes twice—first at a low temperature, then at a high temperature—will cook them through first, then make them golden brown and completely addictive.

---

5 pounds russet or Yukon Gold potatoes (8 to 10 large)
Peanut oil (or canola oil), for frying
Sea salt

TIP: *For a completely delicious twist, toss the cooked fries with ⅓ cup grated Parmesan cheese and 2 tablespoons finely diced fresh chives. Incroyable!*

1. Wash and scrub the potatoes to remove any excess dirt.

2. Cut the potatoes into ¼-inch-thick sticks and place them in a large bowl filled with cold water. Cover the bowl with plastic wrap and refrigerate for 1 hour.

3. Line a baking sheet with paper towels and set a wire rack on top.

4. In a large Dutch oven or a high-sided saucepan, heat 3 inches of oil to 325°F. Drain the potatoes and pat them dry with paper towels.

5. Working in batches, fry the potatoes for 5 to 6 minutes, turning them every minute or so. The fries will be lightly colored at this point. Transfer the partially cooked fries to the rack while you carry on frying the remaining batches.

6. Increase the oil temperature to 375°F. Working in batches, cook the fries again for 2 to 4 minutes, until golden brown and crispy. Drain any excess grease on paper towels, toss with sea salt, and serve immediately.

3

Pasta!

COMFORT HAS A FIRST NAME.

SO HERE'S THE THING ABOUT PASTA. IT'S HEAVEN, BUT YOU ALREADY KNOW THAT. DUH.

It's also the first thing I truly learned how to cook properly, partially because it's cheap as chips and I could afford it on a musician's salary and partially because I'm all kinds of addicted to the overpowering allure of carbs, but mostly because my favorite foods to prepare are the dishes that make people happy. And pasta most certainly makes folks happy. I've learned a few helpful tips along the way to help you cook the best pasta ever.

HOW MUCH WATER?

In this case, more is always better. A general rule of thumb when cooking pasta is 1 quart of water for every 3.5 ounces of pasta. This will give the noodles plenty of room to dance in the boiling water.

SALTED BOILING WATER, SURE, BUT HOW MUCH SALT?

There's a world of opinions on this, but one thing is certain: We tend to undersalt pasta water. For every 5 quarts of water, add 2 tablespoons of salt. Best practice for this is letting the water come to a boil, then adding the salt. The H_2O will chill out for a moment or two, collect its thoughts, and then come back to a rapid boil. When it does, it's go time.

PASTA WATER IS LIQUID GOLD

Shout out and major thanks to Mr. Jamie Oliver for teaching me the glories of pasta water. It used to go straight down the sink, and (no coincidence) my pasta stuck together and my sauce was far too thick and difficult to work with. But adding a little splash or two of that liquid gold to your noodles and sauce is genius, and results in the silkiest, most luxurious pasta ever. Please start doing this immediately.

AL DENTE

You've no doubt heard the term *al dente* before, and if you're anything like I was before I started cooking, you didn't think too much about it. *Al dente* literally means "to the tooth," and it describes perfectly cooked pasta: soft yet with a bit of bite, and firm enough to hold up nicely when removed from the water.

Mushy pasta is the absolute worst. Al dente, friends. Always al dente.

TRUE OR FALSE: IF I THROW A NOODLE AT THE WALL AND IT STICKS, IT'S COOKED AL DENTE . . .

False. Okay, let's just stop right here. Why are you letting your wall dictate

your cooking? Just as you should taste a soup or a sauce throughout the cooking process to check the seasoning and flavor development, your mouth is the tool you need to check for pasta doneness. Learning to taste food at many stages throughout the cooking process will make you a better taster and a better home cook. When there's any chance of your pasta being ready, carefully remove a noodle from the boiling water with some tongs and give it a bite. Repeat this process until it's perfect. Best of all—you're eating pasta!

HOMEMADE FRESH PASTA

MAKES 4 TO 6 SERVINGS • Homemade pasta was sky high on my wish list of things to make when I first started cooking. I remember watching an episode of Mr. Oliver's *The Naked Chef* and being overcome with inspiration (and hunger). I was astonished at how quickly and easily he was able to bang out a batch of noodles! Incredible. Fresh pasta is such a joy. And once you've taken the plunge, you'll be a pasta champ in no time flat.

This fresh pasta recipe assumes that you own an old-school pasta roller (or a super-fancy stand mixer attachment). I'm a proud, longtime owner of the old-school kind and highly recommend investing in one if you don't currently own a pasta machine. It's an inexpensive sidekick that will bring ease and enjoyment to your pasta making.

400 grams "00" flour (see page 29)
½ teaspoon sea salt
4 large free-range eggs
1 tablespoon olive oil

1. Combine the flour and salt on a work surface and make a well in the center (think volcano). Crack the eggs into the well. Pour in the olive oil and lightly beat the oil and eggs together with a fork. Start to pull flour from the outside of the well into the center, gradually mixing it together with the eggs. After a few minutes, when the dough is too thick to work with a fork, get those hands in there and start working the dough with your fingertips. When the dough starts to come together, switch to kneading the dough with the palms of your hands.

Or . . .

If you happen to be especially short on time, pop all the ingredients in a food processor and blitz until the dough resembles fresh bread crumbs. Give the flour a squish with your fingertips. If it seems dry, add a very small amount of water. Tip out onto your work surface.

2. Knead, bash, stretch, hit, yell at, and pummel the dough for about 10 minutes, until the dough ball is elastic and smooth. It's hard work, but it counts as going to the gym. Right? Place

This dough is best fresh, but if you're like me and love being a step ahead of the game, you're in luck! Fresh pasta can be prepared in advance, rolled out, and cut before cooking. Wrap the dough in plastic wrap and refrigerate it for up to 24 hours or freeze it for up to 2 months. If working with refrigerated dough, let the dough come to room temperature on the counter, 2 to 3 hours, then roll it out. If working with frozen dough, thaw it in the fridge, then let it come to room temperature on the counter before rolling it out.

the dough ball on a floured surface, cover with a damp cloth, and let stand at room temperature for 1 hour before rolling. This will help the dough relax and make it much easier to work with. (If you're thinking ahead for tomorrow's dinner, the dough can be wrapped in plastic wrap and chilled in the fridge overnight at this point.)

3. Divide the dough in half. Lightly flour and cover one piece with a damp towel to keep it from drying out. Flatten the other piece into a disc and use a rolling pin to roll the dough into a long, ¼-inch-thick rectangle that's no wider than your pasta maker. With the pasta machine on the thickest setting, feed it through the rollers. Repeat.

4. Fold the rolled-out piece into thirds and press it between your hands once again into a disc. This process will ensure silky smooth, lighter-than-air pasta noodles.

5. Continue passing the dough sheet through the machine, sending it through twice and then lowering the setting. If the dough sheet becomes too long or hard to manage, cut it in half. I tend to stop at the second-to-last setting on my machine, which works best for tagliatelle or pappardelle. But the thickness is most definitely up to you and the requirements of the recipe. Repeat with the second piece of dough.

6. Shape and cut the pasta into noodles by hand or with your chosen pasta cutters. Toss the cut pasta in a little flour to keep the noodles from sticking together.

7. When the pasta (and your sauce of choice) is ready to rock, bring a large pot of salted water to a rapid boil (see page 82 for tips). Add the pasta. Fresh pasta cooks at lightning speed, between 1 and 3 minutes, so watch it like a hawk. To check if it's finished, remove a piece with a pair of tongs and take a bite.

MARINARA SAUCE

MAKES ABOUT 3½ CUPS • Marinara, you're a treasure. Timeless, ready in a flash, and so versatile, this saucy business slays on almost everything. Try adding your favorite veggies, like red peppers or zucchini, or use it to dunk mozza sticks, or serve it alongside crispy calamari, or simply toss it as is with pasta—the possibilities are endless. Whatever your goal, you'll be properly started on a direct path toward deliciousness.

¼ cup olive oil

5 garlic cloves, minced

1 (28-ounce) can crushed tomatoes

1 teaspoon minced fresh basil stems

1 teaspoon kosher salt

¼ teaspoon red pepper flakes

1. In a 3-quart saucepan, heat the olive oil over medium heat. When hot, add the garlic and sauté for 30 seconds, taking care that the garlic does not brown.

2. Stir in the tomatoes, basil, salt, and red pepper flakes and bring to a simmer. Let the sauce simmer away for 10 minutes, stirring every now and then, until thickened.

3. This marinara stores perfectly! Let cool to room temperature, then store in an airtight container in the fridge for up to 1 week or in the freezer for up to 3 months.

Pasta & Sauce
THE BEST OF FRIENDS

In the world of pasta, certain noodles marry exceptionally well with certain sauces, like they were meant to be together. Of course, most every combination will taste delicious, but properly pairing pasta with its intended saucy counterpart will result in next-level *mangiare*. Here are some of the sauce recipes featured in this book, highlighting sauce-and-noodle best friends, with a few bonus options to help keep things fun and fresh in the kitchen.

BASIL PESTO SAUCE (page 106). I love pesto tossed with pasta, dolloped on a pizza, stirred into risotto, spooned over fish, or served with a killer steak. When served with pasta tubes like rigatoni, penne, or macaroni, pesto works its way into every nook and cranny, guaranteeing perfection with each and every bite.

LEMON GARLIC AND WHITE WINE SAUCE (page 90). Tailor-made for long, flat noodles, this sauce is incredible served with steamed white fish or mussels. The recipe also works perfectly with seared scallops, lobster, or haddock.

ROASTED GARLIC CREAM SAUCE

(page 102). This recipe works smashingly with long, flat noodles like linguine, spaghetti, and vermicelli. If you're feeling up for a challenge, might I recommend homemade lemon and ricotta-filled ravioli tossed in this sauce, with extra Parmesan and a nice glass of white wine? Date-night-at-home perfection.

MARINARA SAUCE (page 87). What a

hero! The Sinatra of sauces. Perfect with spaghetti, gnocchi, penne, or cheese-filled ravioli; for dunking calamari (page 235); or even for spooning over crispy chicken Parmesan, marinara does it all.

BOLOGNESE SAUCE (page 92). Spaghetti

with bolognese is as classic a combination as they come, but let's not stop there. I love pairing this weeknight hero sauce with hearty noodles like pappardelle or fettuccine, tossed with penne and baked with a covering of fresh mozzarella, or as a base sauce for homemade lasagna.

CHEESE SAUCE (page 96). Cheese sauce is

everything, and the absolute height of comfort food. A perfect match with almost every noodle in your pantry. For non-pasta-related eats, this sauciness is incredible on nachos, spooned over grilled brats, with garlicky flatbread, or as a warm pretzel dip.

HOMEMADE TAGLIATELLE WITH SHRIMP, ASPARAGUS, AND CHERRY TOMATOES

MAKES 4 TO 6 SERVINGS • First off, you've made homemade pasta. That's so awesome! Now go one step further and truly finish that experience with a bang. This rustic cracker of a dish comes together like a dream, is light and fragrant, and tastes of summertime at the sea. A guaranteed-to-impress, knockout dish.

1 recipe Homemade Fresh Pasta dough (page 84)

All-purpose flour, for the pasta

¼ cup olive oil

1 pound jumbo shrimp, peeled and deveined (see opposite)

4 garlic cloves, thinly sliced

½ cup dry white wine

¼ teaspoon red pepper flakes

1 tablespoon lemon zest

2 cups cherry tomatoes, halved

10 asparagus spears, trimmed and cut into 2-inch pieces

4 tablespoons (½ stick) butter, at room temperature

½ teaspoon sea salt

¼ teaspoon freshly cracked black pepper

1 tablespoon fresh lemon juice

¼ cup fresh flat-leaf parsley leaves, minced

1. Prepare the pasta dough, rolling it out to the second-to-lowest thickness setting (or the thickness of your choice). Fold the long pasta sheets over themselves and cut them into flat, ¼-inch-wide noodles. Don't worry too much about precision—rustic noodles are kind of awesome.

2. Toss the pasta with a little flour to keep the noodles from sticking together, then curl them into five or six pasta nests. Cover with a damp cloth and set aside.

3. Bring a large pot of salted water to a boil (see page 82 for tips).

4. In a large skillet, heat the olive oil over medium heat. Add the shrimp and cook for 3 to 4 minutes, turning halfway through, until they start to turn pink. Remove with a slotted spoon and set aside, reserving the oil in the pan.

5. Add the garlic and sauté for 30 seconds. Add the wine, red pepper flakes, lemon zest, cherry tomatoes, and asparagus and bring to a simmer. Cook for 4 to 5 minutes, until the asparagus is softened but still firm to the bite—al dente all around!

6. Meanwhile, cook the pasta in the boiling water for 2 minutes. While the pasta is cooking, stir the butter, sea salt, black pepper, lemon juice, and shrimp into the sauce. Use tongs to transfer the pasta directly from the boiling water to the skillet and toss it with the sauce.

7. Sprinkle the parsley on top and serve.

Deveining is removing the dark-colored intestinal tube from the back of a shrimp. Using a sharp knife, carefully make a slight incision through the back of a shrimp, then use the knife tip to remove the "vein" itself. Your fishmonger may have already done this, or might be happy to do so.

SPAGHETTI BOLOGNESE

MAKES 4 TO 6 SERVINGS • All Hail the King of the Weeknight Meal, Spaghetti Bolognese! Families all over the world rely on this humble dish week in and week out because it's a breeze to throw together, you can sneak so many delicious and healthy vegetables into that gorgeous sauce, it easily feeds a crowd, and the sauce freezes perfectly. So much win!

3 tablespoons olive oil

3 garlic cloves, minced

1 large onion, diced fine

2 large carrots, finely diced

3 celery stalks, finely diced

Leaves from 2 rosemary sprigs, minced

1 tablespoon minced fresh basil stems

½ teaspoon red pepper flakes

1 pound best-quality ground beef

½ teaspoon sea salt, plus more as needed

2 cups red wine

1 cup beef stock

1 (28-ounce) can diced tomatoes

1 pound uncooked spaghetti

1 cup grated Parmesan cheese, plus more for serving

½ cup fresh basil leaves, cut into chiffonade, plus a few whole leaves for serving

½ teaspoon freshly cracked black pepper

Fresh parsley

1. In a large stockpot or Dutch oven, heat 2 tablespoons of the olive oil over medium heat. Add the garlic and sauté for 30 seconds, keeping a close watch so it doesn't burn. Stir in the onion, carrots, celery, rosemary, basil stems, and red pepper flakes and cook for 5 to 6 minutes, until the vegetables have started to soften. Add the beef and salt and cook, breaking up the meat with a wooden spoon as it cooks, for 5 minutes or until the meat is browned. Add the wine and bring to a simmer. Cook until the liquid has reduced by half, about 5 minutes.

2. Add the stock and tomatoes and bring to a simmer. Reduce the heat to medium-low and let the sauce bubble away, uncovered, for 40 minutes, giving it a stir every now and then so it doesn't stick to the pan.

3. When the sauce has about 15 minutes of cooking time remaining, bring a pot of salted water to a boil (see page 82 for tips) and cook the pasta according to the package directions. Drain, reserving ¼ cup of the cooking liquid.

4. When the sauce is done, remove it from the heat and stir in the cheese and basil leaves. Give the sauce a taste and season with a pinch each of salt and black pepper. Add the reserved cooking liquid and the pasta and toss to combine.

5. Transfer to a serving dish, drizzle with the remaining 1 tablespoon olive oil, and top with a bit more grated cheese, a few whole basil leaves, and fresh parsley.

SUMMERTIME PASTA SALAD

MAKES 6 TO 8 SERVINGS • Though we first met at French camp (yes, that's a real thing), my wife and I started properly hanging out in high school (insert hard-core high school sweetheart humblebrag here).

One of Leanne's absolute favorite things growing up, and the first dish I had to eat at her parents' house, was her mom's pasta salad—super quick, easy, and a family reunion staple. Here is my pimped-out version of the salad I've eaten every summer for almost twenty years. It's delicious warm but perfect if prepared in advance and given a cool home in the fridge for a few hours.

SAUCE

¾ cup ketchup

½ cup packed dark brown sugar

½ cup sunflower oil

2 tablespoons fresh lemon juice

¼ cup apple cider vinegar

¼ teaspoon sea salt

¼ teaspoon freshly cracked black pepper

PASTA

1 pound uncooked fusilli or rotini pasta

1 cup diced bell red pepper

1 cup diced bell green pepper

1 cup diced bell yellow pepper

1 cup cherry tomatoes, halved

1 cup diced cucumber

½ cup finely diced red onion

⅓ cup chopped fresh basil leaves, plus more for garnish

⅓ cup chopped fresh flat-leaf parsley leaves, plus more for garnish

1 cup bocconcini (mini mozzarella balls), halved

1. Make the sauce: Combine the ketchup, brown sugar, sunflower oil, lemon juice, and vinegar in a bowl and whisk until the sauce starts to thicken. Season with the salt and pepper.

2. Make the pasta: Bring a large pot of salted water to a boil (see page 82 for tips) and cook the pasta according to the package directions. Drain and run under cold water to chill and stop the cooking process. Transfer the pasta to a large bowl.

3. Add the bell peppers, tomatoes, cucumber, onion, and sauce to the bowl with the pasta. Stir to combine, then stir in the basil and parsley. Transfer to a large serving dish and top with the bocconcini and more basil and parsley leaves.

4. This salad can be served immediately, but it's particularly delicious when chilled in the fridge for a few hours. If you preplan like a boss, this recipe can be made a day in advance and kept in an airtight container in the fridge.

CREAMY LOBSTER MAC AND CHEESE

MAKES 4 TO 6 SERVINGS • Mac and cheese is the undefeated reigning champ of pasta-grade comfort food. It's everything that a big bowl of happy, euphoric food should be: extra saucy, extra cheesy, and perfectly carb loaded. As a lad who was raised on the boxed stuff poorly attempting to impersonate a proper mac, I can unequivocally guarantee this: Scratch-made is infinitely, life-changingly better. One bite of real and fake is forever ruined.

Here is my go-to mac, Maritime-style. Loaded with fresh lobster and topped with a lemony bread crumb crunch, this is the ultimate feel-good dish.

LOBSTERS AND PASTA

2 (1¼-pound) live lobsters (about ¾ pound lobster meat)

1 pound uncooked pasta shells

1 tablespoon olive oil

SAUCE

3 tablespoons butter, at room temperature

1 garlic clove, minced

2 tablespoons all-purpose flour

3 cups whole milk

½ teaspoon Dijon mustard

¼ teaspoon cayenne pepper

½ teaspoon smoked paprika

½ teaspoon sea salt

½ teaspoon freshly cracked black pepper

2 cups grated aged cheddar cheese

2 cups grated Gruyère cheese

½ cup grated Parmesan cheese

1. Preheat the oven to 350°F.

2. Cook the lobsters and pasta: Bring a large pot of salted water to a boil and prepare an ice bath in a large bowl. Carefully submerge the live lobsters in the boiling water (you can do it!!), cover, and boil for 8 to 10 minutes, until the lobster shells have turned bright red. Immediately transfer the cooked lobsters to the ice bath to cool.

3. Crack the lobster shells and remove the meat from the bodies, claws, knuckles, and anywhere else lobster meat is hiding. Cut it into ½-inch chunks, leaving the claw meat whole if possible (they're the prize at the bottom of the Cracker Jack box). Transfer the meat to a bowl and set aside.

4. Bring the lobster cooking liquid back to a boil. Add the pasta and cook according to the package directions (al dente, of course). As the pasta cooks, it will soak in all that lobstery goodness. Drain and toss with the olive oil. Pour the pasta into a large casserole dish.

5. Make the sauce: In a 3-quart saucepan, melt the butter over medium-low heat. Add the garlic and gently cook for 30 seconds. Add the flour and cook, stirring continuously,

for 2 minutes, or until it begins to brown and develops a nutty aroma. Still stirring, add the milk in a slow and steady stream, making sure that all the flour has worked its way into the milk. Stirring away, let the sauce come to a gentle simmer and thicken, 4 to 5 minutes.

6. Turn the heat to low and stir in the mustard, cayenne, paprika, salt, and pepper. Stir in the cheeses, 1 cup at a time, until they have melted and the sauce is silky smooth.

7. Pour the sauce over the cooked pasta, add the lobster, and fold the lot together.

BREAD CRUMB CRUNCH

- **½ cup grated Parmesan cheese**
- **½ cup panko bread crumbs**
- **1 teaspoon lemon zest**
- **½ teaspoon freshly cracked black pepper**
- **1 tablespoon chopped fresh flat-leaf parsley, plus more leaves for garnish**
- **3 tablespoons olive oil**

8. Make the bread crumb crunch: In a small bowl, combine all the ingredients and stir to combine.

9. Top the pasta with the bread crumb mixture and bake for 15 to 20 minutes, until the bread crumbs have turned golden brown. Garnish with fresh parsley and serve immediately.

HOMEMADE GNOCCHI

MAKES 6 TO 8 SERVINGS • Gnocchi is love. Soft little pillows of heavenly love. My first almost-romantic encounter with a luxurious plate of gnocchi took place in Washington, DC, while en route to Nashville and our big move to Music City. It was a terrifying/surreal/wonderful time in my life, and well before I was able to cook, well . . . anything.

We were in a small, quaint, and all-too-dreamy Italian joint—dark and moody with candlelight and Chet Baker giving us the major feels. Maybe it was the ambience, maybe it was the food, maybe it was the accordion player who randomly appeared halfway through our dinner to serenade us with old-school Italian classics, but it was one of the most memorable and inspiring meals of my life.

Gnocchi is proof that the best things in life are simple, humble, and well prepared, with an extra pinch of love and care.

2¼ pounds russet potatoes (about 4 large)

1¾ cups all-purpose flour, plus more for dusting

2 large free-range egg yolks

1½ teaspoons kosher salt

1. Wash and scrub the potatoes (do not peel—the skin helps to ensure that the potatoes don't absorb too much water). Place the spuds in a large pot of cold water and bring to a boil over medium-high heat. Cook for about 20 minutes, until fork-tender. Drain and let the potatoes cool until they are still warm but workable.

2. Peel the potatoes—the skins will easily rub off using your hands or a kitchen towel. Using a potato ricer, rice the potatoes into a large bowl. (If you don't have a potato ricer, the small holes of a box grater will do in a pinch.) Turn the potatoes out onto a lightly floured surface and shape into a mound.

3. Using your hands, make a well in the center of the potatoes. Whisk the egg yolks lightly and pour them into the well along with the flour and salt. Using a fork, start to pull the flour and potatoes into the yolks until combined. Using your hands, pull together the ingredients and knead just until a smooth, soft dough forms. Keep a little flour and water at the

ready, just in case. If the dough is too wet, add a little flour. Too dry, add a little water.

4. Divide the dough into six pieces. Using the palms of your hands and working on a floured surface, gently roll each piece into a long rope that's about 1 inch around. Slice the rope on an angle into ½-inch-wide gnocchi.

5. Bring a large pot of salted water to a rapid boil (see page 82 for tips) and gently add the gnocchi. Cook until they start to float to the surface, about 2 minutes. Remove with a slotted spoon or very gently drain, taking care to not break the gnocchi.

6. Toss with your sauce of choice, or make the Cheesy Marinara Gnocchi Bake (page 100). *Mangia. Bellissimo!*

CHEESY MARINARA GNOCCHI BAKE

MAKES 4 TO 6 SERVINGS • If gnocchi, pizza, and baked pasta started hanging out (a party we'd all love to be invited to, right? Right!), this is what they'd dream up. This dish is best served on a cool evening with a nice glass of wine while binge-watching your favorite show and sporting a solid pair of stretchy pants.

¼ **cup plus 2 teaspoons olive oil**

5 **garlic cloves, finely minced**

1 **(28-ounce) can crushed tomatoes**

1 **cup chicken stock, store-bought or homemade (page 149)**

¼ **teaspoon dried oregano**

1 **teaspoon red pepper flakes plus more for serving**

1 **teaspoon sea salt**

¾ **teaspoon freshly cracked black pepper**

1 **recipe Homemade Gnocchi (page 98), prepped and ready**

7 **ounces fresh mozzarella cheese**

Handful of fresh basil leaves, for garnish

Grated Parmesan cheese, for serving

1. Preheat the oven to 350°F.

2. In a large high-sided skillet, heat ¼ cup of the olive oil over medium heat. When hot, add the garlic and sauté it for 30 seconds (keep a close watch so that it doesn't burn). Stir in the tomatoes, stock, oregano, ½ teaspoon of the red pepper flakes, the salt, and ½ teaspoon of the black pepper and bring to a simmer. Cook for 5 minutes, then set aside off the heat.

3. Bring a large pot of salted water to a rapid boil (see page 82 for tips), gently add the gnocchi, and cook until they start to float to the surface, about 2 minutes. Remove with a slotted spoon or very gently drain, taking care not to break the gnocchi.

4. Gently add the gnocchi to the warm marinara sauce and fold them together. Break the fresh mozzarella into small pieces and scatter them on top. Sprinkle on the remaining ½ teaspoon red pepper flakes and ¼ teaspoon black pepper, and drizzle the remaining 2 teaspoons olive oil on top.

5. Bake for 15 to 20 minutes, until the cheese has melted and you almost can't stand how mouthwatering your house smells.

6. Top with fresh basil and an extra hit of red pepper flakes. Serve with grated Parmesan cheese.

CRISPY PORK BELLY LINGUINE

MAKES 4 TO 6 SERVINGS • Crispy pork belly and fragrant roasted garlic in a rich and cheesy cream sauce. Sweet mercy! Has there ever been a more beautifully mouth-watering sentence uttered on this planet? Alfredo-style and cream-based sauces are my love language. They're almost universally adored and so easy to customize, with many of the veggies or meats already camping out in your fridge pairing perfectly well with the sauce.

This dish will most certainly never show up on a weight-loss diet plan, but we all need to let our hair down and binge on goodness every once in a while.

ROASTED GARLIC

1 large garlic head, unpeeled
1 teaspoon olive oil
Pinch of sea salt
Pinch of freshly cracked black pepper

PASTA

1 tablespoon olive oil
½ pound best-quality pork belly, cut into ½-inch chunks
1 tablespoon minced fresh oregano leaves
½ cup dry white wine, such as Pinot Grigio
1½ cups heavy cream
1 teaspoon lemon zest
¼ teaspoon sea salt
1 pound uncooked linguine noodles
⅓ pound Broccolini
¼ teaspoon freshly cracked black pepper
½ cup grated Parmesan cheese
2 tablespoons chopped fresh flat-leaf parsley leaves

1. Make the roasted garlic: Preheat the oven to 400°F.

2. Using a sharp knife, slice about ⅛ inch off the top of the garlic head (leaving the root end intact), exposing the individual garlic cloves. Drizzle the olive oil on top and season with the salt and pepper. Tightly wrap the bulb in aluminum foil and roast for 30 to 35 minutes, until the cloves are soft. Set aside.

3. Make the pasta: Heat a large skillet over medium heat. Add the olive oil and pork belly and cook, stirring often, until crispy, 8 to 10 minutes.

4. Set the pork aside on a plate and drain the excess grease from the skillet, reserving 1 tablespoon in the pan.

5. Squeeze the roasted garlic from the bulb and transfer it to a cutting board. Mash the garlic into a paste with a fork.

6. Add the pork belly, oregano, and garlic paste to the pan and fry over medium heat, stirring continuously, for 1 minute. Add the wine, bring to a simmer, and cook until reduced slightly, 2 minutes. Stir in the cream, lemon zest, and salt and bring back to a simmer. Turn the heat to medium-low and gently simmer until the sauce is thick and gorgeous, 5 to 6 minutes.

7. Bring a large pot of salted water to a boil (see page 82 for tips) and cook the pasta according to the package directions.

8. Remove and discard ½ inch from the tough ends of the Broccolini stalks. When there's about 4 minutes of cooking time left on the pasta, add the Broccolini to the pasta pot to cook. Scoop out 2 to 3 tablespoons of the cooking water and reserve.

9. Drain the pasta and Broccolini and mix the reserved cooking liquid into the sauce. Add the pasta and Broccolini to the sauce and toss with the pepper, Parmesan, and parsley.

RISOTTO WITH BACON, MUSHROOMS, AND THYME

MAKES 4 TO 6 SERVINGS • Risotto may very well be the most romantic dish on the planet. It's all about time, love, and tenderness (if you're now humming a Michael Bolton song, that's my bad. I'm truly sorry #notsorry). It's really low and slow cooking that takes a little extra time and patience—risotto is the ultimate glass-of-wine-in-hand-while-listening-to-a-fantastic-record dish. Pro tip—I highly recommend Miles Davis, John Coltrane, or anything by Chet Baker. Perfect risotto-ing tunes. You sip, you hum, you stir, you sip a little more, you stir a little more.

Making risotto takes a little practice. The key is in gently cooking the rice, letting it soak in all that gorgeous broth while stirring almost continuously. Don't rush or increase the heat to try to cut down on the cooking time. Be patient with it. And be sure to taste the risotto at several stages along the way, so you know exactly where the rice is in the cooking process and how the flavors are developing.

MUSHROOMS

- 3 smoked bacon slices, diced
- 4 cups thinly sliced mixed mushrooms
- 2 teaspoons fresh thyme leaves
- 1 garlic clove, minced
- ½ teaspoon sea salt
- ½ teaspoon freshly cracked black pepper

RISOTTO

- 8 cups chicken stock, store-bought or homemade (page 149)
- 3 tablespoons butter
- 2 tablespoons olive oil
- 2 garlic cloves, minced
- 3 medium celery stalks, finely diced

1. Make the mushrooms: Heat a large high-sided skillet over medium heat and fry the bacon, turning often, until crispy, 5 to 6 minutes. Add the mushrooms, thyme, and garlic and season with the salt and pepper. Cook the mushrooms for 5 minutes, until they have started to brown and soften. Transfer to a dish and set aside.

2. Make the risotto: In a medium saucepan, heat the stock until simmering, then reduce the heat to low to keep warm.

3. Heat a large skillet over medium heat and add 2 tablespoons of the butter and the olive oil. When the butter has almost finished melting, add the garlic and sauté for 30 seconds, taking care that it doesn't burn. Add the celery and onion, season with the sea salt, and cook for 5 to 6 minutes, until the onion is translucent.

4. Add the rice and cook, stirring continuously to let the rice soak in that delicious butter and oil, for about 30 seconds.

1 medium onion, finely diced

¼ teaspoon sea salt

2 cups risotto rice

2 cups dry white wine,
   such as Pinot Grigio or
   Sauvignon Blanc

½ cup grated Parmesan
   cheese, plus more for
   serving

Freshly cracked black pepper

Fresh parsley, for garnish

5. Add the wine and cook, stirring, until it has almost entirely been absorbed into the rice. Turn the heat to medium-low. While stirring slowly and almost continuously, add about ½ cup of the stock. Continue stirring until most of the stock has been absorbed by the rice, then add another ½ cup and stir. Repeat, and repeat again. The risotto should never be dry. Keep repeating until about 7 cups of the stock have made their way into the rice. The entire process should take around 30 minutes, the perfect time to enjoy a nice jazz record and a glass of the good stuff.

6. Check on the risotto—at this point it should still have a little bite but be tender and almost ready to rock. Stir in the remaining 1 cup stock and let it reduce and thicken.

7. Remove the risotto from the heat and fold in the mushrooms, cheese, remaining 1 tablespoon butter, and pepper. Garnish with fresh parsley and serve with extra cheese. Heaven.

RIGATONI WITH RICOTTA AND BASIL PESTO

MAKES 4 SERVINGS • Confession time: I do not have a green thumb. I genuinely aspire to gardening greatness, and have mad love for home cooks and chefs who grow their own veggies. Up to this point in my life, though, epic fail. My tomatoes, beets, green peas . . . no love whatsoever. Recently, though, the times are a-changing, thanks to homegrown herbs, which I've been (shockingly) successful at keeping alive, including thyme, rosemary, mint, chives, and my forever love, basil. Being able to walk a few short steps to my backyard garden and pick fresh herbs is a dream come true.

My love of pesto was a big driver in my attempts to grow herbs. Homemade pesto is super quick and easy to assemble and absolutely bursting with fresh, vibrant flavors. Ready and on the table in about 20 minutes, this rigatoni with pesto is tailor-made for a quick weeknight meal at home.

PESTO

2 cups packed fresh basil leaves

2 garlic cloves, coarsely chopped

¼ cup pine nuts

¼ teaspoon sea salt

⅔ cup extra-virgin olive oil

½ cup grated Parmesan cheese

¼ teaspoon freshly cracked black pepper

PASTA

1 pound dried rigatoni

1 tablespoon fresh lemon juice

1 cup ricotta cheese

Red pepper flakes

Extra-virgin olive oil

⅓ cup grated Parmesan cheese

1. Make the pesto: In a food processor, combine the basil, garlic, pine nuts, and sea salt. Pulse until finely chopped, scraping down the sides of the bowl if necessary. With the processor running on low, slowly drizzle in the oil until the pesto is smooth and creamy. Transfer to a bowl and fold in the Parmesan and black pepper.

2. Make the pasta: Bring a large saucepan of salted water to a boil (see page 82 for tips) and cook the pasta according to the package directions. Drain, reserving 2 tablespoons of the cooking liquid.

3. Transfer the pasta to a large bowl and toss with the pesto, reserved cooking liquid, and lemon juice.

4. Portion the pasta into four bowls and top each bowl with ¼ cup of the ricotta, red pepper flakes, and a drizzle of olive oil. Top with the grated Parmesan and serve.

When summer basil is in perfect form, I love to make a few batches of pesto and freeze them for later use. Just prepare the pesto, omitting the cheese and using ½ cup (rather than ⅔ cup) of oil in the food processor. Transfer the pesto to an airtight container, cover with a couple tablespoons of olive oil to prevent oxidation, and freeze for up to 3 months. When ready to use, thaw and stir in the cheese.

So you've grown your very own herb garden, but the seasons are a-changing and frost is imminent. How do you save your hard-grown work, ensuring that your kitchen tastes of summertime all year round? Grab some ice cube trays. Fill the wells two-thirds full of herbs (whatever combination suits your fancy), then top with extra-virgin olive oil. Freeze overnight. Transfer the cubes to freezer bags and use to your heart's delight. Perfect in sautés, soups, stews, roasts, pastas . . . you get the point.

4

Pizza. I Love You.

PIZZA. IT'S THE BEST THING. EVER.

Whether you're winning life in ancient Napoli with a classic Margherita, enjoying a slice of the Big Apple's finest, or face-diving into a Chicago-style deep dish, pizza is almost universally loved and undeniably delicious. Over the past few years I've enjoyed a slice of the good stuff in New York City, Toronto, London, Nairobi, Addis Ababa, and even in a hotel in Hargeisa, Somaliland. Some slices where certainly more memorable than others, but each was full of comfort and nostalgia, and absolutely bursting with happiness and good vibes. I've got mad love for you, pizza. Thanks for making the world a better place.

Perfect pizza at home is all about the crust. That crisp on the outside, soft as a pillow on the inside, restaurant style, bad-to-the-bone crust. I've found these three simple tips to be absolute musts for game-changing crust at home.

1. YOU NEED A PIZZA STONE.

The better the crust, the better the pie—it's that simple. The recipes in this chapter assume that you have a pizza stone (or a baking stone or Baking Steel) at the ready in your home. Pizza stones get wicked hot, retain heat perfectly, and help to perfectly capture the balance of a crispy outer crust with a soft, heavenly inner crust. It's the closest thing to a wood-fired oven that most of us will have available.

2. HIGH HEAT.

Sky high, in fact: 550°F. Using a pizza stone preheated in super-high heat is how home cooks are able to develop that slightly charred, bubbling top crust and perfect crisp bottom crust. For best results, allow the stone to heat for 30 minutes prior to baking. If your oven doesn't go as high as 550°F, fear not! Just turn up that dude as high as it'll go and add a couple of minutes onto the cooking time, keeping an eye on your pie.

3. A PIZZA PEEL AND SOME PARCHMENT PAPER = A STRESS-FREE COOK.

This is my go-to method for transferring pizza in and out of the oven (thanks, Internet, you're awesome). Place a piece of parchment paper that's slightly larger than the width of the pizza dough on top of a pizza peel. Top the parchment paper with the rolled-out dough and build the pie. When the pizza is ready to go, slide it (along with the parchment paper) into the preheated oven. The parchment will help the pizza slide easily off the peel. Close the oven door and wait for 45 seconds to 1 minute. Using a pair of oven mitts, quickly and carefully slide the parchment out from underneath the pizza, bracing the pizza crust with the peel to keep the pie where it is while you remove the parchment. Quick and easy in one fluid motion should get the job done. Carry on cooking the pizza and remove it with the pizza peel when done.

PIZZA DOUGH (ALL ABOUT THAT BASE)

MAKES TWO 12-INCH PIES • I look forward to Friday evening every week, and not because I have a curmudgeon of a boss barking orders at me on the daily. In fact, I'm madly in love with my job (hey, writing this is work! Cray). And not because the stresses of work life are quelled by a weekend evening full of chill and a nice glass of red. No, I look forward to the weekend for one simple reason: Every Friday night at the Prescott house is pizza night. Like clockwork. Delicious, rapturous, hella awesome clockwork. For years now we've been rocking this steadfast tradition, with zero plans of breaking the mold any time soon. This is our go-to pizza dough recipe. Tried, tested, and true blue.

2 teaspoons active dry yeast

1 tablespoon honey

1 cup plus 5 tablespoons lukewarm water

1½ cups all-purpose flour, plus more for dusting

1½ cups "00" flour (see page 29)

2 tablespoons olive oil

1 teaspoon sea salt

1. In a large bowl, combine the yeast, honey, and water and stir well. Let the yeast activate, bubble, and come to life, about 10 minutes.

2. Add the flours, olive oil, and salt and stir with a wooden spoon until a mass of dough begins to form. Turn the dough out onto a floured surface and get those arm muscles ready. Knead away until a soft dough ball forms, about 10 minutes.

3. Transfer the dough to a lightly oiled bowl and cover with plastic wrap. Give the bowl a home in a warm spot in the kitchen and let the dough double in size, about 1½ hours. (If you're a planner, this can also be done the night before. At this point, cover with plastic wrap and chill in the fridge overnight. The next day, warm the dough on the counter for 30 minutes before proceeding to step 4.)

4. Punch down the dough and transfer to a lightly floured surface. Divide the dough into two equal portions and shape into individual balls of dough.

5. Working one a time, roll the dough out with a rolling pin into two 12-inch circles. If they're not perfect circles, no worries— your pizzas will still taste delicious.

6. Now build your pizzas. Top/cook/enter pizza happy zone.

THE PIZZA SAUCE OF YOUR DREAMS

MAKES ABOUT 2 CUPS • Pizza sauce is secondary in importance only to the crust in the foundation of a truly legendary pie. The good news? Homemade pizza sauce tastes outstanding and is totally simple to bang together, well worth the small effort. This is my beloved pizza sauce recipe, made each and every week at home. We often have a bit of sauce left over and I love it served alongside grilled shrimp or squid, or slathered on classic chicken Parmesan.

1 tablespoon butter

2 tablespoons olive oil

½ cup onion, diced

1 garlic clove, minced

1½ cups crushed tomatoes or tomato puree

¼ cup tomato paste

2 tablespoons grated Parmesan cheese

1 teaspoon dried oregano

½ teaspoon sea salt

½ teaspoon freshly cracked black pepper

1 bay leaf

1. In a 3-quart saucepan, melt the butter with the olive oil over medium heat. Stir in the onion and garlic and sauté for 5 minutes, until softened. Add the remaining ingredients and bring the sauce to a simmer. Reduce the heat to medium-low and gently simmer for 30 minutes.

2. Remove from the heat and discard the bay leaf, then puree the sauce directly in the pot with an immersion blender until smooth. (Alternatively, carefully transfer the sauce to a regular blender and puree until smooth; be careful when blending hot liquids.) The sauce will keep in an airtight container in the fridge for several days.

PROSCIUTTO, FRESH MOZZARELLA, AND BASIL PIE

MAKES TWO 12-INCH PIES • I've learned that simple dishes made with top-quality ingredients (and an extra dash of love) are always best. They're the joy makers, laced with nostalgia, and the dishes that tend to find a permanent home on family meal plans. Made with fresh mozzarella, prosciutto, and fragrant basil leaves, this pie is simply spectacular.

1 recipe Pizza Dough (page 112)

1 cup The Pizza Sauce of Your Dreams (page 113)

½ teaspoon dried oregano

8 ounces fresh mozzarella cheese

2 teaspoons olive oil

3½ ounces thinly sliced prosciutto

¼ cup fresh basil leaves, finely sliced

1. Place a pizza stone in the oven and preheat the oven to 550°F for at least 30 minutes (if your oven doesn't go that high, see page 110).

2. Roll out the dough into two 12-inch rounds and transfer to parchment paper according to the directions on page 112. Spread ½ cup of the pizza sauce on each dough round, leaving 1 inch around the edges bare.

3. For each pie, sprinkle ¼ teaspoon of the oregano over the sauce, break up the mozzarella with your hands and scatter it over, and drizzle with the olive oil.

4. Working one at a time, transfer the pies to the preheated oven as directed on page 110 and bake for 6 to 8 minutes, until the cheese has melted and the crust is nice and crispy.

5. Top the cooked pizzas with the prosciutto and basil. Cut into slices with a pizza cutter and enjoy.

MEATBALL PIZZA, THE FRIEND MAKER

MAKES TWO 12-INCH PIES • Of course two of the world's greatest comfort foods—meatballs and pizza—were predestined to be together. It was fate! I've named this recipe the Friend Maker because, like it or not, if you start making food like this at home, your popularity is bound to skyrocket.

MEATBALLS

1 pound best-quality ground beef (80% lean)

1 large free-range egg

½ cup panko bread crumbs

¼ cup whole milk

¼ cup grated Parmesan cheese

1 teaspoon dried oregano

½ teaspoon garlic powder

½ teaspoon red pepper flakes

¼ teaspoon onion powder

½ teaspoon sea salt

¼ teaspoon freshly cracked black pepper

PIES

1 recipe Pizza Dough (page 112)

1 cup The Pizza Sauce of Your Dreams (page 113)

8 ounces fresh mozzarella cheese

4 teaspoons olive oil

¼ cup fresh basil leaves, cut into chiffonade

¼ cup grated Parmesan cheese

1. Place a pizza stone in the oven and preheat the oven to 450°F. Line a large baking sheet with parchment paper.

2. Make the meatballs: Combine all the meatball ingredients in a large bowl and mix gently with your hands. Roll the mixture into golf ball–size balls in the palms of your hands (you'll end up with 14 to 16 meatballs). If the meatballs look a little big, fear not! They will shrink as they cook. Set the meatballs on the prepared baking sheet, leaving at least 1 inch of space between each, and bake for 15 minutes, or until nicely browned and cooked through. Set aside.

3. Make the pizza: Increase the oven temperature to 550°F and let the pizza stone preheat for 30 minutes.

4. Roll out the dough into two 12-inch rounds and transfer to parchment paper according to the directions on page 112. Spread ½ cup of the pizza sauce on each dough round, leaving 1 inch around the edges bare. Divide the meatballs between the pizzas and break the mozzarella over the top. Drizzle 2 teaspoons of the olive oil over each pizza.

5. Working one at a time, transfer the pizzas to the preheated oven as directed on page 110 and bake for 6 to 8 minutes, until the crust is perfectly crisp, the cheese is melted, and your taste buds are going bananas.

6. Top with the basil and Parm, serve, and become a neighborhood legend.

PEAR, PROSCIUTTO, AND ARUGULA PIZZA WITH BALSAMIC REDUCTION

MAKES TWO 12-INCH PIES • This dish just screams summertime—al fresco dining with a cold beer in hand and a strong desire to chill. I love grilling this pie outside (which I highly recommend!), but it's perfectly delicious all year round. The combination of sweet honey and pear, spicy arugula, and rich balsamic reduction is just unreal.

1 recipe Pizza Dough
(page 112)

3 tablespoons olive oil

2 Bartlett pears, cored and
cut into thin slices

⅔ cup ricotta cheese

2 tablespoons honey

3½ ounces prosciutto, thinly
sliced

1 cup baby arugula

2 tablespoons balsamic
reduction (see Note)

1. Place a pizza stone in the oven and preheat the oven to 550°F for at least 30 minutes.

2. Roll out the dough into two 12-inch rounds and transfer to parchment paper according to the directions on page 112. Brush 1½ tablespoons of the olive oil on each dough round, leaving 1 inch around the edges bare.

3. Arrange the pear slices on the pies. Crumble the ricotta on top and drizzle the pies with the honey.

4. Working one at a time, transfer the pies to the preheated oven as directed on page 110 and bake for 6 to 8 minutes, until the pears have softened and the crust is browned and crispy.

5. Top each pizza with half the prosciutto and ½ cup of the arugula and drizzle on 1 tablespoon of the balsamic reduction.

NOTE: *Balsamic reduction can be made easily at home. Simply bring 1 cup balsamic vinegar to a simmer, then reduce to medium-low heat. Cook for about 30 minutes, or until the vinegar has reduced to ⅓ cup and thickened beautifully. You're cooking the vinegar down, so don't spend a fortune at the grocery store. A basic balsamic will work great and taste incredible. If you're short on time, most quality grocery stores or specialty shops now stock a good balsamic reduction option.*

If the sun is shining and the grill is free, try your hand at grilling this pie. Preheat the grill to the hottest temperature possible (550°F is genius), with one side of direct heat and one side of indirect heat. Blooming hot, y'all.

Prepare the dough as usual, brushing the top of each dough rough with olive oil. Working one at a time, slide the pizza onto the hot grill with a pizza peel, oil-side down, and brush the top of the pie with olive oil. Grill, uncovered, for 2 to 3 minutes on each side, until grill marks just start to form. Remove the pizza crust and quickly top with the pears, ricotta, and honey. Place the pizza back on the grill, cover, and grill until the pears have softened and the crust is golden brown and gorgeous, 3 to 5 minutes, keeping an eye on them so that the crust doesn't burn. If the crust seems to be inching toward the burn zone, shift the pizza to indirect heat. Repeat to make the second pie. Finish the pies with the rest of the toppings and serve.

BRUSCHETTA PIZZA

MAKES TWO 12-INCH PIES • Our hometown's local microbrewery has been killing it in the wood-fired pizza game for years. Back in 2005, we set up camp in Moncton, New Brunswick, and recorded the drums for my band's debut record. Every single evening we would convoy to the Pump House Brewery to chow down on pizza, drink brewskis, and laugh our faces off into the wee hours of the morning. Since then, we've adopted the joint as our local watering hole.

After eating more Pump House Margherita pizzas than I care to admit, I came up with this little doozy of a recipe. If you love bruschetta and you love pizza (so, everyone), then you're going to freak for this pie. This recipe is especially fantastic during the summer months, when local tomatoes and basil are at their peak.

4 Roma (plum) tomatoes

2 garlic cloves, minced

1 tablespoon plus 2 teaspoons olive oil

1 teaspoon balsamic vinegar

2 tablespoons finely sliced fresh basil leaves, plus whole leaves for garnish

¼ cup finely grated Parmesan cheese

⅛ teaspoon sea salt

1 recipe Pizza Dough (page 112)

1 cup The Pizza Sauce of Your Dreams (page 113)

8 ounces fresh mozzarella cheese

⅛ teaspoon freshly cracked black pepper

1. Place a pizza stone in the oven and preheat the oven to 550°F for at least 30 minutes.

2. Finely dice the tomatoes, discarding the seeds and excess tomato juice, and transfer to a large bowl. Add the garlic, 1 tablespoon of the olive oil, the balsamic vinegar, sliced basil, Parmesan, and sea salt. Mix well and set aside.

3. Roll out the dough into two 12-inch rounds and transfer to parchment paper according to the directions on page 112. Spread ½ cup of the pizza sauce on each dough round, leaving 1 inch around the edges bare.

4. Spoon half the bruschetta mixture over each pie, spreading it as evenly as possible over the pizza sauce while keeping the 1-inch edge clear. Break half of the mozzarella over each pie, dotting it in seven or eight places, drizzle over the remaining 2 teaspoons olive oil, and top with the pepper.

5. Working one at a time, transfer the pies to the preheated oven as directed on page 110 and bake for 6 to 8 minutes, until the cheese has melted and the crust is nice and crispy.

6. Top the pizzas with fresh basil leaves and serve. Delish!

ROASTED VEGGIE AND GOAT CHEESE PIZZA

MAKES TWO 12-INCH PIES • What's up, veggie lovers! Occasionally pizza night needs a little shakeup, a break from the same ol' (albeit delicious) red sauce routine we tend to get ourselves into. This garlic béchamel white sauce pie is chock-full of mouth-watering roasted veggies and topped with creamy goat cheese and fresh mozzarella. Divine! And all those veggies make this pizza healthy. Right?

ROASTED VEGGIES

4 ounces Broccolini

1 small red onion, halved and cut into half-moons (½ cup)

½ cup julienned red bell pepper

1 zucchini, sliced into rounds

1 cup Brussels sprouts, halved

2 tablespoons olive oil

½ teaspoon sea salt

½ teaspoon freshly cracked black pepper

GARLIC BÉCHAMEL

1½ tablespoons butter

1½ tablespoons all-purpose flour

2 garlic cloves, minced

1¼ cups whole milk

½ teaspoon sea salt

¼ teaspoon freshly cracked black pepper

PIES

1 recipe Pizza Dough (page 112)

4 ounces goat cheese, crumbled

4 ounces buffalo mozzarella cheese, torn

½ teaspoon red pepper flakes

2 teaspoons olive oil

1. Place a pizza stone in the oven and preheat the oven to 400°F.

2. Make the roasted veggies: In a large bowl, toss the veggies with the olive oil and season with the salt and pepper. Spread them on a large baking sheet and roast for 20 minutes, turning halfway through, or until the veggies are softened and starting to crisp on the edges. Set aside.

3. Increase the oven temperature to 550°F. Let the stone preheat for 30 minutes at this temperature.

4. Meanwhile, make the béchamel: In a small saucepan, melt the butter over medium heat. Whisk in the flour and garlic and cook for 1 minute, whisking to keep the garlic from burning. Whisking continuously, pour in the milk and bring it to a simmer. Cook, whisking away, for 5 minutes, until the sauce has thickened. Season with the salt and pepper and set aside.

5. Make the pies: Roll out the dough into two 12-inch rounds and transfer to parchment paper according to the directions on page 112. Spoon ½ cup of the béchamel sauce onto each pie, leaving 1 inch around the edges bare. Arrange half the veggies on each pie and top with the goat cheese, mozzarella, and red pepper flakes. Drizzle 1 teaspoon of the olive oil over each pie.

6. Working one at a time, transfer the pies to the preheated oven as directed on page 110 and bake the pizzas for 6 to 8 minutes, until the cheese has melted and the crust is gloriously golden brown.

BBQ CHICKEN PIZZA

MAKES TWO 12-INCH PIES • Leanne and I were married on a cold, snowy, all-too-romantic Canadian evening in early January, and the next morning we boarded a plane destined for sunny, gloriously beach-laden Santa Monica, California. We chose a local joint for our first West Coast meal. It was the first time I'd heard of BBQ chicken pizza. No doubt I was quite unfashionably late to the party, but that dish rocked my red sauce–lovin' pizza socks off. I've eaten many BBQ chicken pizzas since then, and this recipe combines all my favorite qualities—spicy, smoky, sweet, and cheesy. In other words, all things good and wonderful.

1 large boneless, skinless chicken breast, cut into thin strips

1 teaspoon chili powder

½ teaspoon smoked paprika

1 teaspoon lemon zest

Pinch of sea salt

1 tablespoon plus 2 teaspoons olive oil

1 medium red onion, sliced into half-moons

1 recipe Pizza Dough (page 112)

1 cup BBQ sauce, store-bought or homemade (page 75)

8 ounces fresh mozzarella cheese

1 cup baby arugula

1 teaspoon red pepper flakes

2 tablespoons balsamic reduction (see page 118)

1. Place a pizza stone in the oven and preheat the oven to 550°F.

2. In a medium bowl, toss the chicken, chili powder, smoked paprika, lemon zest, and salt.

3. In a medium skillet, heat 1 tablespoon of the olive oil over medium heat. Add the chicken and onion and cook, turning often, for 8 to 10 minutes, until the chicken is cooked through and starting to crisp and the onion is beautifully browned. Transfer to a bowl and set aside.

4. Roll out the dough into two 12-inch rounds and transfer to parchment paper according to the directions on page 112. Spread ½ cup of the BBQ sauce on each dough round, leaving 1 inch around the edges bare. Divide the chicken and onion between the pies and break up the mozzarella, sprinkling it over the pies. Drizzle 1 teaspoon of the olive oil over each pie.

5. Working one at a time, transfer the pies to the preheated oven as directed on page 110 and bake for 6 to 8 minutes, until the cheese has melted and the crust is perfectly golden brown.

6. Top each pizza with ½ cup of the baby arugula, ½ teaspoon of the red pepper flakes, and a drizzle of balsamic reduction.

CHEESY GARLIC FINGERS WITH DONAIR SAUCE, A MARITIME CLASSIC

MAKES TWO 12-INCH PIES • When I was enrolled at Mount Allison University (to say I was attending would mean that I actually went to class. Sorry, Mom and Dad), I survived off basically two things: pasta with butter and Joey's Restaurant's garlic fingers and Donair sauce. (How I dodged scurvy, I'll never know.) As quintessentially Maritime as maple syrup or lobster, garlic fingers are the pinnacle of late-night East Coast chow (second only to the Zeus of Maritime Comfort, the almighty Donair). Garlic fingers, a loveable cousin to garlic knots, are cheesy, buttery pizza sticks cut into perfect dunkable-size slices. Nom!

This recipe is *all* about the sauce, an East Coast shout-out to the garlic sauce traditionally served with shawarma—super sweet, a little savory, and the perfect friend for cheesy garlic fingers.

DONAIR SAUCE

- ⅔ cup sweetened condensed milk
- ¼ cup distilled white vinegar
- ½ teaspoon garlic powder

GARLIC FINGERS

- 3 tablespoons butter
- 4 garlic cloves, minced
- ½ teaspoon dried basil
- 1 recipe Pizza Dough (page 112)
- 1 pound mozzarella cheese, grated

1. Place a pizza stone in the oven and preheat the oven to 550°F.

2. Make the Donair sauce: In a small dish, stir together the sweetened condensed milk, vinegar, and garlic powder until smooth. Refrigerate until the garlic fingers are ready.

3. Make the garlic fingers: In a small saucepan, melt the butter over medium-low heat. Turn off the heat and stir in the garlic and basil. Set aside.

4. Roll out the dough into two 12-inch rounds and transfer to parchment paper according to the directions on page 112. Baste each dough round with the garlic butter, leaving 1 inch around the edges bare. Sprinkle half the mozzarella over each pie.

5. Working one at a time, transfer the pies to the preheated oven as directed on page 110 and bake for 6 to 8 minutes, until the cheese has melted and the crust is golden brown.

6. Slice the pies into 1-inch fingers and serve with the killer Donair sauce. Ultimate Maritime happiness.

5
Noodles.
HAPPY IN A BOWL.

NOODLES ARE PROOF THAT GOD LOVES US AND WANTS US TO BE HAPPY.

What began as a regional staple food has positively exploded into a global superpower, with folks from all corners of the earth happily slurping away on big bowls of nourishing goodness.

Noodles offer us endless flavor possibilities and ingredient combinations.

From ramen to pad thai, *dan dan* to honey garlic, there's literally a noodle dish for every person, every season, and every situation.

Here are a few of my favorite noodle dishes, guaranteed to cure your constant noodle craving.

NOODLE BOWLS WITH CRISPY CHICKEN AND PEANUT SAUCE

MAKES 4 TO 6 SERVINGS • Occasionally in our kitchen journeys we run headfirst into a recipe that we never quite recover from. As I was creating the recipes for this book, I simply could not shake this one. It was love at first bite, craving the combination of the salty, sweet peanut sauce, crispy stir-fried chicken, and refreshing veggies. Delicious!

This recipe requires some marinating time for the chicken, letting it soak in all those gorgeous flavors. After that, it comes together in a flash. Perfect for a quick, nourishing, delish weeknight meal at home.

CHICKEN AND MARINADE

- 1 pound boneless, skinless chicken breasts, cut into long ½-inch strips
- 3 tablespoons soy sauce
- 2 tablespoons fish sauce
- 1 tablespoon toasted sesame oil
- 1 tablespoon rice vinegar
- 1 tablespoon brown sugar
- 2 garlic cloves, minced
- 1 tablespoon minced fresh ginger

PEANUT SAUCE

- 1½ cups canned coconut milk
- ¾ cup creamy peanut butter
- 1½ tablespoons fish sauce
- 1½ tablespoons sriracha
- 1 tablespoon honey
- 1 garlic clove, minced

(Ingredients continue on the next page.)

1. Make the chicken and marinade: Arrange the chicken in a single layer in a casserole dish. Whisk together all the marinade ingredients in a bowl and pour the marinade over the strips. Cover with plastic wrap and chill in the fridge overnight, or for at least 1 hour if you're short on time.

2. Make the peanut sauce: Combine the peanut sauce ingredients in a 2-quart saucepan and cook over medium-low heat, stirring every couple of minutes, until the peanut butter has melted and the sauce is creamy and smooth, 4 to 5 minutes. Lower the heat and keep the sauce warm, checking occasionally to make sure it doesn't burn.

3. Make the noodles: Bring a large saucepan of water to a boil and cook the vermicelli according to the package directions. Drain and set aside.

NOODLES

1 (8.8-ounce) package rice vermicelli

1 tablespoon vegetable oil

2 carrots, julienned

1 English cucumber, sliced into thin rounds

½ cup roasted salted peanuts, chopped

1 to 2 fresh red chiles, sliced

¼ cup fresh mint leaves

¼ cup fresh basil leaves

1 lime, cut into wedges

4. Heat a large wok or skillet over medium-high heat and add the vegetable oil. When the oil is hot, add the chicken strips (reserving any leftover marinade) and cook, tossing often, for 5 to 6 minutes, until cooked through. Add the reserved marinade and cook for 1 to 2 minutes, until thickened.

5. Divide the noodles into individual serving bowls and top with the chicken, carrots, and cucumber. Sprinkle the peanuts and chiles on top and serve with the mint, basil, and lime wedges.

PULLED PORK RAMEN

MAKES 4 TO 6 SERVINGS, WITH LEFTOVER PORK • Pulled Pork Ramen—come on! This recipe was born with two things in mind:

PULLED PORK is the food of the gods.

NOT everyone lives in a major city center and has easy access to many of the traditional ingredients required in the superhero dishes found around the world.

This ramen recipe is far from traditional, but makes up for it in spades by being a soul-satisfying flavor bomb of a dish. And we know there's only one thing that truly matters: deliciousness.

Heads up! This recipe takes several hours to prepare, so it's best served on a cool, Netflix-binge-watching kinda day. You'll need the biggest Dutch oven (or high-sided oven-safe pan) you can get your hands on, awesome ramen-loving friends, and a strong desire to chill.

1 (3-pound) bone-in pork shoulder

1 tablespoon vegetable oil

1 teaspoon sea salt

2 sweet (Vidalia) onions, sliced into half-moons

1 thumb-size knob ginger, peeled and minced

5 garlic cloves, minced

¼ cup white miso paste

1 cup dried shiitake mushrooms

1 (12-ounce) bottle of your favorite beer

2 quarts chicken stock, store-bought or homemade (page 149)

2 tablespoons soy sauce

6 large free-range eggs, at room temperature

(Ingredients continue on page 135.)

1. Preheat the oven to 325°F.

2. Heat a very large (minimum 5-quart) high-sided oven-safe stockpot or Dutch oven over medium-high heat. Rub the pork all over with the vegetable oil and season with the salt. Sear the pork on all sides until browned, 6 to 8 minutes total. When the last side is searing, add the onions to sear along with the pork, 2 minutes. Add the ginger and garlic, toss with the onions, and cook for 30 seconds, keeping an eye on it so that the garlic doesn't burn.

3. Stir in the miso paste, add the shiitakes, and pour in the beer and stock. Bring the mixture to a boil, then very carefully transfer the pot to the oven and braise for 3½ hours, until the pork easily shreds and falls away from the bone.

4. Transfer the pork to a cutting board, remove any fat, and shred the meat with two forks.

7 ounces ramen noodles or thin egg noodles

6 heads baby bok choy, ends trimmed and leaves separated

1 teaspoon togarashi spice

1 bunch fresh cilantro

2 scallions, thinly sliced

1 or 2 fresh red chiles, thinly sliced

5. Skim the fat from the top of the stock left in the pot and discard it. The clearer, the better. Pour the stock through a fine-mesh sieve set over a large bowl and discard the solids.

6. Pour the stock into a large pot and add the soy sauce and pulled pork. Bring to a simmer over medium heat and let simmer away for 30 minutes.

7. Soft-boil the eggs as directed on page 8.

8. Bring a large saucepan of water to a boil and cook the noodles according to the package directions. Drain and set aside.

9. After the pork and stock have been simmering for 30 minutes, turn off the heat and stir in the bok choy.

10. Divide the noodles among individual serving bowls and pour over a hearty portion of the ramen stock and pork. Slice the eggs in half. Place one whole sliced egg in each bowl, and sprinkle the eggs with togarashi spice.

11. Top each ramen bowl with fresh cilantro, sliced scallions, and sliced red chiles.

MARINATED MISO SALMON NOODLES

MAKES 4 SERVINGS • Sometimes a simple discovery changes everything. A few years ago I was cooking away at a catering gig in beautiful Southampton, New York, and stumbled across the happiest of kitchen accidents. The revelation? A marinade can make the best sauce ever. With zero prep time available and in desperate need of an extra dish to feed a hungry crowd of sun-soaked vacationers, I made a split decision. Two pounds of salmon had soaked overnight in a gorgeous marinade that I had thankfully set aside, and I had a pack of simple egg noodles in hand. So without much thought, I got that leftover marinade simmering away, tossed some cooked noodles in the glorious sauce, and never looked back. Life-changing! I've been doing this ever since.

This little dish is a tribute to my original marinade awakening and highlights the almighty miso paste—gatekeeper of umami heaven. The overnight marinade ensures that the salmon will soak in that game-changing flavor bomb. Healthy, packed with flavor, and perfect for a weeknight meal at home. No waste, only deliciousness.

MARINADE

2 tablespoons white miso paste

½ cup soy sauce

¼ cup mirin

¼ cup rice vinegar

1 tablespoon sriracha

1 tablespoon minced fresh ginger

2 garlic cloves, minced

2 tablespoons pure maple syrup

2 teaspoons cornstarch

1. Make the marinade: In a medium bowl, whisk together all the marinade ingredients except the cornstarch until combined. In a small bowl, stir the cornstarch with 2 tablespoons water until dissolved, then whisk it into the marinade.

2. Make the salmon and noodles: Place the salmon in a casserole and top with the marinade. Cover with plastic wrap and give the salmon a home in the fridge for 24 hours, turning the fish once or twice.

3. Preheat the oven to 350°F and line a baking sheet with parchment paper.

4. Place the salmon skin-side down on the baking sheet, reserving the marinade. Bake for 25 to 30 minutes, or until the fish is easily flaked with a fork. With about 5 minutes of time remaining, drizzle the honey over the salmon. The honey will caramelize like a boss.

SALMON AND NOODLES

4 (6-ounce) skin-on salmon fillets

1 tablespoon honey

12 ounces egg noodles

2 teaspoons vegetable oil

7 ounces Broccolini or broccoli florets

4 ounces spinach

2 scallions, finely sliced

1 or 2 red chiles, finely sliced

1 bunch fresh cilantro

1 lime, cut into wedges

5. Meanwhile, when the salmon is about halfway done cooking, bring a large pot of salted water to a boil. Cook the egg noodles according to the package directions, drain, and set aside.

6. Heat a large wok over medium heat and add the vegetable oil. When the oil is hot, add the Broccolini and cook for 2 minutes, keeping it moving the entire time. Pour the reserved marinade into the wok and bring to a simmer. Add the noodles and give everything a toss to coat well. Stir in the spinach, scallions, and chiles and give the pan one last toss.

7. Portion the noodles into four serving bowls and top with the salmon fillets. Serve with the fresh cilantro and lime wedges.

SUPER-SPICY DAN DAN NOODLES

MAKES 4 TO 6 SERVINGS • *Dan dan!!* Sichuan street food done right. This fiery flavor bomb is not for the faint of heart. It's the benchmark noodle bowl for the chile lovers of the world and ticks every single box for me. Hot, hot, hot, and absolutely exploding with flavor.

As with all wok-cooked dishes, when the stir-frying starts, this recipe comes together with lightning speed. *Mise en place* is crucial here—get all those veggies chopped, spices measured, and sauces ready to go before you start cooking. Your dish and stress level will be well chuffed that you did.

SAUCE

½ cup chile oil

½ cup chicken stock, store-bought or homemade (page 149)

3 tablespoons soy sauce

2 teaspoons sugar

½ teaspoon five-spice powder

1½ teaspoons Szechuan peppercorns, ground with a mortar and pestle

2 garlic cloves, finely minced

2 tablespoons tahini

1 scallion, finely sliced

PORK AND NOODLES

2 tablespoons sesame oil

1 pound best-quality ground pork

1 tablespoon chili bean sauce

2 teaspoons sherry

1 teaspoon soy sauce

½ teaspoon five-spice powder

8 ounces egg noodles

3 heads baby bok choy, stems removed and leaves separated

2 scallions, finely sliced

¼ cup crushed roasted salted peanuts

1. Make the sauce: In a small saucepan, whisk together all the sauce ingredients except the scallion. Heat over medium-low heat just until the sauce starts to simmer. Remove from the heat and whisk in the scallion. Set aside.

2. Make the pork and noodles: Heat a wok over medium-high heat and add the sesame oil and pork. Cook for 5 minutes, stirring often, until the pork is browned all over. Add the chili bean sauce, sherry, soy sauce, and five-spice and cook for 3 minutes. The sauce will have found a home in the pork and almost disappeared at this point, leaving the pork perfectly crispy and tasting like gold. Set aside.

3. Bring a large pot of salted water to a boil and cook the noodles according to the package directions. When about 1 minute of cook time remains, add the bok choy to cook with the noodles. Drain.

4. Divide the sauce among four to six large noodle bowls. Portion the noodles over the sauce, then add the crispy pork. Top each bowl with the scallions and crushed peanuts and serve immediately.

ROAST CHICKEN PHO

MAKES 4 TO 6 SERVINGS • Bless you, pho. You're a superstar. Anytime I'm feeling a tad under the weather, it's dark and dreary outside, or I'm just in need of a big ol' food hug, pho to the rescue. Truth be told, this is our go-to chicken noodle soup—it's a bowl of soul-satisfying, deeply flavorful broth loaded with crispy roast chicken, noodles, and crunchy, spicy toppings. Pho for the forever win.

ROAST CHICKEN

1 (3-pound) free-range chicken

1 tablespoon olive oil

½ teaspoon sea salt

¼ teaspoon freshly cracked black pepper

1 lime, halved

1 garlic head, halved

PHO BROTH

1 cinnamon stick

1 (2-inch) piece fresh ginger, peeled

1 (2-inch) piece lemongrass, lightly smashed

1 teaspoon whole black peppercorns

5 whole cloves

2 teaspoons fennel seeds

1 star anise

1 tablespoon vegetable oil

4 garlic cloves, minced

1 large leek, rinsed well and finely diced

12 cups chicken stock, store-bought or homemade (page 149)

2 tablespoons fish sauce

8 ounces dried rice noodles

1. Preheat the oven to 450°F.

2. Make the roast chicken: Pat the chicken dry with paper towels and massage it with the olive oil, sea salt, and pepper. Stuff the lime and garlic head halves in the bird's cavity. Transfer the chicken to a cast-iron pan or roasting pan.

3. Roast for 10 minutes, then lower the oven temperature to 400°F. Roast for about 1 hour, or until the chicken reaches an internal temperature of 165°F, the juices run clear, and the chicken legs basically fall away from the bird. Set the pan aside to cool.

4. Make the pho broth: Prepare a bouquet garni by bundling the cinnamon stick, ginger, lemongrass, peppercorns, cloves, fennel, and star anise in a piece of cheesecloth and tying off the bundle with kitchen twine. Set aside.

5. In a large stockpot, heat the vegetable oil over medium heat. When hot, add the garlic and sauté for 30 seconds (don't let it burn). Add the leek and cook, stirring often, for 5 minutes, or until the leek has started to soften and become translucent. Add the stock, fish sauce, and bouquet garni.

6. Remove the crispy skin, leg bones (not the meat), and wings from the roast chicken and add them to the pot. Bring the soup to a simmer, letting that delicious broth bubble away for 15 minutes.

TOPPINGS

½ **cup fresh basil leaves**

½ **cup fresh mint leaves**

1 small red onion, halved and sliced into thin half-moons

4 scallions, finely sliced

2 cups bean sprouts

1 or 2 jalapeños, thinly sliced

2 or 3 limes, cut into wedges

Garlic chile sauce, for spicy lovers

7. Meanwhile, bring a pot of water to a boil and cook the noodles according to the package directions. Drain and immediately run under cold water to shock and stop the cooking process. Set aside.

8. While the broth is simmering away, use two forks to shred the meat from the roast chicken.

9. Set a fine-mesh sieve over a large bowl and strain the broth into the bowl. Discard the solids. You want a smooth, clear broth. Pour the broth back into the (clean) pot and stir in the shredded chicken. Bring to a simmer over medium heat and cook for 5 minutes.

10. Divide the noodles among four to six serving bowls. Top with the broth and garnish with all the toppings.

HONEY-GARLIC NOODLES

MAKES 4 TO 6 SERVINGS • One of the first ever Dennis the Prescott recipes, this little noodle dish is still crushing it on the Prescott family at-home bestseller list. This recipe was born as a way to cope when our beloved local noodle chef, Ming, traveled home to China every winter, leaving us almost losing our noodle-loving minds.

These honey-garlic noodles are perfect as is, or as a side dish served with chicken, steak, or a fried egg or tossed with your favorite stir-fried veggies. The recipe comes together very quickly, so get everything diced, sliced, minced, and prepped first.

HONEY-GARLIC SAUCE

⅓ cup soy sauce

½ cup mirin

1 tablespoon toasted sesame oil

4 garlic cloves, minced

1 or 2 fresh bird's-eye chiles, finely diced

1 tablespoon honey

NOODLES AND FRIENDS

12 ounces thin egg noodles

2 tablespoons sunflower or vegetable oil

1 tablespoon minced fresh ginger

6 scallions, thinly sliced

2 limes: 1 halved, 1 cut into wedges for serving

1 tablespoon sesame seeds

Fresh cilantro or your favorite spicy herbs, for serving

1. Make the sauce: In a small bowl, combine the sauce ingredients. Stir and set aside.

2. Make the noodles and friends: Bring a large pot of salted water to a boil and cook the noodles according to the package directions. When 1 minute of cooking time remains and the noodles are softened but firm, drain.

3. In a wok, heat the sunflower oil over medium-high heat. When the oil is hot, add the noodles and ginger and stir-fry for 2 minutes, keeping the noodles moving the entire time.

4. Pour in the sauce and cook for 1 minute, tossing to ensure that the noodles are completely coated. Turn off the heat.

5. Toss in the scallions, squeeze the juice of the halved lime on top, and sprinkle on the sesame seeds. Give everything a good toss to mix and combine.

6. Serve with the lime wedges and fresh cilantro or spicy greens.

SHRIMP AND TOFU PAD THAI

MAKES 4 SERVINGS • Of all the food on God's green earth, pad thai is my wife's favorite dish. Her constant craving, her forever love. The combo of sweet, savory, and spicy is so next-level—a delicious force to be reckoned with.

This is another dish that was added to the Prescott family repertoire out of necessity. Every year, our favorite local food truck serves up delicious Thai food all around the city. The only problem? The owners take a much-deserved snow-free winter break and travel eastward to Thailand. If we were going to get our fix during the cold weather months, I was going to have to learn to do it myself. As with everything, try, taste, fail (that's okay!), try again, learn, and repeat. You'll become a better taster and a better cook. Almost anything a restaurant can make, you can cook at home.

This recipe is fantastic with shrimp, but if you're not a fan of our crustacean friends, feel free to use chicken instead. Just slice the chicken into very thin strips and wok-fry it in oil for 3 to 4 minutes until browned before starting this recipe. Then, when the recipe calls for adding shrimp, add the chicken instead. Awesome.

SAUCE

¼ cup vegetable stock

3 tablespoons fish sauce

2 tablespoons dark brown sugar

1 tablespoon tamarind paste

1 to 2 tablespoons garlic chili sauce

PAD THAI

10 ounces medium rice stick noodles

¼ cup peanut oil

4 garlic cloves, minced

½ medium onion, very thinly sliced

1. Make the sauce: Combine all the sauce ingredients in a small saucepan and heat over medium-low heat. Cook, stirring often, until the sugar has dissolved, 2 to 3 minutes. Set aside.

2. Make the pad thai: Bring a large pot of water to a rapid boil. Remove from the heat and submerge the noodles. Let the noodles soak for 8 to 10 minutes, until softened but firm (think al dente).

3. In a large wok, heat the peanut oil over medium-high heat. Add the garlic, onion, and tofu and stir-fry, turning often, until the tofu starts to turn golden brown, 2 to 3 minutes. Add the shrimp and cook, turning several times, until they start to turn pink. Push everything in the wok to one side and pour in

7 ounces extra-firm tofu, cut into ½-inch cubes (about 2 cups)

1 pound jumbo shrimp, peeled and deveined

2 large free-range eggs, lightly whisked

1 carrot, grated on the large holes of a box grater

4 scallions, thinly sliced

TOPPINGS

2 cups bean sprouts

¼ cup roasted salted peanuts, chopped

1 or 2 red chiles, diced

1 small bunch fresh cilantro

1 lime, cut into wedges

the eggs. Cook, stirring often, until the eggs are just starting to set, then stir to combine them with the shrimp and tofu mixture.

4. Stir in the sauce, noodles, carrot, and scallions, tossing the stir-fry several times to coat the noodles.

5. Immediately divide the noodle mixture among individual serving bowls. Top each bowl with some of the bean sprouts, peanuts, chiles, cilantro, and a wedge of lime.

Stir-fries work best when the ingredients have a little room to breathe in the pan. I have a crazy-big wok that I found at a New York market a few years ago. It's large enough to cook multiple servings at a time— perfect for feeding a hungry crowd. If the wok or skillet you plan to use is on the smaller side, divide the ingredients in half and cook in batches.

6

Warm Bowls of Comfort

SOUP. THE ULTIMATE FEEL-GOOD DISH.

It's the go-to meal of choice when we're feeling more zero than hero, when rainy or snow-packed weather rears its ugly head, or when we just need a warm bowl of comfort in our lives. Since the start of my culinary journey, I've been consistently drawn to soups and stock-based recipes. They're delicious, yes, but also a fantastic way to experiment with different meat and veggie combinations or sneak extra veggie goodness into a dish (don't tell my nieces and nephews). But wait, there's more! Soups are easy on the pocketbook and go a long way in feeding a crowd. So rad.

From Maple Coconut Curry Squash to Roasted Tomato, here are some of my favorite soup recipes. Perfect for every cozy occasion.

HOMEMADE CHICKEN STOCK

MAKES ABOUT 5 QUARTS • Chicken stock is an essential kitchen ingredient, used in countless recipes from sauces to soups to risotto. As with everything else under the sun, homemade is best. The first time you scratch-make chicken stock is the last time you'll choose store-bought. Guaranteed.

Every time I roast a bird, I make chicken stock with the carcass, but you can make stock with fresh chicken too. And it freezes perfectly, so you'll always be well stocked.

1 large leftover chicken carcass, or 1 (4- to 5-pound) fresh chicken (see Note)

2 large onions, halved

2 large carrots, coarsely chopped

3 celery stalks, coarsely chopped

1 garlic head, halved crosswise

½ teaspoon whole black peppercorns

2 bay leaves

2 fresh rosemary sprigs

2 fresh thyme sprigs

5 fresh flat-leaf parsley sprigs

5 large fresh sage leaves

1. Combine all the ingredients in a large stockpot and cover with 6 quarts cold water. There's no need to peel anything—just toss it in there. The bones (or chicken) should be covered by at least 2 to 3 inches of water.

2. Bring the stock to a gentle simmer and cook, uncovered, for 4 hours, skimming the fat from the top of the stock every hour or so.

3. Let the stock cool slightly, then strain it through a fine-mesh sieve set over a large bowl. Discard the solids.

4. Use it immediately or let cool and store for later use. The stock will keep awesomely in an airtight container in the fridge for up to 3 days. If you don't plan on using it right away, this bad boy will also freeze perfectly for 2 to 3 months. I typically portion the cooled stock into zip-top freezer bags, about 3 cups per bag.

NOTE: *If using a whole chicken, in step 2, remove the chicken from the pot at the 2-hour mark and remove the meat. Return the bones to the liquid. Carry on simmering for 2 hours more. Save the cooked chicken meat for something delicious, like chicken noodle soup, a killer sandwich, or a stir-fry.*

MISO CHICKEN NOODLE SOUP

MAKES 4 TO 6 SERVINGS • Not your average feel-better broth, this chicken soup is packing serious heat. The flavor weapon of choice? Mighty miso. Full-bodied and rich, miso, along with its mates soy sauce and bok choy, propels the classic chicken noodle soup that we all know and love into the stratosphere.

1 tablespoon vegetable oil

1 cup finely diced red onion

1 tablespoon minced fresh ginger

2 garlic cloves, minced

2 large carrots, finely sliced

2 celery stalks, finely diced

2 cups thinly sliced cremini mushrooms

2 tablespoons white miso paste (or other miso paste, for a stronger flavor)

3 tablespoons soy sauce

8 cups chicken stock, store-bought or homemade (page 149)

12 ounces chicken breasts

7 ounces medium-thickness egg noodles

3 heads baby bok choy, trimmed and leaves separated

Salt and freshly cracked black pepper

Handful of fresh cilantro sprigs, for garnish

1. In a large stockpot, heat the vegetable oil over medium heat. When hot, stir in the onion, ginger, and garlic and sauté until the onion has softened, about 5 minutes. Add the carrots, celery, and mushrooms and cook, stirring often, for 5 minutes. Stir in the miso paste and soy sauce and add the chicken stock and chicken breasts, making sure they are submerged. Bring the soup to a boil, then reduce the heat to maintain a simmer and cook for 20 minutes.

2. Meanwhile, bring a large pot of salted water to a boil and cook the noodles according to the package directions. Drain and set aside.

3. Turn the heat off under the soup. Using a pair of tongs, transfer the chicken breasts to a plate. Let them cool for a minute, then shred the meat with two forks.

4. Add the shredded chicken and bok choy leaves to the soup and stir to combine. Give the soup a quick taste to check the seasoning and add a pinch of salt and pepper.

5. Divide the noodles among serving dishes and pour the soup on top. Garnish with fresh cilantro and serve immediately.

MAPLE COCONUT CURRY SQUASH SOUP

MAKES 6 TO 8 SERVINGS • I've always been partial to fall. Sorry, summertime, I still love you. But there's just something undeniably magical about apple season, harvest vegetables, the bright red landscape, and the crisp, refreshing fall air. And with the arrival of autumnal splendor, the Prescott household eagerly moves into soup season.

Butternut squash is one of my all-time favorite veggies. I love it roasted, pureed in soups, or mixed with potatoes for the most incredible mash on the planet. It's super healthy and loaded with vitamins and antioxidants. Good gravy, if butternut squash isn't officially a superfood, it darn well should be.

This recipe is autumn in a bowl, and as long as I've been cooking, I've made a version of it. Tastes just like home. Your family will adore this soup.

1 (2-pound) butternut squash, halved lengthwise and seeded

1 tablespoon olive oil

1 teaspoon kosher salt, plus more as needed

1 teaspoon freshly cracked black pepper, plus more for serving

3 tablespoons butter

2 garlic cloves, minced

1 cup finely diced red onion

1 cup finely diced Spanish onion

2 large carrots, finely diced

1 tablespoon finely minced fresh sage leaves

1 tablespoon coriander seeds, bashed in a mortar and pestle

¼ teaspoon red pepper flakes

2 yellow-fleshed potatoes (such as Yukon Gold), peeled and diced

1. Preheat the oven to 350°F.

2. Put the squash on a baking sheet, skin-side down, and brush both halves with the olive oil. Season with ½ teaspoon each of the salt and pepper. Bake for 1 hour 15 minutes, or until fork-tender. Spoon the flesh into a bowl and discard the skin.

3. In a large stockpot, melt the butter over medium heat. Add the garlic and sauté for 30 seconds, taking care that it doesn't burn. Add the onions, carrots, sage, coriander, and red pepper flakes and cook, stirring often, for 8 to 10 minutes, until the vegetables are softened.

4. Stir in the squash, potatoes, curry powder, turmeric, and stock and season with the remaining ½ teaspoon each salt and pepper. Bring the soup to a simmer and cook for 20 minutes, until the potatoes are very tender.

5. Remove the soup from the heat and puree it directly in the pot with an immersion blender. (Alternatively, working in batches, carefully transfer the soup to a regular blender

1 teaspoon mild curry powder

½ teaspoon ground turmeric

8 cups vegetable or chicken stock

1 cup heavy cream, plus more for garnish

1 tablespoon pure maple syrup

Extra-virgin olive oil, for garnish

and puree—be careful when blending hot liquids.) Stir in the cream and maple syrup and give the soup a taste to check the seasoning. Add a pinch each of salt and pepper if needed. Garnish each serving with an extra bit of cream, a drizzle of extra-virgin olive oil, and some freshly cracked black pepper.

BRAISED BEEF SHANK FRENCH ONION SOUP

MAKES 8 TO 10 SERVINGS • Sometimes inspiration strikes at the most un-expected of times, and this little recipe is literally a dream come true. (Yes, I have, in fact, started sleep-cooking. This is a judgment-free zone, y'all.) Two of my forever comfort food loves are French dip sandwiches and French onion soup. They're the total package—heartwarming, taste bud–tingling deliciousness. This recipe was born out of the idea of smashing those two glorious dishes together and creating something otherworldly. Twice the flavor, twice the awesome.

Heads up! This soup needs a quiet home on the stove where it can simmer away for several hours, so plan ahead. Awesome is on the way.

BEEF

2 pounds bone-in beef shank

1½ tablespoons olive oil

½ teaspoon sea salt

½ teaspoon freshly cracked black pepper

1 tablespoon butter

2 large leeks, rinsed well and thinly sliced

1 red onion, thinly sliced

1 white onion, thinly sliced

2 garlic cloves, minced

3 cups beef stock

1 bay leaf

2 fresh thyme sprigs

1. Make the beef: Heat a large heavy-bottomed Dutch oven over medium heat. Massage the beef with the olive oil and season with the salt and pepper. Brown the beef well, about 4 minutes per side, then transfer to a plate.

2. Melt the butter in the hot pot and add the leeks and onions. Cook, stirring often, for 10 minutes, until the vegetables are softened and beginning to brown. Stir in the garlic and cook for 30 seconds.

3. Return the beef shanks to the pot and add the stock, bay leaf, and thyme. Reduce the heat to medium-low, cover, and cook for 3 hours, until the beef easily falls away from the bone, stirring occasionally to make sure nothing burns. If the liquid gets a tad low, top it off with more stock (or water). The beef should be almost entirely submerged at all times. Remove from the heat and transfer the beef to a cutting board to cool slightly.

4. Shred the beef with two forks. Discard the bones and any excess fat. Transfer the shredded beef to a large bowl along with the contents of the pot. Set aside.

5. Soup time! In the same Dutch oven, melt the butter with the olive oil over medium heat. Add the onions, season

SOUP

2 tablespoons butter

1 tablespoon olive oil

2 pounds mixed onions (red, Spanish, leeks—a mixture is best!), sliced into thin half-moons

¾ teaspoon sea salt

1 cup dry white wine

1 tablespoon all-purpose flour

1 quart beef stock, plus more as needed

½ teaspoon freshly cracked black pepper, plus more for serving

1 crusty baguette, sliced

3 cups grated Comté cheese

1 teaspoon fresh thyme leaves

with ¼ teaspoon of the salt, and give the onions a toss to coat them in oil. Cover and cook for 30 minutes, stirring a few times throughout the cooking process to help keep the onions from sticking to the bottom of the pot.

6. Pour in the wine to deglaze the pot, scraping up all the delicious browned bits from the bottom. Stir in the flour and stock. Add the shredded beef and onion mixture and season with the remaining ½ teaspoon salt and the pepper. Bring to a gentle simmer over medium-low heat and cook, uncovered, for 45 minutes, or until reduced and thickened.

7. Preheat the oven to broil. Portion the soup into oven-safe serving dishes. Top each dish with 1 or 2 baguette slices, a heaping handful of the grated cheese, a pinch of the thyme leaves, and black pepper. Heat under the broiler until the cheese is bubbling and serve immediately.

ROASTED TOMATO SOUP WITH ROSEMARY CROUTONS

MAKES 6 TO 8 SERVINGS • Elegant. Timeless. Classic.

It doesn't get much more nostalgic than tomato soup. Many of us were raised on the stuff, with a crispy grilled cheese sandwich on the side. But this most definitely isn't a Warhol-style soup in a can from yesteryear. This is tomato soup jacked to 10.

Roasting tomatoes brings out remarkably fragrant and full-bodied flavors, and this recipe truly shines when local tomatoes are at their best and in peak season. One of the greatest soups ever. Period.

ROASTED VEGGIES

2 pounds whole mixed tomatoes, as many varieties as you can find

1 large red onion, chopped

6 garlic cloves, unpeeled

2 tablespoons olive oil

1 teaspoon sea salt

1 teaspoon freshly cracked black pepper

1 tablespoon fresh rosemary leaves

1 tablespoon fresh thyme leaves

ROSEMARY CROUTONS

8 ounces crusty sourdough bread, cut into ½-inch pieces

2 tablespoons olive oil

1 tablespoon minced fresh rosemary leaves

¼ teaspoon sea salt

¼ teaspoon freshly cracked black pepper

1. Make the roasted veggies: Preheat the oven to 375°F.

2. Spread the tomatoes, onion, and garlic cloves on a large rimmed baking sheet and drizzle the olive oil on top. Season with the salt and pepper and sprinkle on the herbs. Roast for 45 minutes to 1 hour, or until the tomatoes are broken down, the garlic is soft, and the onion is starting to crisp, giving the pan a shake halfway through. Remove and discard any tomato stems and the garlic skins. Set aside. Keep the oven on.

3. Make the croutons: Spread the bread on a rimmed baking sheet and toss with the olive oil, rosemary, salt, and pepper. Bake until golden brown, about 15 minutes. Set aside until the soup is ready to rock.

4. Make the soup: In a large pot, heat the olive oil over medium heat. When hot, add the leek, red pepper flakes, and basil stems and cook for 5 minutes, stirring often, until the leek is softened. Add the roasted tomatoes, garlic, and onion, and the stock, season with the salt and pepper, and bring to a boil over medium-high heat. Reduce the heat to medium and simmer, stirring often, for 20 minutes, or until reduced and thickened slightly.

SOUP

1 tablespoon olive oil

1 large leek, rinsed well and thinly sliced

¼ teaspoon red pepper flakes, plus more as needed

1 tablespoon minced fresh basil stems

2 cups chicken stock, store-bought or homemade (page 149)

½ teaspoon sea salt, plus more as needed

¼ teaspoon freshly cracked black pepper, plus more as needed

1 tablespoon red wine vinegar

1 tablespoon fresh lemon juice

1 tablespoon honey

2 tablespoons minced fresh basil leaves, plus whole leaves for serving

Extra-virgin olive oil, for serving

5. Turn off the heat under the soup and stir in the vinegar, lemon juice, honey, and basil leaves. Blend directly in the pot with an immersion blender. (Alternatively, working in batches, carefully transfer the soup to a regular blender and puree—be careful when blending hot liquids.) Take a quick taste to check the seasoning and add a pinch of salt and pepper if needed.

6. Serve up the soup with a nice drizzle of extra-virgin olive oil, the toasty croutons, basil leaves, and an extra hit of red pepper flakes.

SMOKY BEEF AND BEER CHILI

MAKES 6 TO 8 SERVINGS • Winter is coming—give me all the chili.

There's a direct correlation between the onset of wintery weather patterns and my desire to face-dive into a giant bowl of homemade chili. A big, nourishing, hearty bowl of happy to make you feel like all's right and well in the world. Chili was one of the first things I learned to cook while living in a small sublet apartment in Brentwood, Tennessee (615, represent!). Now that I'm back in the Great White North, I love making chili for friends on game day or when we're snowed in with little to do but get cozy and binge-watch classic films.

This chili recipe is completely heartwarming, stick-to-your-ribs goodness. It's perfectly delicious on its own or piled high atop a plate of nachos, split baked potatoes, hot dogs, or even French fries.

CHILI

- 3 smoked bacon slices, cut into ¼-inch pieces
- 1 large onion, diced
- 1 large red bell pepper, diced
- 4 garlic cloves, minced
- 1 tablespoon finely minced fresh cilantro stems
- 2 pounds best-quality ground beef (80% lean)
- 3 tablespoons chili powder
- ½ teaspoon smoked paprika
- ½ teaspoon ground cumin
- ½ teaspoon dried oregano
- 1 teaspoon sea salt
- 1 (12-ounce) bottle of your favorite dark beer
- 1 (28-ounce) can diced tomatoes
- ½ cup beef stock
- 1 (19-ounce) can red kidney beans, drained and rinsed
- 1 teaspoon freshly cracked black pepper

1. Heat a Dutch oven or stockpot over medium heat. Fry the bacon until the fat has rendered and the bacon is starting to crisp, about 5 minutes. Stir in the onion, bell pepper, and garlic and cook for 5 minutes, or until the onion has softened. Add the cilantro stems, beef, and spices and season with ½ teaspoon of the sea salt. Cook for 5 to 6 minutes, breaking up the beef with a wooden spoon until it has started to brown, with very little pink remaining.

2. Add the beer, tomatoes, stock, and beans and season with the remaining ½ teaspoon sea salt and the pepper. Increase the heat to medium-high and bring the chili to a boil, then reduce the heat to medium and simmer, stirring occasionally, for 30 to 35 minutes, until the chili is thickened and wonderful.

3. Top bowls of chili with some of the sour cream, cheddar, avocado, onion, and cilantro and serve.

TOPPINGS

½ cup sour cream

1 cup grated cheddar cheese

1 large ripe avocado, pitted, peeled, and diced

½ cup finely diced red onion

Fresh cilantro

7

THE

Family Meal

MEALTIME. SUCH A SIMPLE YET LOADED WORD—ONE THAT CAN HAVE DRASTICALLY DIFFERENT SIGNIFICANCE TO ANY TWO PEOPLE.

To some, mealtime means quickly grabbing takeout while on the move from one activity to the next. To others, mealtime means family or friends gathered around the communal table, indulging in great food and fellowship. And to yet others, mealtime doesn't come often enough, with an all-too-real daily challenge of working to provide healthy, abundant food for their family. Still, beyond our bodies' physical needs, we all love delicious food. As I've traveled the globe, I've loved asking folks about their favorite thing to eat, and no matter where I roam—whether the next town over or halfway around the world—there's an immediate answer. From camel in Somaliland to lobster in Shediac, a town in New Brunswick, we all love delicious.

A recent mealtime in the most unexpected of surroundings changed my life forever. On a rainy afternoon in the northwestern Kenyan highlands, I learned how to prepare mutton stew over an open flame, then sat to break bread with Catherine, Andrew, and their children, along with my family from World Vision's Hunger Free initiative. They speak Swahili, I speak English. They live in Kenya, I live

in Canada. I love cheeseburgers, they've never heard of a cheeseburger. But it didn't matter. The very moment that Catherine and I began to prepare that meal together, an invisible wall of hesitation was broken and we were able to connect on a real level. We sat to eat, we laughed and joked, the family asked me questions about my Canadian homeland and about my tattoos, and I was able to ask them about their daily lives. Food is community.

The past few decades have been rough on the North American family table. It's increasingly difficult to ease our rat-race schedules and really prioritize family mealtime. But what's of critical importance is real, honest connection that helps our relationships grow and our communities thrive. My hope is that the recipes in this chapter inspire you to throw dinner parties, host holiday meals, enjoy date night at home, or simply prepare a delicious and healthy weeknight meal. Whatever the occasion, the goal is an incredible meal and an even more memorable evening with loved ones.

Mealtime! Get into it, friends.

HOW TO COOK THE PERFECT STEAK

A perfectly cooked, juicy, restaurant-style steak is an absolute joy, and much easier to make at home than you might think. Here are some tips to help you cook the best steak you've ever tasted.

BEST QUALITY

Note, the above reads best *quality* and not best cut. Yes, the sirloins and tenderloins of the world are delicious, but often it's the lesser-known cuts that are the most flavorful. Best quality means finding a local butcher (they're the expert) who really invests the time and care in producing the best-fed, most-loved, and ultimately best-tasting beef possible. Absolutely well worth the effort, and the results are staggeringly delicious.

ROOM TEMPERATURE

Letting the steak come to room temperature is essential to ensure that the steak cooks properly and evenly. For best results, let the beef sit on the counter for 1 hour prior to cooking.

OIL

Grab your favorite oil (for me it's a top-quality olive oil) and rub the steak to coat it (don't add so much oil that it's dripping off the beef).

SEASONING

Seasoning is make or break in cooking steak. Remember, you can't season the inside of the beef, so very generously season both sides of the steak with coarse salt and freshly cracked black pepper. You should be able to easily see the salt on the steak. Seasoning = flavor.

HOT PAN

Like, crazy hot. Smoking hot, even. If your steak doesn't sizzle and hiss when it hits the pan, quickly remove the beef and let the pan get as hot as the sun. Crack the window, get the fan on, ignore the smoke detector, and get that pan blazing. Essential in developing that wicked outer crust we all know and love.

RESTING

Resting your steak is absolutely essential. As it rests, all those juices will do their thing, settling and soaking into the beef, resulting in the juiciest, most tender and flavorful steak experience of your life. Fight the urge to immediately cut into that beef. You spent your hard-earned cash on a top-quality cut of steak and cooked it to perfection. Finish strong and rest that dude. Repeat after me: I will always rest my steak.

PLATE JUICES

After resting a steak, you'll notice the juices left on the plate. Never waste this liquid gold. After you carve a steak, pour the plate juices on top and enter beef nirvana.

THE METHOD

Each cut of beef should be treated differently, but here's a general method for a 1½-inch-thick steak, such as a sirloin:

1. Preheat a cast-iron pan over medium-high heat until it's smoking hot, 5 to 8 minutes.

2. Set a timer for 8 minutes. Add the oiled and seasoned steak to the pan. After 1 minute, grab some tongs and flip the steak. Continue flipping the steak every minute, cooking for a total of 8 minutes for medium-rare. To ensure the steak is cooked precisely to your liking, insert a meat thermometer into the beef. If the temperature reads between 120°F and 125°F, you're golden (after resting it will go to 135°F). Perfect medium-rare steak.

3. Transfer to a plate and top with any juices left in the skillet. Tent the steak loosely with aluminum foil and let rest for at least 6 minutes before carving. Slice up, plate up, and drizzle all those gorgeous juices on top.

A Kiss of Butter, Rosemary, and Garlic. For next-level steak action, try this. With 4 minutes of cooking time remaining, spoon 2 tablespoons butter into the pan and add a few rosemary sprigs and garlic cloves on top of the butter. Baste the flavored butter all over the steak as it cooks. There's just no reason not to.

CORIANDER-ESPRESSO-RUBBED SIRLOIN WITH NEW POTATOES, CORN, AND CHIMICHURRI

MAKE 4 TO 6 SERVINGS • We all have our favorites—the recipes that speak to our soul and bring us back time and time again. If I've got a hankering for steak, this is the one: strip (also known as striploin) steak with My Favorite Spice Rub (page 168), paired with a killer chimichurri and roasted veggies. Steak night at home just got extra tasty.

This recipe is delicious all year round, but is especially great during the summer months when local new potatoes and corn are readily available at the farmers' market. Be sure to plan ahead for the overnight marinade.

2 (10-ounce) strip (striploin) steaks, 1½ inches thick

1 tablespoon olive oil

2 tablespoons My Favorite Spice Rub (page 168)

2 pounds new potatoes

2 tablespoons duck fat (olive oil will also work well here, but duck fat is king)

2 tablespoons minced fresh rosemary leaves

½ teaspoon sea salt

¼ teaspoon freshly cracked black pepper

1. Massage the steaks with the olive oil, then coat with the spice rub. Transfer to a plate, cover with plastic wrap, and refrigerate overnight.

2. Let the steaks come to room temperature on the counter for about 1 hour prior to cooking.

3. Preheat the oven to 400°F.

4. Wash and scrub (but do not peel) the potatoes. Transfer the spuds to a large stockpot of water and bring to a boil over medium-high heat. Boil the potatoes until just fork-tender, 8 to 10 minutes. Drain, then return the potatoes to the pot, off the heat. Give the potatoes a few shakes, to help fluff the outsides and achieve crispy spud perfection (thanks for the tip, Mr. Oliver).

5. Spoon the duck fat onto a large rimmed baking sheet and place it in the oven to melt. When it has melted, immediately spread the potatoes over the baking sheet, sprinkle the rosemary, sea salt, and pepper on top, and give the sheet a shake to coat the potatoes in the duck fat. Extra-crispy spuds

CHIMICHURRI

- **2 tablespoons finely chopped fresh basil leaves**
- **2 tablespoons finely chopped fresh flat-leaf parsley**
- **1 tablespoon very finely diced shallot**
- **1 garlic clove, minced**
- **¼ cup extra-virgin olive oil**
- **2 tablespoons apple cider vinegar**
- **2 tablespoons fresh lime juice**
- **¼ teaspoon sea salt**
- **⅛ teaspoon freshly cracked black pepper**

- **3 ears corn, shucked**
- **2 tablespoons butter, at room temperature**

are on their way! Roast for 45 to 50 minutes, giving the pan a few shakes throughout the cooking process.

6. Make the chimichurri: Combine the basil, parsley, shallot, and garlic in a mortar and pestle. Smash the lot together for about 1 minute. Drizzle in the olive oil, vinegar, and lime juice and season with the salt and pepper. Give the chimichurri a good mix and set aside. Bonus: This sauce can be prepared the evening before serving and stored in an airtight container in the fridge. Just give it a good mix when plating up. Presto!

7. When the potatoes have about 20 minutes left to roast, use a very sharp knife to carefully cut the corn into 3-inch pieces. Fill the stockpot with water and bring it to a rapid boil over medium-high heat. Add the corn and boil for 3 minutes, or until the kernels have just started to soften. Drain and set aside. When the potatoes have 10 minutes left to roast, add the corn to the sheet with the potatoes to cook with them.

8. Start cooking the steak when the potatoes and corn are almost done. Heat a cast-iron pan over medium-high heat.

When smoking hot, set a timer and add the steak to the pan. Cook, turning every minute, 8 minutes total for medium-rare (cook longer if you prefer your steak more well done). When there are 2 minutes of cooking time remaining, spoon the butter into the pan. Baste the melted butter all over the steak. See my steak tips on pages 163–165. Transfer the steak to a plate to rest for at least 6 minutes.

9. Carve the steak against the grain into thin strips, top with the chimichurri, and serve with the roasted veggie goodness. Best steak ever!

MY FAVORITE SPICE RUB

MAKES ABOUT ⅓ CUP • This is my all-time favorite, desert island, do-it-all spice rub, with bold flavors like coriander, espresso, and cayenne paired with brown sugar and lemon sweetness. I love it to bits and would gladly smother almost anything it in, from Coriander-Espresso-Rubbed Sirloin (page 166) to grilled shrimp, or even use it as a glass rimmer for brunchtime Caesars (page 48).

This spice rub will store well for several weeks in an airtight container, but I guarantee it won't last that long.

1 tablespoon coriander seeds
1 teaspoon lemon zest
1 tablespoon kosher salt
2 teaspoons freshly cracked
    black pepper
½ teaspoon paprika
1 tablespoon ground espresso
1 tablespoon brown sugar
¼ teaspoon cayenne pepper
1½ teaspoons chili powder
½ teaspoon ground cumin

In a mortar and pestle, bash the coriander seeds until they're broken down but still resemble seeds. Combine all the remaining ingredients and transfer to an airtight container. Done and done.

GOCHUJANG MAPLE SURF AND TURF

MAKES 4 TO 6 SERVINGS • Living a stone's throw from the Atlantic Ocean, East Coasters have direct access to top-quality beef and award-winning seafood that are an integral part of Maritime cuisine. Most definitely not your parents' surf and turf, this recipe trades in the classic seasonings for a sweet-and-spicy Korean-infused combination of bold flavors, marinated to perfection overnight (so plan ahead!).

TURF

- 3 tablespoons soy sauce
- 3 tablespoons pure maple syrup
- 3 tablespoons chicken stock, store-bought or homemade (page 149)
- 1 tablespoon gochujang hot pepper paste
- 1 teaspoon toasted sesame oil
- 2 garlic cloves, grated
- 1 tablespoon grated fresh ginger
- 2 (1-pound) boneless rib-eye steaks, 1½ inches thick
- 1⅓ cups jasmine rice, rinsed
- 2 tablespoons butter

SURF

- 1 pound raw jumbo shrimp, peeled and deveined
- 5 ounces Broccolini
- 1 lime, cut into wedges
- ¼ cup fresh cilantro

1. Make the turf: In a small bowl, whisk together the soy sauce, maple syrup, stock, gochujang, sesame oil, garlic, and ginger. Pour into a large freezer bag, add the steak, and massage it with the marinade, turning to coat all sides. Cover and refrigerate overnight.

2. Let the steak come to room temperature on the counter 1 hour before cooking.

3. Cook the rice according to the package directions. Cover and set aside to keep warm.

4. Heat a large cast-iron skillet over medium-high heat and let it get super hot. Reserving the marinade, cook the steaks for 8 minutes, flipping every minute for medium-rare (cook longer if you prefer your steak more well done). See How to Cook the Perfect Steak on page 163.

5. When there are 2 minutes of cooking time remaining, spoon the butter into the pan. Baste the melted butter all over the steak. Transfer the steaks to a plate, pour the pan juices on top, and rest for at least 6 minutes.

6. Make the surf: With the pan still on medium-high heat, add the shrimp and Broccolini and cook for 1 minute. Flip the shrimp and pour in the reserved marinade from the beef. Cook for 1 minute more, or until the shrimp have turned pink and are cooked through, then transfer to a plate.

7. Slice the steak into thin strips against the grain and serve with the shrimp, Broccolini, rice, lime wedges, and cilantro.

FIVE-SPICE BEEF AND BROCCOLINI

MAKES 4 SERVINGS • In my past life, before I started cooking, I was completely in love with takeout beef and broccoli, so delicious and soul-satisfying. Knowing that a better, healthier, scratch-made version was possible, I got to work, and this dish quickly made its way into our meal-plan lineup.

After an overnight marinade in the fridge, this dish comes together in mere minutes. Perfect for a quick weeknight meal at home or anytime you want to crush the local takeout competish.

MARINADE

½ cup beef stock (or chicken stock, in a pinch)

1 tablespoon sesame oil

3 tablespoons Shaoxing wine or dry sherry

3 tablespoons honey

1 tablespoon sriracha

3 garlic cloves, minced

1 tablespoon minced fresh ginger

½ cup soy sauce

½ teaspoon five-spice powder

3 tablespoons potato starch

STIR-FRY

1 pound flank steak

1⅓ cups jasmine rice

1 tablespoon sunflower or vegetable oil

7 ounces Broccolini, or 1 head of broccoli, cut into florets

¼ cup salted cashews

4 scallions, thinly sliced

1 or 2 red chiles, finely diced

Handful of fresh cilantro sprigs

1 lime, cut into wedges

1. Make the marinade: Whisk all the marinade ingredients together in a medium bowl.

2. Make the stir-fry: With a sharp knife, cut the steak against the grain into thin ¼-inch strips. Transfer the beef to a sealable freezer bag and pour the marinade into the bag. Seal and shake well to ensure that the beef is well coated. Refrigerate overnight. Let the beef and marinade come to room temperature on the counter for 30 minutes before cooking.

3. Cook the rice according to the package instructions. Set aside and cover to keep warm.

4. In a wok, heat the sunflower oil over medium-high heat. When the oil is super hot, add the steak, reserving the marinade. Cook, tossing often, for 3 minutes, or until the steak is cooked through and seared on all sides. Add the reserved marinade and the Broccolini. Give the beef and Broccolini a toss and bring the marinade to a boil to cook and thicken, about 2 minutes. Remove from the heat and toss with the cashews and scallions.

5. Serve with steamed jasmine rice and top with the chiles, cilantro, and lime wedges.

SAUCY ITALIAN-STYLE MEATBALLS

MAKES 12 TO 15 LARGE MEATBALLS, IN SAUCE • Like the wheel, the pyramids, the smartphone, and a strong IPA, meatballs are one of humanity's greatest achievements—transcendent little balls of joy that remind you that everything will be a-okay. These meatballs are fantastic with crusty bread, over pasta, on a pizza, in a sandwich, over polenta, as a burger, and a million other ways I've yet to think of.

If you're a plan-ahead rock star, these meatballs can be prepped a day early. Just form and shape the meatballs, set them on a baking sheet (lined with parchment paper), cover with plastic wrap, and refrigerate until ready to cook.

MEATBALLS

¾ cup bread crumbs (see page 253)

½ cup dry red wine

1 pound best-quality ground beef

12 ounces best-quality ground pork

½ cup grated onion

3 garlic cloves, minced

1 large free-range egg, beaten

2 tablespoons minced fresh oregano leaves

2 tablespoons minced fresh flat-leaf parsley

½ teaspoon red pepper flakes

¼ cup grated Parmesan cheese

¼ teaspoon freshly cracked black pepper

½ teaspoon sea salt

1. Make the meatballs: Preheat the oven to 450°F. Line a baking sheet with parchment paper.

2. In a large bowl, combine the bread crumbs and red wine and stir until all the bread crumbs are bright purple. Add the rest of the meatball ingredients and mix well but gently.

3. Using the palms of your hands, roll the meatball mixture into 12 to 15 balls, each using about 3 tablespoons of the mixture. Arrange them on the prepared baking sheet, leaving 1 inch between each meatball.

4. Bake the meatballs for 10 minutes. Set aside.

5. Meanwhile, crack on with the sauce: In a large pot, heat the olive oil over medium heat. When the oil is hot, fry the garlic for 30 seconds, keeping a close eye on it to make sure it doesn't burn. Add the tomatoes, wine, stock, basil stems, red pepper flakes, salt, and black pepper and bring the sauce to a simmer. Let the sauce bubble away for 10 minutes.

6. Transfer the meatballs to the sauce and cook, stirring gently every few minutes, for 10 minutes, or until the meatballs are cooked through. Stir in the Parmesan and basil leaves. Serve as desired!

TOMATO SAUCE

¼ cup olive oil

5 garlic cloves, minced

1 (28-ounce) can crushed tomatoes

1 cup dry red wine

½ cup beef stock (or chicken stock, in a pinch)

1 tablespoon minced fresh basil stems

¼ teaspoon red pepper flakes

1 teaspoon sea salt

½ teaspoon freshly cracked black pepper

¼ cup grated Parmesan cheese

¼ cup finely chopped fresh basil leaves

BEEF BULGOGI

MAKES 4 SERVINGS • While living in Nashville and spending my days torn between playing guitar and dreaming of pulled pork, sweet tea, and biscuits, I had my food world rocked to the core. One unexpected meal transformed my culinary outlook entirely. Our dear friend Esther, who'd taught for years in South Korea, suggested that we absolutely *had* to try proper Korean food (not yet a thing in my Maritime homeland). I was completely destroyed by the sweet, spicy, tangy, pickle-y, fermented goodness. The especially incredible beef bulgogi was a game changer, and I've been making a version of this dish ever since.

1 pound beef tenderloin or sirloin

½ cup grated peeled pear

¼ cup grated onion

4 garlic cloves, finely minced

2 scallions, finely sliced

2 tablespoons soy sauce

2 tablespoons dark brown sugar

1 tablespoon toasted sesame oil

1½ cups uncooked jasmine rice

1 large carrot, sliced ⅛ inch thick on an angle

1 cup thinly sliced napa cabbage

1 cup broccoli florets

TO SERVE

2 scallions, finely sliced

1 tablespoon sesame seeds

1 cup spicy greens, such as baby arugula or mizuna

1 or 2 red chiles, thinly sliced

1. Pop the beef in the freezer for about 1 hour (this will help you to slice it super thin).

2. Thinly slice the cold beef into ⅛-inch-thick pieces and transfer them to a freezer bag. Add the pear, onion, garlic, scallions, soy sauce, brown sugar, and sesame oil, seal the bag, and give it several vigorous shakes to mix. Refrigerate overnight or for at least 1 hour, if you're short on time.

3. This dish comes together with lightning speed (the best!). Prepare the rice according to the package instructions. Cover and set aside to keep warm.

4. Meanwhile, heat a grill pan or skillet over medium-high heat. Toss the beef and veggies together to mix well. When smoking hot, grab some tongs and grill the beef, carrot, cabbage, and broccoli for 3 to 4 minutes, turning often so they develop a nice char on both sides. Pour in any remaining marinade and grill for 1 minute, then remove from the heat.

5. Toss the scallions and sesame seeds with the beef and veggies and serve with the rice, greens, and chiles (for spicy lovers after my own heart).

CHRISTMAS DINNER: ROAST BEEF WITH CRISPY SPUDS AND GREEN BEANS

MAKES 8 TO 10 SERVINGS • I love Christmas. I love every single awesome thing about it. The family time, the food, decorating the tree, singing carols, getting presents (whatever, I'll admit it. Don't judge). But above all, the most cherished moments during the holidays are those spent intentionally slowing down, spending time reconnecting with those near and dear, and appreciating a wonderfully blessed year with good friends and great family.

Often these moments happen while you're in the kitchen preparing the family meal. If you're responsible for cooking the big show this holiday season, fear not! Everything is going to be okay. Repeat after me: *Everything is going to be okay.* Take a deep breath.

All right, now let's get to work. This recipe is all about timing, planning ahead, and having everything you need locked and loaded and at the ready. If you've got everything well prepped and planned, it's a breeze to prepare. Happiest of holidays, friends!

BEEF

- 1 (5- to 6-pound) standing beef roast, trimmed
- 1 teaspoon kosher salt
- 1 teaspoon freshly cracked black pepper
- 5 garlic cloves, coarsely chopped
- 2½ tablespoons fresh thyme leaves
- 2½ tablespoons fresh rosemary leaves
- Zest of 1 lemon
- ¼ cup Dijon mustard
- 1 tablespoon olive oil
- 2 red onions, quartered

1. Make the beef: Let the beef stand at room temperature for at least 2 hours prior to cooking. Rub the roast all over with the salt and pepper.

2. Preheat the oven to 400°F.

3. Pop the garlic, thyme, and rosemary in a food processor and pulse until finely minced. Add the lemon zest, mustard, and olive oil, and pulse until combined and smooth. Rub the Dijon mixture all over the beef, coating it evenly. Perfect.

4. Place the red onions in a roasting pan fitted with a rack and set the beef on the rack. Roast for exactly 30 minutes—set a timer! When the timer goes off, immediately reduce the oven temperature to 350°F. Roast the beef for 30 minutes more.

GARLIC AND SHALLOT POTATOES

4 pounds russet potatoes, unpeeled, cut into 1½-inch chunks

10 medium shallots

1 garlic head, cloves separated but left unpeeled

2 tablespoons finely diced fresh rosemary

⅓ cup olive oil

1 teaspoon salt

½ teaspoon freshly cracked black pepper

(Ingredients continue on page 181.)

5. Meanwhile, make the potatoes: Place the potatoes in a large stockpot of cold salted water and bring the water to a boil over medium-high heat. Cook for 8 to 10 minutes, or until the potatoes start to become tender. Drain, return the potatoes to the pot off the heat, and give the lot a shake or two to chuff up the sides (a must for the crispiest spuds ever). Potato heaven.

6. Transfer the potatoes to a large baking dish (but one that will fit into the oven with the roasting pan) and add the shallots, garlic, and rosemary. Pour the olive oil over the veggies, season with the salt and pepper, and give everything a good mix.

7. Pop the potatoes into the oven to roast alongside the beef.

8. After about 30 minutes (1½ hours total roasting time for the beef), pop an instant-read thermometer into the thickest part of the beef to check the progress (see Note, page 181). For a medium-rare roast, the thermometer should read 130°F (the internal temperature will rise as it rests). If the beef is not quite there yet, continue roasting, checking every 10 minutes

GREEN BEANS

3 pounds green beans, ends trimmed

3 tablespoons olive oil

Juice of 1 lemon

½ teaspoon smoked paprika

½ teaspoon kosher salt

½ teaspoon freshly cracked black pepper

GRAVY

2 tablespoons butter

2 tablespoons all-purpose flour

1 garlic clove, minced

1½ cups red wine (or use more beef stock for an alcohol-free gravy)

1½ cups beef stock

Kosher salt and freshly cracked black pepper

NOTE: *An instant-read thermometer is absolutely essential for accuracy in this recipe. Standing rib roasts are far too expensive for guesswork!*

until the roast reaches the desired doneness (cook the beef longer if you prefer your meat more well done). Transfer the roast to a cutting board, reserving the liquid and onions in the pan. Cover loosely with aluminum foil and let stand for 20 minutes.

9. Give the potato pan a shake to flip the spuds and let them carry on roasting away for 30 minutes more, or an hour in total if you kept the beef in longer.

10. Make the green beans: Bring a large saucepan of salted water to a boil. Add the green beans and cook until tender, 8 to 10 minutes. Drain. Toss the green beans with the olive oil, lemon juice, paprika, salt, and pepper.

11. Meanwhile, make the gravy: Set the beef roasting pan over medium heat and add the butter to the juices in the pan. When it has melted, whisk in the flour and garlic and cook for 1 minute. Slowly and steadily whisk in the wine to deglaze the pan, scraping up all the heavenly browned bits from the bottom. Whisk in the stock, season with a pinch of salt and pepper, and bring the mixture to a boil. Let the gravy simmer until reduced by half, 8 to 10 minutes. Pour through a fine-mesh sieve to remove any lumps, then pour into a gravy boat, cover, and set aside to keep warm.

12. Using a long carving knife, slice the beef into thin portions, ¼ to ½ inch thick. Serve that incredible roast beef with the gravy, roasted spuds, and green beans.

Deglazing means to add a liquid (such as broth, beer, water, or wine) to a pan that food was cooking in, then scraping up all the browned bits from the bottom of the pan and stirring them into a sauce or gravy. You can then carry on reducing the liquid to the desired consistency to help in developing the boldest, most intensely delicious flavor possible.

LEMON-THYME ROAST CHICKEN

MAKES 4 TO 6 SERVINGS • From Los Angeles to London to Timbuktu, there are few things as unanimously crowd pleasing as a succulent, golden brown, crispy-skinned roast chicken. It is one of life's simple joys and the perfect main event dish for Sunday lunch or holiday meals. Best of all, with only a few simple steps, it's a total breeze to prepare—as long as you throw it in the brine before roasting.

This chicken is especially delicious served with Garlic and Rosemary Hasselback Potatoes (page 276) or Tuscan-Style Panzanella Salad (page 292).

BRINE

½ cup kosher salt

½ cup sugar

¼ cup apple cider vinegar

4 fresh thyme sprigs

4 fresh rosemary sprigs

1 lemon, halved

1 garlic head, halved

2 tablespoons whole black peppercorns

ROAST CHICKEN

1 (3½- to 4-pound) best-quality free-range chicken

2 large carrots, coarsely chopped

1 large onion, cut into 1-inch chunks

2 tablespoons olive oil

1 lemon, halved

1 garlic head, halved crosswise

1 tablespoon fresh thyme leaves

1 tablespoon lemon zest

1 teaspoon sea salt

1 teaspoon freshly cracked black pepper

1. Make the brine: In a large stockpot, combine the salt, sugar, and 1 gallon of water and bring it to a boil over medium-high heat. Set aside to cool completely. Stir in the remaining brine ingredients.

2. Make the roast chicken: Submerge the chicken in the brine. Cover and refrigerate for at least 4 hours and up to 8 hours.

3. Drain the chicken and discard the brine. Pat the bird completely dry with paper towels and transfer to a board. Let stand at room temperature for 30 minutes.

4. Preheat the oven to 450°F.

5. Arrange the carrots and onion in a large cast-iron pan, Dutch oven, or other oven-safe pan. Massage the chicken all over with the olive oil and set it on top of the veggies. Stuff the lemon and garlic head halves in the bird's cavity. Sprinkle the thyme, lemon zest, sea salt, and pepper on the bird, getting all areas nicely coated.

6. Roast the chicken for 15 minutes, then reduce the oven temperature to 375°F and roast for 1 hour 15 minutes more, or until an instant-read thermometer inserted into the thickest part of the thigh registers 165°F. If the temperature has not quite reached 165°F, continue roasting and check the temperature of the bird every 10 minutes until it does.

Brining is a flavor enhancer. I call it the delicious maker. As meat cooks, it shrinks and loses moisture as the muscle fibers get all science-y. Brining actually increases the moisture within the meat, so that less is lost during the cooking process and you get a much juicier final product.

Brining is especially important when cooking poultry or pork. It's a smart and easy habit to get into.

7. Loosely tent the chicken with aluminum foil and let it rest on a cutting board for 15 minutes, then carve and serve. (Save the carcass and any leftover bones for Homemade Chicken Stock, page 149.)

MAPLE-BUTTERMILK FRIED CHICKEN WITH A WICKED MAPLE-DIJON SLAW

MAKES 6 TO 8 SERVINGS • Let's just stop here for a minute and really, wholeheartedly thank the genius who created the masterpiece that is fried chicken—the Sistine Chapel of all comfort food dishes. As far as I'm concerned, it doesn't get any more delicious than crunchy, fried, buttermilk-soaked goodness.

I ate my fair share of fried chicken growing up. It came in a big bucket with a drawing of a vintage-looking dude on the side, and for all I knew, that was a proper, legit representation of the dish. Then I moved to the blessed South and experienced the rapturous bliss that is legit, home-style, fried-to-perfection chicken.

As with everything, scratch-made at home is always best, and this recipe is proof positive (just be sure to account for the overnight marinade—it will be worth it!). Spiked with a maple-buttermilk marinade and served with a killer maple-Dijon slaw, this recipe is a guaranteed hit.

CHICKEN

3½ **pounds chicken drumsticks and thighs**
⅓ **cup pure maple syrup**
2½ **cups buttermilk**
½ **teaspoon cayenne pepper**
1 **teaspoon finely minced fresh thyme leaves**
1 **teaspoon sea salt**

SLAW

½ **large red cabbage, thinly sliced (about 8 cups)**
2 **large carrots, grated on the large holes of a box grater**
1 **cup grated Brussels sprouts, grated on the large holes of a box grater**
⅓ **cup whole-grain Dijon mustard**

(Ingredients continue on page 187.)

1. Make the chicken: In a large bowl or freezer bag, combine the chicken, maple syrup, buttermilk, cayenne, thyme, and sea salt and massage together. Cover with plastic wrap and refrigerate overnight, or for a minimum of 8 hours.

2. Preheat the oven to 225°F. Let the chicken come to room temperature on the counter for 20 to 30 minutes prior to cooking.

3. Make the slaw: In a large bowl, toss the cabbage, carrots, and Brussels sprouts. In a small dish, whisk together the mustard, maple syrup, vinegar, and lemon juice. While whisking continuously, slowly stream in the vegetable oil until all the oil has worked itself into the silky-smooth dressing. Season with the salt and pepper. Pour the dressing over the veggies and give everything a mix. Cover and refrigerate (see Note).

4. Make the seasoned flour: In a large bowl, combine all the ingredients and toss to mix.

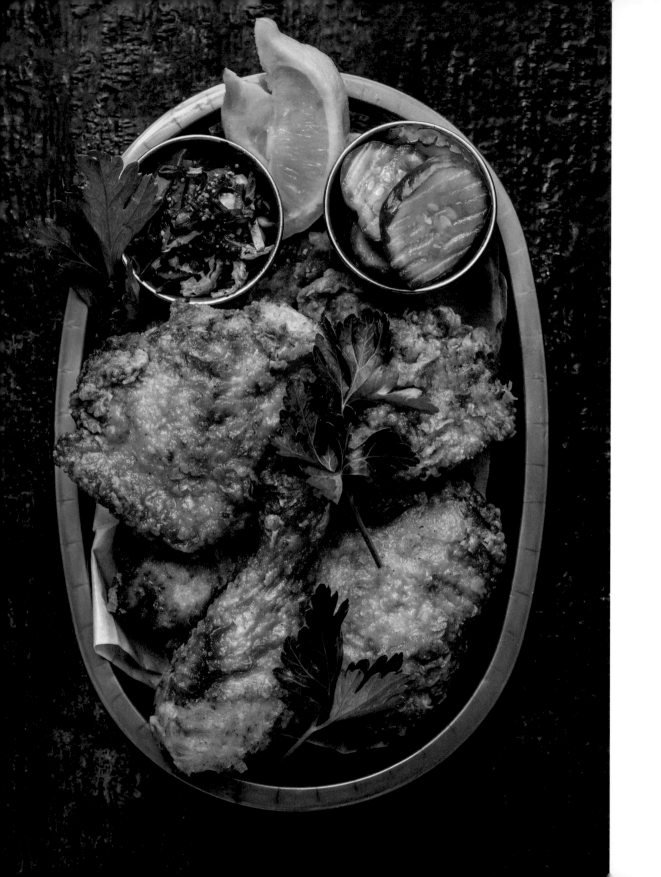

- ¼ cup pure maple syrup
- ¼ cup apple cider vinegar
- 2 tablespoons fresh lemon juice
- ¼ cup vegetable oil
- ¼ teaspoon sea salt
- ¼ teaspoon freshly cracked black pepper

SEASONED FLOUR

- 2 cups all-purpose flour
- 1 teaspoon sea salt
- ½ teaspoon garlic powder
- ½ teaspoon cayenne pepper
- ½ teaspoon smoked paprika
- ½ teaspoon chili powder
- ½ teaspoon freshly ground white pepper
- 1 tablespoon lemon zest

- Canola oil, for frying
- Your favorite bread and butter pickles, for serving
- Fresh lemon wedges, for serving

5. Fry the chicken: In a high-sided Dutch oven or stockpot, heat 3 inches of canola oil to 350°F. Set a rack over a large rimmed baking sheet.

6. Give the chicken pieces a gentle shake to remove any excess marinade, then dredge them in the seasoned flour, coating them well. Working in batches, fry the chicken for 15 to 18 minutes, turning the pieces a couple of times, until they are golden brown and full of happy. The internal temperature of the chicken should be 165°F on an instant-read thermometer. If so, good to go. Transfer the cooked chicken to the rack and set the baking sheet in the oven to keep warm. Continue to fry the rest of the chicken.

7. Serve with the slaw, some nice pickles, and fresh lemon wedges.

Dredging is lightly coating a food, in this case chicken, in a flour or bread crumb mixture. When the food is fully coated, give it a shake or two to remove any excess before frying.

NOTE: *If planning ahead, combine the veggies in one bowl and the dressing in another. Cover each with plastic wrap and chill in the fridge for up to 24 hours. Before serving, give the dressing a good whisk, then toss with the shredded veggies. Done and done.*

CRISPY LEMON-OREGANO CHICKEN TRAY BAKE

MAKES 4 TO 6 SERVINGS • Tray-baked recipes are weeknight heroes: fabulous, easy-to-assemble, family-style meals that let you cook for a crew with very little cleanup required (best thing ever). Roasting all that deliciousness together in one baking pan really encourages those beautiful flavors to hang out, shake hands, and become the best of friends. And it looks super impressive, y'all! Total win. So grab your camera and get Insta-ready.

This dish does require an overnight marinade—but that makes it all the simpler when it comes time to cook.

6 large bone-in, skin-on chicken thighs

2 tablespoons olive oil

1 tablespoon lemon zest

1 teaspoon smoked paprika

½ teaspoon dried oregano

½ teaspoon sea salt

¼ teaspoon freshly cracked black pepper, plus more as needed

2 pounds new (baby) potatoes, scrubbed

1 cup sparkling white wine

1 cup chicken stock, store-bought or homemade (page 149)

3 garlic cloves, minced

10 ounces cherry tomatoes, on the vine if possible

½ teaspoon smoked (or regular) sea salt

1 tablespoon minced fresh oregano leaves

6 slices cured coppa ham or prosciutto

½ cup crumbled feta cheese

Fresh parsley, for serving

Lemon wedges, for serving

1. Place the chicken thighs in a large freezer bag and add the olive oil, lemon zest, paprika, oregano, sea salt, and pepper. Massage the marinade all over the chicken, seal the bag, and refrigerate overnight.

2. Dinnertime! Preheat the oven to 400°F.

3. Put the potatoes in a large pot of cold water. Bring to a boil and cook for 8 to 10 minutes, until just fork-tender. Drain.

4. Heat a 3-quart oven-safe pan over medium-high heat. When the pan is banging hot, add the chicken, skin-side down, and cook for 3 to 4 minutes, until the skin is golden brown and super crispy. Turn the chicken over and add the wine, stock, and garlic. When the liquid comes to a simmer, use tongs to arrange the potatoes underneath the chicken. Add the cherry tomatoes and season with the smoked sea salt and some pepper. Scatter the oregano on top and roast for 35 to 40 minutes, or until the chicken is cooked through and an instant-read thermometer inserted into the thickest part registers 165°F.

5. Top each piece of chicken with a slice of ham, crumble the feta on top, and sprinkle with parsley. Serve with lemon wedges.

1 (2-inch) piece cinnamon
    stick

8 garlic cloves, minced

1 tablespoon minced fresh
    ginger

½ teaspoon fenugreek seeds

1 or 2 red chiles, diced

¼ cup tomato paste

1 (28-ounce) can crushed
    tomatoes

1 teaspoon red (Kashmiri)
    chile powder

3 cups chicken stock, store-
    bought or homemade
    (page 149)

1 teaspoon sea salt

1 tablespoon pure maple
    syrup

1 tablespoon crushed dried
    fenugreek leaves (find
    these at a specialty grocer
    or online)

1 cup heavy cream

1 tablespoon garam masala

TO SERVE

Heavy cream

Fresh cilantro

Sliced red chiles

Rice or naan (such as Chile-
    Coriander Naan, page 267)

the garlic, ginger, fenugreek seeds, chiles, and tomato paste and cook for 2 minutes, stirring often. Stir in the tomatoes and chile powder and cook, stirring often to keep the sauce from sticking to the pot, for 20 minutes.

6. Turn off the heat and puree the sauce directly in the pot with an immersion blender. (Alternatively, carefully transfer the sauce to a regular blender and puree—be careful when blending hot liquids.) Turn the heat to medium and stir in the stock and sea salt. Bring to a simmer and cook for 15 minutes, or until the sauce has started to thicken beautifully.

7. Remove the chicken pieces from the skewers and stir them into the curry, along with the maple syrup and dried fenugreek leaves. Cover and cook for 8 minutes. Turn the heat to medium-low and stir in the cream and garam masala. Simmer the sauce for a final 5 minutes.

8. Top each bowl of curry with a drizzle of cream, fresh cilantro, and sliced red chiles, if you like it spicy. Serve with rice or naan. Immediately enter comfort food heaven.

HOISIN CHICKEN DRUMSTICKS

MAKES 4 TO 6 SERVINGS • I have a major soft spot for extra-saucy, BBQ-style anything. These Hoisin Chicken Drumsticks are a wicked weeknight meal option, and fit that bill to a T. Hoisin is a bit like a Chinese BBQ sauce and pairs wonderfully well with chicken or beef or tossed with egg noodles. A weekly recipe staple in our home when Leanne and I were first married was her classic BBQ chicken, an extra-saucy chicken dish spooned over rice. This is my pimped-out version of that old-school Prescott family staple.

Chicken drumsticks are an inexpensive protein option and, in my opinion, far more flavorful than their boneless, skinless cousin. After a flavor brine in the fridge, this recipe will be ready and on the table in under an hour. Awesome.

CHICKEN AND BRINE

½ cup sugar

½ cup kosher salt

Juice of 1 lime

1 garlic head, halved horizontally

2 tablespoons whole black peppercorns

10 skin-on chicken drumsticks

2 tablespoons peanut oil

SAUCE

⅓ cup hoisin sauce

⅓ cup chicken stock, store-bought or homemade (page 149)

3 tablespoons soy sauce

3 tablespoons ketchup

1 tablespoon garlic chili sauce

1 tablespoon rice vinegar

1 tablespoon honey

3 garlic cloves, minced

3 cups chicken stock, store-bought or homemade (page 149)

1. Brine the chicken: In a large saucepan, combine the sugar, salt, and 8 cups water and bring to a boil over medium-high heat. Remove from the heat and stir in the lime juice, garlic, and peppercorns. Let cool to room temperature, then submerge the chicken in the brine, cover, and refrigerate for 3 to 4 hours.

2. Chicken time! Preheat the oven to 425°F.

3. Drain the chicken and discard the brine. Pat the chicken completely dry with paper towels and transfer to a large bowl. Massage the drumsticks with the peanut oil.

4. Heat a large high-sided oven-safe pan over medium heat. When hot, add the chicken and cook until golden brown on all sides, 5 to 6 minutes.

5. While the chicken is getting its crispy on, make the sauce: In a small bowl, whisk together all the sauce ingredients.

6. Pour the sauce into the pan and toss to coat the chicken on all sides. Transfer the pan to the oven and roast for 30 to 35 minutes, until the meat easily pulls away from the bone and has reached an internal temperature of 165°F as measured on an instant-read thermometer.

- 1½ cups jasmine rice, rinsed
- 7 ounces baby bok choy, trimmed, leaves separated
- 3 scallions, finely sliced, for serving
- 1 or 2 red chiles, finely diced, for serving
- 1 tablespoon sesame seeds, toasted (see below), for serving
- 1 lime, halved, for serving

7. While the chicken is roasting, bring the stock to a boil in a 3-quart saucepan over medium heat. Add the rice and cook according to the package directions. Cover and set aside to keep warm.

8. Add the bok choy leaves to the pan with the chicken to wilt.

9. Spoon the cooked rice onto a serving tray, top with the chicken and bok choy, and pour the saucy pan juices on top. Sprinkle the chicken with the scallions, chiles, and sesame seeds, and serve with the lime halves.

Toasting sesame seeds couldn't be easier. Simply heat a dry skillet over medium heat and add the sesame seeds. Toast, tossing often, for 3 to 5 minutes, until lightly browned and fragrant. Done! Awesome.

PAPRIKA-CORIANDER CHICKEN WITH APRICOT COUSCOUS

MAKES 4 TO 6 SERVINGS • Paprika, coriander, apricots, and goat cheese. This recipe just sells itself—spicy, savory, and sweet, with crispy chicken and a flavorful but light couscous. This is one of my favorite recipes in this book. Your family will go completely bananas for it.

CHICKEN

4 whole bone-in chicken legs (thighs and drumsticks)

2 tablespoons olive oil

1 tablespoon paprika

1 tablespoon coriander seeds, bashed in a mortar and pestle

½ tablespoon sea salt

½ tablespoon freshly cracked black pepper

1 large red onion, sliced into thin half-moons

3 fresh ripe apricots, halved and pitted

COUSCOUS

1 tablespoon olive oil

2 garlic cloves, minced

¼ cup dried apricots, thinly sliced

2½ cups chicken stock, store-bought or homemade (page 149)

2 cups couscous

½ teaspoon ground cumin

¼ teaspoon sea salt

¼ teaspoon freshly cracked black pepper

½ cup crumbled goat cheese

¼ cup chopped fresh flat-leaf parsley, plus more for serving

1. Make the chicken: Preheat the oven to 400°F.

2. In a large bowl, massage the chicken legs with the olive oil, paprika, coriander, salt, and pepper.

3. Heat a large oven-safe skillet over medium-high heat. When the pan is sizzling hot, brown the chicken legs on both sides, 3 to 4 minutes total. Remove the chicken from the pan.

4. Using tongs, lay the onion on the bottom of the pan and top with the chicken. Roast for 40 to 45 minutes, or until the chicken reaches an internal temperature of 165°F on an instant-read thermometer, the skin is super crispy, and the meat easily falls away from the bone. With about 5 minutes of cooking time left, pop the fresh apricot halves into the pan.

5. While the chicken is cooking, make the couscous: In a 3-quart saucepan, heat the olive oil over medium heat. When hot (but not smoking), add the garlic and cook for 30 seconds, watching closely so it doesn't burn. Stir in the dried apricots and stock and bring to a boil. Stir in the couscous, cumin, salt, and pepper. Remove from the heat, cover, and let the couscous sit for 5 minutes to soak in all that beautiful stock. Fluff with a fork and fold in the goat cheese and parsley.

6. Spoon the couscous onto a large serving platter and top with the chicken, onion, and apricots. Pour the delicious pan juices over the top and sprinkle with the parsley.

GENERAL TSO'S CHICKEN

MAKES 4 SERVINGS • When I was a kid, my family ate Chinese takeout. A lot. And of all the delicious combination plate options at the local Silvery Moon Restaurant, their General Tso's will forever have my heart. The marriage of sweet-and-spicy sauce with super-crispy chicken is just perfection.

This is my homemade version of a childhood classic. And it's baked, not fried—so it's much healthier than the old standard—bonus! No MSG, only goodness. Serve it up with rice and some steamed broccoli or Super-Quick Garlic Bok Choy (page 275), and it'll quickly become a household favorite.

CHICKEN

⅓ cup all-purpose flour

2 large free-range eggs, beaten

1 cup bread crumbs (see page 253)

1 cup panko bread crumbs

2 teaspoons lime zest

½ teaspoon kosher salt

1½ pounds boneless, skinless chicken breasts, cut into ½-inch cubes

SAUCE

1½ cups chicken stock, store-bought or homemade (page 149)

⅓ cup hoisin sauce

1½ tablespoons soy sauce

¼ cup rice vinegar

3 tablespoons dark brown sugar

2 teaspoons cornstarch

1 large red bell pepper, julienned

4 scallions, finely sliced

2 tablespoons sesame seeds

Steamed rice, for serving

Handful of fresh cilantro

1 or 2 red chiles, finely sliced

1. Make the chicken: Preheat the oven to 450°F. Fit a rack over a large baking sheet lined with parchment paper.

2. Prepare three bowls: one with the flour, one with the beaten eggs, and one with a mixture of the bread crumbs, panko, lime zest, and salt. Working with one or two pieces at a time, dredge the chicken in the flour, then dunk it in the egg wash, and finally drop it into the bread crumb mixture, getting each piece completely coated.

3. Transfer the chicken to the prepared baking sheet and bake for 20 minutes, turning halfway through.

4. When the chicken has 10 minutes left to cook, make the sauce: In a large saucepan, combine the stock, hoisin, soy sauce, vinegar, brown sugar, and cornstarch. Give the sauce a good whisk and bring it to a boil over medium heat, stirring often. Reduce the heat to medium-low and simmer for 2 to 3 minutes, until thick and glossy.

5. Toss the chicken and bell pepper in the sauce. Remove from the heat and toss with the scallions and, sesame seeds.

6. Serve up with steamed rice, then garnish with the fresh cilantro and chiles.

CHICKEN WINGS, THREE WAYS

MAKES 5 POUNDS CHICKEN WINGS • My good friend, former bandmate, and probable marketing genius Matt Sutherland once told me that he wanted to start a band called 10 Cent Wings. His plan? Advertise the band and capitalize on the hordes of wing-loving crazies who would no doubt swarm the pub thinking they were in for a delicious, non-music-related treat.

The moral of this story? Almost everybody loves chicken wings.

Chicken wings are handheld happiness. They're a total treat to make at home and so much better than store-bought. This is one wing recipe with three sauce options, tailor-made to customize wing night to your liking. Awesome.

½ cup sugar

1 cup kosher salt

1 lemon, halved

4 fresh thyme sprigs

1 garlic head, cut crosswise

2 tablespoons whole black peppercorns

5 pounds chicken wings, split into drums and flats

3 tablespoons vegetable oil

Sauce of your choice (see pages 199–201)

1. In a large stockpot, combine 1 gallon water, the sugar, and the salt. Stir and bring to a boil over medium-high heat. Turn off the heat and stir in the lemon, thyme, garlic, and peppercorns. Let cool to room temperature. Submerge the wings in the brine, cover, and give the bowl a home in the fridge. Leave the brine to work its magic for 2 to 4 hours. (If the stockpot is too large for your fridge, transfer the brine to an airtight container that will fit all the wings and brine.)

2. Preheat the oven to 425°F. Line two large baking sheets with parchment paper and top each with a rack.

3. Drain the wings and discard the brine. Pat them completely dry with paper towels, and place them in a large bowl. Massage the wings all over with the vegetable oil.

4. Arrange the wings in a single layer on the racks and bake for 45 to 50 minutes, turning halfway through, until they're golden brown, crispy, and have reached an internal temperature of 165°F (using an instant-read thermometer).

5. Sauces! While the wings are rocking away, prepare the sauce-weapon of your choice.

6. Generously baste both sides of each wing with the sauce and bake for 5 minutes more.

KOREAN GOCHUJANG SAUCE

MAKES ABOUT 2½ CUPS

½ cup gochujang hot pepper paste

¼ cup soy sauce

6 tablespoons pure maple syrup

2 tablespoons rice vinegar

2 tablespoons fresh lime juice

2 tablespoons sesame oil

½ cup (1 stick) butter, melted

4 garlic cloves, grated

1 tablespoon grated fresh ginger

¼ cup crushed roasted salted peanuts

¼ cup finely sliced scallions

2 tablespoons sesame seeds

1 lime, cut into wedges, for serving

Handful of fresh cilantro, for serving

1. In a large bowl, whisk together the gochujang, soy sauce, maple syrup, vinegar, lime juice, sesame oil, butter, garlic, and ginger until well combined, about 30 seconds.

2. Generously baste the wings with the sauce and bake a final 5 minutes. Transfer the wings to a large bowl and toss them together the peanuts, scallions, and sesame seeds.

3. Serve with the lime wedges, fresh cilantro, and any leftover sauce for dipping.

BUFFALO SAUCE

⅔ cup (1⅓ sticks) butter

½ cup of your favorite hot sauce (such as Frank's RedHot)

2 tablespoons fresh lemon juice

½ teaspoon garlic powder

1. In a medium saucepan, melt the butter over medium-low heat. Whisk in the hot sauce, lemon juice, and garlic powder.

2. Generously baste the wings with the sauce and bake for 5 minutes more.

STICKY BBQ SAUCE

1½ cups packed dark brown sugar

1¼ cups ketchup

1½ tablespoons molasses

3 tablespoons apple cider vinegar

1 tablespoon fresh lemon juice

1 tablespoon lemon zest

2 teaspoons ground mustard

1½ teaspoons paprika

½ teaspoon chili powder

½ teaspoon garlic powder

½ teaspoon onion powder

¼ teaspoon cayenne pepper

1½ teaspoons kosher salt

1½ teaspoons freshly cracked black pepper

1. Combine all the ingredients in a medium saucepan over medium heat and bring the mixture to a simmer. Cook until the sauce has thickened slightly, about 5 minutes. Remove from the heat.

2. Generously baste the wings with the sauce and bake for 5 minutes more. Easy, peasy, lemon squeezy.

CRISPY PORK TONKATSU

MAKES 4 SERVINGS • Fried pork. Isn't it marvelous?

In Japan, tonkatsu is serious comfort food business, with everyone from Michelin-starred restaurants to vending machine sandwiches (*katsu-sandos*) and all points in between offering their version to the masses. This genius little dish consists of a super-crispy breaded and fried pork cutlet with a sweet-and-savory sauce and is typically served with rice and shredded cabbage. Best of all, because the pork is pounded into submission, this recipe is quick as a wink.

TONKATSU SAUCE

¾ cup ketchup

2 tablespoons Worcestershire sauce

3 tablespoons soy sauce

2 tablespoons fresh lemon juice

1 garlic clove, grated

1 teaspoon grated fresh ginger

1 teaspoon Dijon mustard

1 tablespoon mirin

1 tablespoon pure maple syrup

1. Make the tonkatsu sauce: Combine all the sauce ingredients in a medium saucepan, stir well, and bring to a simmer over medium heat. Gently simmer for 5 minutes, until thickened slightly, then remove from the heat and run through a fine-mesh sieve set over a bowl. Cover with plastic wrap and set aside.

2. Make the pork: Working with one chop at a time, sandwich the pork between two pieces of plastic wrap. Pound the meat with the palm of your hand, a rolling pin, or a wine bottle until each piece is ½ inch thick. Sprinkle both sides of the pork chops with salt and pepper.

3. Prepare three bowls: one with a mixture of the flour, salt, and pepper; one with the eggs; and one with the panko.

4. In a heavy-bottomed Dutch oven, heat 2 inches of oil over medium heat to 350°F. Working one at a time, dredge the pork chops in the flour, then the egg, and then the bread crumbs, making sure all sides are well coated. Working in batches as necessary, fry the pork, turning once or twice, for 8 to 10 minutes, until the crust is golden brown and the juices run clear. Slice each chop into 5 or 6 long strips.

5. Plate up each serving with a 1-cup mountain of the rice, 1 cup of the cabbage, and 1 sliced pork cutlet. Pour a heaping spoonful of the tonkatsu sauce on top, sprinkle with sesame seeds, and add your favorite greens.

4 (6-ounce) boneless pork loin chops

1 cup all-purpose flour

1 teaspoon kosher salt, plus more for sprinkling

1 teaspoon freshly cracked black pepper, plus more for sprinkling

2 large free-range eggs, lightly whisked

2½ cups panko bread crumbs

Vegetable oil, for frying

4 cups cooked short-grain rice

4 cups shredded napa cabbage

1 tablespoon sesame seeds

2 cups of your favorite greens or sprouts

PAN-ROASTED PORK CHOPS WITH MAPLE-SAGE APPLES AND CAULIFLOWER MASH

MAKES 4 TO 6 SERVINGS • Pork, sage, and apples are the best of friends, and the combination is magic during harvest season when local apples are at their peak. Combined with a creamy cauliflower mash and salty feta, this may just be your new favorite pork recipe.

With pork chops there is very little gray zone. When cooked properly, they are juicy, mouth-watering pieces of meaty heaven. When cooked poorly, you're left with shoe leather. Brining your chops, searing them in a super-hot skillet, and then pan roasting (with an instant-read thermometer at the ready) will guarantee you perfectly juicy pork chops every single time.

PORK AND BRINE

¼ cup kosher salt

½ cup pure maple syrup

2 cups apple cider

2 tablespoons apple cider vinegar

1½ teaspoons whole black peppercorns

2 fresh sage sprigs

4 (1-pound) bone-in center-cut pork chops, 1 inch thick

CAULIFLOWER MASH

1 cauliflower head

3 tablespoons whole milk

3 tablespoons sour cream

1 tablespoon butter

½ teaspoon sea salt

¼ teaspoon freshly cracked black pepper

2 tablespoons olive oil

Salt and freshly cracked black pepper

(Ingredients continue on page 206.)

1. Brine the pork: Combine the salt, maple syrup, and 6 cups water in a medium saucepan over medium heat, stirring often. When the salt has completely dissolved, let the brine cool to room temperature. Add the apple cider, vinegar, peppercorns, and sage.

2. Submerge the pork chops in the brine. Cover and refrigerate for 45 minutes to 4 hours.

3. Remove the chops from the brine and pat them completely dry with paper towels (discard the brine). Set the pork on a plate and cover with plastic wrap. Let the pork come to room temperature for 30 minutes before cooking.

4. Preheat the oven to 400°F.

5. Make the cauliflower mash: Bring a large pot of salted water to a boil. Cut the cauliflower into florets and cook them until fork-tender, 5 to 7 minutes, then drain. In a bowl with an immersion blender or in a food processor, pulse the cauliflower, milk, sour cream, and butter until smooth. Season with the salt and pepper, and pulse a few more times to mix. Cover to keep warm and set aside.

MAPLE-SAGE APPLES

1 tablespoon butter

1 tablespoon olive oil

10 fresh sage leaves

½ cup thinly sliced red onion

1 pound Honeycrisp or Gala apples, peeled, cored, and cut into 1-inch-thick wedges

2 tablespoons pure maple syrup

¼ cup crumbled feta cheese

6. Massage the pork with the olive oil and season each chop with a pinch of salt and pepper. Heat a cast-iron skillet or other ovenproof pan over medium-high heat and get it smoking hot. Open the kitchen windows and crank on the oven fan. We need that pan blazing, friends! Add the pork chops and sear on one side, without turning, for 3 minutes. Turn the chops and transfer the pan directly to the oven. Roast for 6 to 10 minutes, or until the pork is at 140°F to 145°F on an instant-read thermometer inserted into the thickest part of the meat. Transfer to a plate, pour any pan juices on top, and tent loosely with foil. Rest for 5 minutes.

7. Meanwhile, make the apples: In a large skillet, melt the butter with the olive oil over medium heat. Add the sage and fry for 1 minute. Remove the sage with a slotted spoon and set aside. Add the onion and cook for 5 minutes, until softened. Add the apples, toss them with the onion, and cook for 6 to 8 minutes, until softened. Add the maple syrup and cook for 1 minute. Remove from the heat and fold in the feta and crispy sage leaves.

8. Portion the cauliflower mash onto individual serving plates, top with a pork chop, and spoon a heaping portion of the maple-sage apples on the side.

Many of the recipes in this book suggest the use of an instant-read thermometer. Why? Because you can't see the inside of a piece of meat (unless you're secretly one of the X-Men, in which case, please disregard). For us mere mortals, thermometers take the guesswork out of cooking and let us know exactly where we stand, guaranteeing perfectly cooked food, every single time.

BANGERS AND MASH

MAKES 4 SERVINGS • One of my most unforgettable experiences in the music business was crossing the pond to have our first record mastered at the incomparable Abbey Road Studios in London. As a lifelong megafan of the Beatles, I could barely contain my excitement. Working in the same studio with the same genius engineer (the late, great Chris Blair), while I sat on the same sofa as bands that changed the musical landscape forever, was completely mind-boggling. And I almost instantaneously fell in love with London. The beer, the culture, the food, the history, the vibe—all incredible. London, you hold a very special place in my heart.

Immediately after stumbling off our red-eye flight, the band made our way to a pub to sample the local fare: my first ever hand-pulled (cask) ale and a big plate of English comfort by way of bangers and mash.

8 pork sausages (about 2 pounds), the best quality you can find

MASH

2 pounds yellow-fleshed potatoes (such as Yukon Gold), peeled and cut into 1-inch chunks

⅓ cup heavy cream

2 tablespoons butter

3 ounces goat cheese

1 teaspoon sea salt

1 tablespoon minced fresh chives

(Ingredients continue on the next page.)

1. Preheat the oven to 400°F.

2. Set the sausages on a baking sheet and cook them in the oven for 30 minutes, turning halfway through.

3. Meanwhile, make the mash: Pop the potatoes into a stockpot full of cold water. Bring to a boil over medium-high heat and cook for about 15 minutes, or until fork-tender. Drain, then return the potatoes to the pot. Let them sit for 5 minutes to help the potatoes dry out. Partially mash the potatoes, then add the cream, butter, goat cheese, and salt. Continue mashing. Once everything is nicely melted and combined, add the chives and whisk the potatoes until smooth.

GRAVY

2 tablespoons butter

1 tablespoon olive oil

2 large white onions, thinly sliced

½ teaspoon sea salt

2 teaspoons all-purpose flour

1 garlic clove, minced

1 cup dark beer

1 cup beef stock

½ teaspoon freshly cracked black pepper

1½ cups frozen peas

1 tablespoon butter

Fresh flat-leaf parsley, for garnish

4. Make the gravy: In a large high-sided nonstick skillet, melt the butter with the oil over medium heat. Add the onions and season with ¼ teaspoon of the sea salt. Cook, stirring often, for 15 minutes, until the onions are softened and starting to caramelize. Stir in the flour and garlic and cook for 1 minute. Stir in the beer and stock and bring the mixture to a boil. Reduce the heat to medium-low and simmer until the gravy is thick and wonderful, about 10 minutes. Season with the remaining ¼ teaspoon salt and the pepper.

5. While the gravy is simmering, bring a small saucepan of salted water to a boil over medium-high heat. Add the peas and cook until tender, 3 to 5 minutes. Drain and toss with the butter. Set aside.

6. Portion the mash onto four plates and top each with 2 sausages, and a generous ladle of the onion gravy. Add the peas, garnish with parsley, and serve immediately.

SZECHUAN-STYLE GREEN BEANS AND PORK

MAKES 4 SERVINGS • Bucket list things I've yet to accomplish: fly in a hot-air balloon, swim with sharks in South Africa, visit New Zealand, successfully grow a vegetable garden. Over the past few years I've successfully whittled away at my travel list, visiting farms in North America, Europe, and Africa, collecting tips and tricks along the way. A total joy when I visit vegetable gardens is picking fresh veggies straight from the plant. My favorite veggie to sample? Green beans. Straight off the vine, they're perfection—crunchy, healthy, and totally addictive.

This recipe is all about those fresh green beans, tossed with crispy Szechuan peppercorn–spiked pork. It's spicy and delish on its own as a light dinner, or served with rice or noodles.

1½ tablespoons toasted sesame oil

10½ ounces green beans, ends trimmed

4 garlic cloves, minced

1 tablespoon minced fresh ginger

½ teaspoon Szechuan peppercorns, bashed in a mortar and pestle

5 ounces best-quality ground pork

¼ cup soy sauce

1 tablespoon black bean sauce

1 tablespoon rice vinegar

¼ cup chicken stock, store-bought or homemade (page 149)

2 heads baby bok choy, trimmed, leaves separated

1 or 2 red chiles

Cooked rice or noodles, for serving (optional)

1. In a wok, heat 1 tablespoon of the sesame oil over medium-high heat. When hot, add the green beans and cook, tossing often, for 2 minutes. Using tongs, transfer the beans to a plate, leaving any oil in the pan.

2. Add the remaining ½ tablespoon sesame oil, the garlic, ginger, and peppercorns to the wok and cook for 30 seconds, then stir in the pork, breaking it up with a wooden spoon. Cook, stirring often, for 3 minutes. Stir in the soy sauce, black bean sauce, vinegar, and stock. Cook, stirring often, for 3 to 4 minutes, until the pork is cooked through and crispy.

3. Add the green beans and bok choy, toss, and cook for 1 minute.

4. Top with the fresh chiles and serve immediately, on its own or with rice or noodles.

LAMB SOUVLAKI KEBABS

MAKES 4 SERVINGS • Montreal, circa 2001. A few friends and I decided to travel by train from Moncton, New Brunswick, to Montreal (go there, trust me) to see the one band that, to this day, still creatively inspires me like no other. Radiohead was touring for their *Amnesiac* record, and a young Dennis took his first trip without parental supervision (thanks, Mom and Dad!).

The show? Spectacular. Mind-blowing. World-changing, even. But, like most kids just out of high school, I was living on dollars and cents. Our best food option was a small, hole-in-the-wall restaurant on the ground floor of the downtown dive where we were staying. I had never tried—or likely even heard of—a lamb kebab before this trip, but I may have eaten one for every single meal during the duration of our Montreal stay. Breakfast included.

Delicious, grilled to perfection, and healthy to boot! We love to make these kebabs in the summer when we're grilling up a storm, but they can easily be made any time in a griddle pan or large skillet.

LAMB AND MARINADE

- **2 pounds lamb shoulder, fat trimmed, cut into 1-inch chunks**
- **1 tablespoon lemon zest**
- **3 tablespoons olive oil**
- **2 tablespoons fresh lemon juice**
- **1 teaspoon smoked paprika**
- **2 garlic cloves, finely minced**
- **½ teaspoon dried oregano**
- **1 teaspoon sea salt**
- **½ teaspoon freshly cracked black pepper**

HUMMUS

- **1 (19-ounce) can chickpeas, drained and rinsed**
- **¼ cup fresh lemon juice**
- **¼ cup olive oil**
- **2 tablespoons tahini**

1. Make the lamb and marinade: In a large bowl, combine the lamb and marinade ingredients. Massage the marinade into the lamb and chill in the fridge for 2 hours or up to overnight.

2. Soak eight bamboo skewers in cold water for 30 minutes (this will keep them from burning).

3. Make the hummus: Combine all the hummus ingredients in a food processor or blender and process until smooth. If you like your hummus a tad thinner, add a small splash of water. Spoon into a serving dish and refrigerate until ready to serve.

4. Make the yogurt sauce: In a small bowl, combine all the yogurt sauce ingredients and stir until smooth. Refrigerate until ready to serve.

5. Make the tomato-cucumber salad: In a small bowl, combine all the tomato-cucumber salad ingredients and toss to mix. Set aside at room temperature.

2 garlic cloves, minced

½ teaspoon ground cumin

½ teaspoon paprika

¼ teaspoon sea salt

¼ teaspoon freshly cracked
black pepper

YOGURT SAUCE

1½ cups Greek yogurt

½ cup finely diced cucumber

2 tablespoons fresh lemon
juice

¼ cup finely chopped fresh
parsley

Pinch of sea salt

Pinch of freshly cracked black
pepper

TOMATO-CUCUMBER SALAD

1 cup finely diced tomatoes,

1 cup finely diced cucumber

½ cup finely diced red onion

2 tablespoons finely chopped
fresh basil

2 tablespoons fresh lemon
juice

2 teaspoons red wine vinegar

Pinch of sea salt

TO SERVE

Olive oil, for grilling

1 cup Kalamata olives, pitted

½ cup crumbled feta cheese

1 lemon, cut into wedges

Pita bread

6. Thread the lamb onto the skewers, leaving 1 inch free at both ends for easy handling. Heat a grill to medium-high heat (or heat a grill pan over medium-high heat). Lightly brush the grates with olive oil. Grill the lamb for 3 to 4 minutes per side for medium, or longer if you prefer it more well done. Transfer to a cutting board, tent with aluminum foil, and let it rest for 3 minutes.

7. Serve the lamb kebabs with the hummus, yogurt sauce, tomato-cucumber salad, olives, feta, lemon wedges, and some pita bread.

An Epic Cheese Board

Okay. So let's all just admit something together, shall we? Rocking a dinner party, an impromptu get-together, or a random drive-by hangout can be a lot of work, and sometimes even a tad stressful. What can you throw together quickly that'll be delicious, satisfying, and dressed to impress? Enter the cheese board.

Cheese boards are one of the greatest things on earth. Small tapas-style portions, beautifully plated and served family-style, are unmatched in their ability to serve a large crew of hungry (and chances are, thirsty) riffraff who drop by for some chill time.

THE DEAL

Here are the elements that make up a truly unforgettable cheese board. There are no hard-and-fast rules here, but some helpful tips from a guy who's been to the bottom of a charcuterie plate or cheese board more times than I'd like to admit.

THE VEHICLE

Cheese, meats, jams, jellies, and the like all need a vehicle. Yes, you could go for a box of premade crackers that have been quietly collecting dust in your cupboard since the Bush administration. Or . . .

Head down to your local bakery and pick up a fantastic, crusty baguette. Cut it into ½-inch-thick pieces and brush both sides with olive oil. Grill over medium heat on a grill or grill pan until charred on both sides (or toast them on a baking sheet in the oven). Peel 2 garlic cloves. Immediately after removing the bread from the grill, gently rub the garlic all over both sides of each piece for an added kiss of awesome. So delicious.

THE CHEESE

There's no such thing as too much cheese, so go for broke here. If by some miracle you happen to find yourself with leftovers, fear not! That cheese will find a very temporary home in your fridge until it's put to good use in midnight snacks, cheesy omelets, quesadillas, grilled cheese sandos, nachos, and things as yet uninvented! Here are some of my favorite cheesy cheeseboard options:

FRESH CHEESE—burrata or fresh mozzarella

SOFT CHEESE—Brie, feta, or Camembert

SEMISOFT CHEESE—Havarti or Gouda

FIRM CHEESE—aged cheddar, Gruyère, or Emmental

HARD CHEESE—Parmesan, Pecorino Romano, or Comté

VEINED CHEESE—blue cheese, Stilton, or Gorgonzola

MEAT

Just like the deliciously varied cheese options above, everyone has a favorite cured meat, so an assortment is welcome. My personal favorites are prosciutto, speck, salumi, and chorizo. Visit your local butcher or the best-quality deli in your town and describe the board that you're looking to create. Butchers and cheesemongers are the experts. They have a wealth of knowledge and are often able to offer hidden gems that you'd never consider.

SIDES

Here are a few side and topping options. I tend to change these up often, depending on what's in season at my local market.

FRESH FRUIT AND VEGGIES— blackberries, figs, seedless grapes, strawberries, and cherry tomatoes are an incredible addition to any board. They're delicious and perfectly sized for eating alone, or when sandwiched between meat and cheese on a slice of toasty baguette.

SOMETHING SPICY—I love Peppadews (or piquanté peppers). They're spicy-and-sweet perfection, and available in most major supermarkets or specialty shops.

OLIVES—An absolute must on any board. I love to plate two different kinds, typically Kalamata olives and spicy green olives. They're game changing.

FRESH HERBS OR SPROUTS—Soft herbs, such as flat-leaf parsley or basil and sprouts, add a hit of freshness to the board, and they look lovely. Garnishing the board with an assortment of both herbs and sprouts will guarantee added deliciousness and chef-level food styling.

JELLY—Jams and jellies are a great addition to any board. I especially love the sweet-and-spicy flavors of red pepper jelly or habanero jelly, or classic quince paste, but pick your favorite and plate away.

Possibly the best part about creating a delicious cheese and charcuterie board is you can prepare it quickly just before or even after your guests arrive. Zero time worrying about burning something on the stove, more time enjoying a nice glass of relaxation with company.

8

From the Sea.

THE KEY TO A MARITIMER'S HEART.

SEAFOOD IS EVERYTHING. AS A PROUD BORN AND RAISED MARITIMER, THE BOUNTY OF THE SEA SINGS HARMONY WITH MY SOUL.

It's a birthright, connecting each coastal-living individual to our local heritage. Lobster, scallops, salmon, mussels, cod, oysters, haddock, and clams—all are synonymous with the seaside, sun-soaked vibes, and unforgettable, family-style feasts.

Buying fish and seafood can be daunting if you're not sure what to look for. Here are a few simple tips to get you started on the seafood journey:

FIND A LOCAL FISHMONGER OR SEAFOOD MARKET

This is essential to guarantee top-quality fish and seafood. Fishmongers have a wealth of knowledge about local, sustainable, fresh, top-quality products. They're your best friends on your fresh path toward deliciousness. As with everything, local is best.

DO A SMELL TEST

Fresh fish should have a "fresh sea" aroma to it. If it smells really fishy or has a strong odor, it's most definitely not fresh, and not worth your hard-earned cash.

DO A TOUCH TEST

The flesh of fresh fish should always be firm and spring back when touched.

BUY THE DAY YOU EAT

Try, if at all possible, to purchase your seafood the day you're planning on cooking it. It will keep chilled in the fridge for a maximum of 24 hours, but same day is always best for guaranteed freshness.

CLASSIC BEER-BATTERED FISH AND CHIPS

MAKES 4 SERVINGS • Every May along the Acadian Coast of New Brunswick, restaurants open their doors to hungry, summer-loving, comfort-seeking Atlantic Canadians. The atmosphere is filled with the overwhelming and intoxicating aroma of seasonal fried fish, shellfish, and "all things from the sea." From May to September, it's like all is well and right in the world. Fresh is the name of the game, direct from the Maritime Northumberland Strait that morning to our bellies later that same day. Really, it's the embodiment of local, heavenly East Coast eating and well worth re-creating at home, no matter where you hang your hat.

From London to Sydney, folks have their own version of this beloved classic recipe. Some love a dill-infused dish, others one served with mushy peas or even malt vinegar. But what will forever remain true is that fish and chips are happy, deep-fried summertime bliss.

TARTAR SAUCE

1 cup prepared mayo

2 tablespoons finely diced cornichons

1 tablespoon finely diced capers

1 tablespoon fresh lemon juice

1 teaspoon Dijon mustard

Pinch of sea salt

Pinch of freshly cracked black pepper

CHIPS

3 pounds russet potatoes, scrubbed (do not peel)

Canola oil, for frying

Sea salt

FISH

1½ pounds cod fillets, skin and bones removed, cut into 4 large pieces

1. Make the tartar sauce: Combine all the tartar sauce ingredients in a small dish and stir well. Cover and refrigerate until ready to serve.

2. Make the chips: Cut the potatoes into ¼-inch-thick matchsticks. Place the fries in a large bowl and cover with cold water. Transfer to the fridge to soak for 1 hour. Drain and pat dry with paper towels.

3. In a large Dutch oven or stockpot with a thermometer attached, heat 3 inches of canola oil to 325°F. Working in batches, cook the fries for 5 minutes, until they are just starting to turn golden brown. Use a slotted spoon to transfer them to a baking sheet lined with paper towels. You'll come back to these later for a double fry, so first crack on with the fish.

4. Make the fish: Pat the fish dry with paper towels and season with a pinch of sea salt and the pepper. In a large bowl, combine 1½ cups of the flour, the baking powder, lemon zest, garlic powder, paprika, cayenne, and 1 teaspoon sea salt. Whisk in the beer until the batter is smooth. Pour the remaining ½ cup flour onto a large plate.

1 teaspoon sea salt, plus a pinch

½ teaspoon freshly cracked black pepper

2 cups all-purpose flour

1 teaspoon baking powder

2 teaspoons lemon zest

½ teaspoon garlic powder

½ teaspoon paprika

¼ teaspoon cayenne pepper

1 (12-ounce) bottle of your favorite stout

1 lemon, cut into wedges, for serving

5. Increase the oil temperature to 375°F.

6. Working in batches, dredge the fish in the plain flour, then dip it in the beer batter, coating it completely. Transfer carefully to the hot oil and fry for 6 to 7 minutes, turning frequently, until deep golden brown and perfectly crispy. Remove with a slotted spoon and drain the excess grease on paper towels.

7. Working in batches, return the fries to the oil and fry until golden brown and crispy, 2 to 4 minutes. Transfer the fries to paper towels and season them with a pinch of sea salt.

8. Serve with the tartar sauce and lemon wedges.

LEMON-GARLIC BUTTER-POACHED LOBSTER ROLLS

MAKES 8 SERVINGS • Confession time . . . I sometimes take lobster for granted. There, I said it. I'm sorry. These little crustaceans are simply a part of daily Maritime life, and I spent my formative years a stone's throw from lobster heaven. Every summer we celebrate with the Shediac Lobster Festival. Fishermen sell daily-caught lobsters from coolers in the cabs of their trucks on the side of the road—and they're as cheap as chips. What I'll never take for granted is how buttery and delicious these little dudes are.

Taking a slight left turn from the classic version, these lobsters are par-cooked, then finished by gently poaching in garlicky lemon butter. Tossed with some fresh chives and served on a toasty bun, this is serious comfort food territory.

8 brioche sub rolls (or potato rolls)

1 cup (2 sticks) butter, plus 2 tablespoons melted butter

4 (1¼-pound) live lobsters

1 garlic clove, minced

½ teaspoon red pepper flakes

2 tablespoons fresh lemon juice

2 tablespoons minced fresh chives, plus more for serving

Flaky sea salt

1. Heat a large grill pan (or skillet) over medium heat. Brush the outside of the rolls with the 2 tablespoons melted butter and toast until charred, about 2 minutes. Set aside.

2. Bring a large stockpot of water to a rapid boil. Prepare an ice bath.

3. Working in batches—one or two lobsters at a time—boil the lobsters for 2 minutes, then immediately transfer them to the ice bath to shock, cool, and stop the cooking process.

4. Carefully and gently crack open the tails, claws, and anywhere else that delicious lobster bits might be hiding. Remove all the meat and cut it into ½-inch chunks.

5. In a small saucepan, gently melt 1 cup butter over medium-low heat. Stir in the garlic, red pepper flakes, and lemon juice.

6. Working in batches, add the lobster chunks to the butter and poach for 5 minutes, turning halfway through.

7. Transfer the cooked lobster to a large bowl and toss with the chives. Portion the buttery lobster into the toasted buns and top with an extra hit of chives and flaky sea salt.

GARAM MASALA AND BEER MUSSELS

MAKES 4 TO 6 SERVINGS • I fell head over heels for mussels by way of *moules frites* several summers ago in beautiful Charlottetown, Prince Edward Island (Google, then immediately add to your bucket list). Eating seafood al fresco with the sun setting over the Atlantic is an experience not to be missed.

These little mollusks are delicious, sustainable, immune-boosting, and inexpensive. Win/win/win/win. Here, mussels are spiked with a sweet curry-beer sauce. Have some extra crusty bread nearby to sop up all that goodness.

For an extra bit of awesomeness, try serving these mussels with homemade French fries, à la *moules frites*. See page 78 for The Perfect French Fry.

3 pounds fresh mussels

1 tablespoon butter

2 garlic cloves, minced

1 cup finely diced red onion

1 cup finely diced celery

1 tablespoon minced fresh ginger

¾ cup sweet Peppadew peppers, thinly sliced

1 cup of your favorite beer

1 teaspoon garam masala

1 tablespoon honey

1 cup heavy cream

½ teaspoon kosher salt

½ teaspoon freshly cracked black pepper

2 scallions, thinly sliced

Handful of fresh cilantro, for garnish (and for deliciousness)

Crusty bread, for serving

1. Scrub the mussels under cold running water and toss any that won't close (see below).

2. In a large stockpot, melt the butter over medium heat. Add the garlic and sauté for 30 seconds, then add the onion, celery, and ginger and cook for 5 minutes, stirring often, until the vegetables have started to soften. Stir in the Peppadews and cook for 1 minute. Pour in the beer and cook until the liquid has reduced by half, about 5 minutes.

3. Add the garam masala, honey, cream, salt, and black pepper and bring to a boil. Add the mussels and cover the pan. Cook for 5 to 6 minutes, until the mussels have opened (discard any mussels that don't open).

4. Transfer the mussels to a serving platter and top with the scallions and cilantro. Serve with crusty bread, a nice pint, and, if you can swing it, a warm sunshine-y day.

To clean mussels, place them in a bowl or colander in the sink under cold, running water. Scrub each mussel thoroughly to remove any barnacles or hangers-on that decided to join the ride from the sea floor. If any of the mussels are partially opened, give them a firm tap. If they close, they're good to go. If they don't close, discard.

DECONSTRUCTED SUSHI BOWLS

• Hands up. Anyone remember the first time they had sushi? Like, proper sushi. Not those rolls deliciously pretending to be sushi. I do. It was my *Fear Factor* moment, and I was equal parts terrified and excited. I may have even plugged my nose (I admit to nothing).

Fresh sushi is the embodiment of simple = best. Get the highest-quality ingredients available, prepared with love and care, and you have yourself a rock-star dish. To find the best sushi-grade fish, become best friends with your local fishmongers. They're the experts with a wealth of knowledge and will be able to direct you to top-quality local fish and seafood.

This recipe is perfect for dinner parties, summer days when you can't bear the idea of turning on the oven, or any time you can get your hands on sushi-grade fish.

2 cups sushi rice, rinsed

2 tablespoons sugar

1 teaspoon salt

⅓ cup rice vinegar

2 pounds mixed sushi-grade fish (salmon, tuna, halibut, or flounder)

2 carrots, julienned or spiralized

1 English cucumber, julienned or spiralized

2 large ripe avocados, pitted, peeled, and sliced into ½-inch wedges

2 teaspoons toasted sesame seeds

1 sheet nori (Japanese seaweed), cut into very small matchsticks

1½ cups of your favorite sprouts

Pickled ginger, wasabi, and soy sauce, for serving

1. Bring 2¼ cups water to a boil in a medium saucepan over medium heat. Add the rice, cover, and reduce the heat to medium-low. Cook for about 20 minutes, until the water has been absorbed and the rice is tender. Transfer the rice to a large bowl and let stand, covered, for 10 minutes.

2. Meanwhile, in a small saucepan, stir together the sugar, salt, and vinegar and heat over medium-low heat until the sugar and salt have dissolved. Pour the mixture into the rice and stir well to combine.

3. Grab a very sharp knife and slice the fish into manageable pieces about 3 x 1 inches and ½ inch thick. No need for precision—you're just looking for small, eatable, chopstick-able pieces.

4. Portion the rice into individual serving bowls. Assemble the fish over the rice on one side of the bowl. On the other side, build a salad of carrots, cucumber, avocados, and nori.

5. Sprinkle the avocados with toasted sesame seeds. Top with your favorite sprouts and serve with pickled ginger, wasabi, and soy sauce.

CRISPY BAJA-STYLE FRIED FISH TACOS

• While on our honeymoon rambling around SoCal, Leanne and I decided to take a day trip to San Diego and visit their world-famous zoo. That day was beyond memorable for several reasons.

1. I met a giraffe, an elephant, and a tiger (from a great distance) for the first time. Legit!

2. I dipped a toe in the Pacific. (Bucket list checked!)

3. We ate the most incredible, life-changing tacos ever.

Fish tacos are an absolute joy and perfect for handheld munching. This recipe is a shout-out to those world-shaping tacos, re-created to make your home feel just like a warm, sunny Californian afternoon. Bless you, tacos.

AVODOBO SAUCE

1 large ripe avocado

½ cup sour cream

1 tablespoon adobo sauce (from a can of chiles in adobo)

2 tablespoons fresh lime juice

¼ teaspoon sea salt

SLAW

3 cups thinly sliced green cabbage

1 small red onion, halved and sliced into thin half-moons

2 carrots, grated on the large holes of a box grater

½ cup finely minced fresh cilantro

1 tablespoon olive oil

2 tablespoons apple cider vinegar

¼ cup fresh lime juice

¼ teaspoon sea salt

¼ teaspoon freshly cracked black pepper

1. Make the avodobo sauce: Combine all the sauce ingredients in a food processor. Process until smooth, then transfer to a serving dish. Refrigerate until ready to serve. (This sauce can be made up to 24 hours before taco-ing. Store in an airtight container in the fridge and stir well before serving.)

2. Make the slaw: In a large bowl, combine the cabbage, onion, carrots, and cilantro. Drizzle in the olive oil, vinegar, and lime juice. Season the slaw with the salt and pepper and get those hands in there and mix. Refrigerate until it's taco time.

3. Make the tacos: Heat a griddle pan, grill, or cast-iron pan over medium-high heat. Working with one at a time, char both sides of the tortillas, about 1 minute per side, then shape them into taco shells. It takes a few minutes, but it's well worth the effort and looks like a million bucks. Set aside.

4. In a high-sided Dutch oven or deep fryer, heat 3 inches of canola oil over medium heat to 375°F.

5. In a large bowl, whisk together the flour, baking powder, lime zest, salt, and pepper. Whisk the beer into the flour until the batter is smooth.

FISH TACOS

12 (6-inch) flour tortillas

Canola oil, for frying

1½ cups all-purpose flour

1 teaspoon baking powder

1 tablespoon lime zest

1 teaspoon sea salt

½ teaspoon freshly cracked black pepper

1 (12-ounce) bottle dark beer

1½ pounds cod fillets

2 jalapeños, thinly sliced

1 lime, cut into wedges

Handful of fresh cilantro, to make those tacos look like little rock stars

6. Slice the cod into 1-inch-thick, taco-able strips. Working in batches, dredge the fish in the beer batter, then transfer to the hot oil. Fry, turning halfway through, for 5 to 6 minutes or until crispy, golden brown, and perfect. Lay the fried fish on paper towels to blot excess oil as you finish.

7. Build the tacos with the fish, slaw, avodobo sauce, sliced jalapeños, lime wedges, and cilantro.

SEAFOOD CHOWDER

MAKES 8 TO 10 SERVINGS • When the weather is cool, the rain is falling, and you desperately need a big ol' food hug, seafood chowder to the rescue. This rich and velvety chowder is chock-full of seafood, vegetables, and all the feels. It's a classic dish in the Maritimes, throughout New England, and anywhere folks truly want to experience the flavors of the gods.

8 smoked bacon slices, cut into ½-inch pieces

2 tablespoons butter

1 large onion, finely diced

2 celery sticks, finely diced

1 large carrot, finely diced

1 bay leaf

1 tablespoon fresh thyme leaves

¾ teaspoon sea salt, plus more as needed

3 garlic cloves, minced

1 tablespoon all-purpose flour

½ cup dry white wine (such as Sauvignon Blanc or Pinot Grigio)

2 medium Yukon Gold or other yellow-fleshed potatoes, peeled and cut into ½-inch cubes

4 cups fish or vegetable stock

3 cups heavy cream

1 tablespoon lemon zest

1 pound fresh mussels

1 pound fresh sea scallops

¼ teaspoon smoked paprika

1 (9-ounce) bottle baby clams and juice

1. Heat a large stockpot over medium heat. Add the bacon and fry for 5 to 6 minutes, until crispy. Using a slotted spoon, transfer the bacon to paper towels and discard the excess grease, leaving 1 tablespoon of the grease in the pot. Add the butter and when it's melted, add the onion, celery, carrot, bay leaf, and thyme. Season with ¼ teaspoon of the salt and cook for 5 minutes, or until softened. Add the garlic and flour and cook, stirring, for 30 seconds, until well blended. Your kitchen smells incredible right now!

2. Add the wine and cook until it has almost entirely evaporated, about 5 minutes. Add the potatoes, stock, cream, lemon zest, and remaining ½ teaspoon salt and bring the chowder to a simmer. Let it gently bubble away for 20 minutes, until the potatoes are very soft.

3. Meanwhile, under cold running water, scrub the mussels (see the tip on page 227). Halve the scallops horizontally to make small discs.

4. Fish time! Stir in the smoked paprika, then layer in the baby clams and juice, scallops, haddock, and mussels. Cover the pot and cook for 5 to 6 minutes over medium heat, until the mussel shells have opened and the fish easily flakes apart.

1 pound skinless haddock fillets, cut into 2-inch pieces

1 pound cooked lobster meat

2 tablespoons minced fresh chives, plus more for serving

2 tablespoons chopped fresh flat-leaf parsley leaves, plus more for serving

1 tablespoon fresh dill leaves

Uncover the pot and carefully fold in the cooked lobster, bacon, chives, and parsley. Taste the soup to check the seasoning. If necessary, hit the chowder with more salt.

5. Divide the chowder among bowls and top them with dill, chives, and parsley.

CRISPY LIME-PEPPER CALAMARI WITH SPICY LIME MAYO

MAKES 4 TO 6 APPETIZER SERVINGS • I love calamari—classic, beloved, and my go-to appetizer on pub night. Add a pint or two to the situation and I'm in my glory!

This recipe comes together in flash. Frying very quickly in hot oil will result in golden brown calamari that's crisped to perfection on the outside and light and tender on the inside. And if you happen to find yourself with a spot of leftover marinara sauce (page 87), tuck it away for the next time you make this recipe. Double the sauce love, double the awesome.

SPICY LIME MAYO

½ cup prepared mayo
1 tablespoon fresh lime juice
1 teaspoon soy sauce
1 tablespoon sriracha
1 garlic clove, minced

CALAMARI

2 pounds whole squid
Canola oil, for frying
2 cups all-purpose flour
1 teaspoon lime zest
½ teaspoon chili powder
¼ teaspoon cayenne pepper
1 teaspoon kosher salt, plus more for serving
1 teaspoon freshly cracked black pepper
Handful of fresh cilantro sprigs, for serving
1 or 2 limes, sliced, for serving

1. Make the spicy lime mayo: In a small bowl, whisk the mayo ingredients together. Cover and give it a home in the fridge until the calamari is ready to rock.

2. Make the calamari: Separate the squid tubes and tentacles by holding firmly on the body while pulling on the head. Rinse the squid tubes under cold running water. Remove the clear, backbone-ish thing from inside the tubes. Rinse out the inside of the tubes and pull off and discard the fins. Remove and discard the eyes and head from the tentacles, keeping the tentacles themselves intact. Peel the purple outer skin from the tubes, then cut them into ½-inch rings.

3. In a high-sided Dutch oven or stockpot, heat 3 inches of canola oil over medium heat to 375°F.

4. In a large bowl, whisk together the flour, lime zest, chili powder, cayenne, salt, and pepper. Working in batches as needed, dredge the calamari in the flour, and fry 1 to 1½ minutes per batch, until golden brown and crispy. Remove the calamari with a slotted spoon and transfer to a baking sheet lined with paper towels to capture any excess grease.

5. Sprinkle over an extra pinch of kosher salt and serve immediately with the mayo, fresh cilantro, and sliced limes.

GRILLED LOBSTER WITH LEMONY HERB COMPOUND BUTTER

MAKES 4 TO 6 SERVINGS • Lobster is delicious six ways to Sunday and incredible paired with everything from pizza to surf and turf, and even as the superhero in mac and cheese (page 96). There are hundreds of ways to prepare this heavenly delicacy, but we tend to gravitate toward the tried-and-true steamed method and serve it with copious amounts of melted butter. Delicious, no doubt, but it's entirely acceptable to expand our lobstery horizons every now and then.

This recipe is perfect for that time of the year when backyard BBQs are the daily MO and lobster season is cranked to 10. Basting the shellfish as it cooks with garlic herb compound butter ensures that every bite is full of happiness.

3 (1¼-pound) live lobsters

½ cup (1 stick) butter, at room temperature

2 tablespoons chopped fresh flat-leaf parsley leaves

1 tablespoon minced shallot

2 garlic cloves, minced

1 tablespoon lemon zest

1 tablespoon fresh lemon juice

½ teaspoon sea salt

¼ teaspoon freshly cracked black pepper

2 tablespoons olive oil

2 lemons, halved

1. Bring a large pot of water to a rapid boil. Prepare an ice bath.

2. Working in batches as needed, submerge the lobsters headfirst in the boiling water and cover the pot (you can do it!). Cook for 5 minutes, then transfer the lobsters to the ice bath to stop the cooking process.

3. In a medium bowl, combine the butter, parsley, shallot, garlic, lemon zest, lemon juice, salt, and pepper and whisk until smooth. Set aside. If making ahead (which I often do), cover with plastic wrap and chill in the fridge.

4. Using a very sharp knife, split the lobsters lengthwise. Clean the tomalley ("lovely" green stuff) from the body and discard. Brush the lobster halves all over with the olive oil.

5. Heat a grill to medium heat (or heat a grill pan over medium heat). When hot, place the lobsters on the grill, cut-side down, and cook for 4 minutes. Flip and spoon about 2 tablespoons of the compound butter over the meat of each lobster half.

As the butter begins to melt, baste with a brush all over the meat. Cook for 3 minutes, until the butter has melted entirely.

6. While the lobsters are getting ready for the runway, pop the lemon halves on the grill, cut-side down, for 30 seconds.

7. Serve the lobster halves immediately with the grilled lemons and more butter, if that suits your fancy.

WICKED OUTDOOR EAST COAST LOBSTER BOIL

MAKES 6 TO 8 SERVINGS • When I imagine what the Kings of the East Coast (yes, I'm aware that's not a real thing, just roll with me) used to eat, it's this. The ultimate seafood party feast! A fitting tribute to the bounty of the sea.

Lobster boils are a stunning treat on a hot and sunny summer's day. Cooking everything together in one massive pot lets all those gorgeous flavors fuse together and makes cleanup a snap.

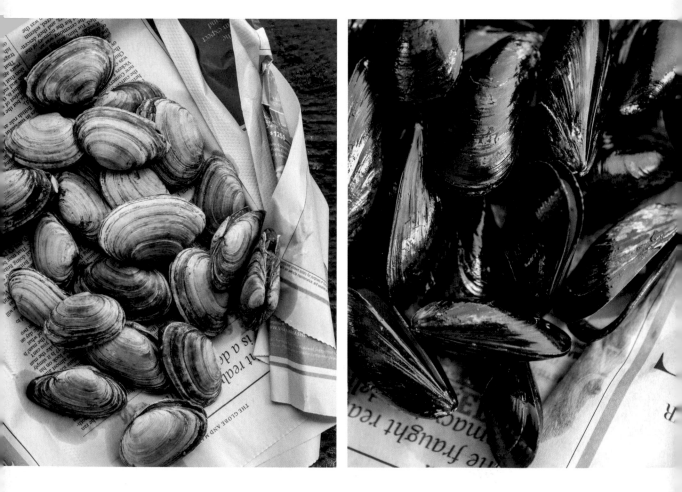

2 pounds baby (new) yellow-fleshed potatoes (such as Yukon Gold)

2 large onions, quartered

1 garlic head, halved crosswise

2 (12-ounce) bottles of your favorite beer

2 tablespoons Old Bay seasoning

2 tablespoons sea salt

6 fresh thyme sprigs

1 bay leaf

1 pound kielbasa sausage, cut into 1-inch chunks

6 ears corn, shucked and cut into thirds

4 (1¼-pound) live lobsters

2 pounds fresh littleneck clams

2 pounds fresh mussels

1 or 2 lemons, cut into wedges, for serving

Melted butter, for serving

Crusty sourdough bread, for serving

1. Combine the potatoes, onions, and garlic in the most ginormous steamer pot you can get your hands on. The bigger, the better here. Pour in the beer and 4 cups water and add the Old Bay, sea salt, thyme, bay leaf, and sausage. Bring the mixture to a boil over medium-high heat, cover, and cook for 15 minutes.

2. Layering time. Add a layer of corn, then the lobsters, then the clams and mussels. Cover and cook until the lobsters have turned bright red and the clams have opened, about 15 minutes. Using a large colander or a slotted spoon and a steady arm, carefully drain the liquid from the pot, reserving the broth.

3. Pour the seafood, potatoes, and corn onto a large picnic table covered with newspaper (or your paper of choice). Serve with lemons, melted butter, the reserved broth, crusty bread, and lots of napkins. This is summer living!

SALMON POKE BOWLS

MAKES 4 SERVINGS • Poke bowls may be *the* "it" dish. So hot right now! They've taken over the urban culinary landscape for the most delicious of reasons. Unreal awesome, this Hawaiian masterpiece is healthy, easily assembled, and a wonderful vehicle for creativity. Top-quality salmon is the hero here, but if it's not easily found where you live, tuna is a fantastic (and maybe more authentic) substitute. (Of course, being a Maritimer, I find salmon is king.) This recipe is perfect any time of the year, but especially great on hot summer days. Very little cooking required, healthy, cooling, and vibrantly fresh.

SALMON AND MARINADE

¼ cup soy sauce

2 tablespoons toasted sesame oil

2 tablespoons olive oil

1 tablespoon rice vinegar

2 tablespoons fresh lime juice

2 garlic cloves, minced

1 pound sushi-grade salmon, skin removed

1 tablespoon sesame seeds, toasted (see page 193)

POKE

1½ cups short-grain white rice

2 teaspoons rice vinegar

2 large ripe avocados, pitted, peeled, and cut into ½-inch chunks

½ English cucumber, cut into very thin matchsticks or spiralized

1 cup ½-inch-dice pineapple

2 scallions, finely sliced

1 or 2 red chiles, finely sliced

1 cup shelled edamame beans

1 cup pea shoots or your favorite sprouts

¼ cup pickled ginger

1. Make the marinade: In a large bowl, whisk together the soy sauce, sesame oil, olive oil, vinegar, lime juice, and garlic.

2. Cut the salmon into ¾-inch chunks and transfer them to the marinade bowl. Sprinkle the sesame seeds on top and stir to combine. Cover with plastic wrap and refrigerate for 2 hours, or up to 24 hours.

3. Make the poke: Cook the rice according to the package directions. Transfer it to a large bowl and stir in the vinegar. Set aside.

4. Poke time! Build each poke bowl with ¼ of the rice, salmon, avocado, cucumber, pineapple, scallion, and red chile goodness. Top each bowl with some of the edamame, pea shoots, and pickled ginger, and drizzle over some extra marinade from the salmon dish. Delicious!

SHRIMP AND THREE-CHEESE GRITS

MAKES 4 SERVINGS • One night around four A.M., after a long evening of bourbon-soaked and cigar-smoked good times, my squad decided to head to a late-night dive restaurant in Franklin, Tennessee. I ordered a bowl of cheesy grits and have not quite recovered. It was creamy, buttery, with a hint of spice—so velvety and luxurious!

This recipe is full of spicy shrimp and crispy bacon in a big bowl of cheesy, comforting, stick-to-your-ribs goodness. Perfect for breakfast, lunch, or dinner.

GRITS

1 cup stone-ground grits

½ teaspoon kosher salt

1 cup whole milk

⅔ cup grated aged cheddar cheese

⅔ cup grated Swiss cheese

¼ cup grated Parmesan cheese

1 tablespoon butter

SHRIMP

4 thick-cut smoked bacon slices, cut into ½-inch pieces

1 pound jumbo shrimp (16 to 20 shrimp total), peeled and deveined

Sea salt and freshly cracked black pepper

2 garlic cloves, minced

2 scallions, finely sliced

Juice of 1 lemon, plus lemon wedges, for serving

½ teaspoon cayenne pepper

Fresh flat-leaf parsley sprigs, for garnish

1. Make the grits: Bring 3 cups water to a boil in a 3-quart saucepan over medium-high heat. Stir in the grits and salt and turn the temperature to medium-low. Gently cook, stirring frequently, for 30 minutes. Stir in the milk and gently cook for 10 minutes more, until tender and super creamy. Remove from the heat. Gradually stir in the cheeses, about ½ cup at a time, until melted and smooth. Stir in the butter and cover to keep warm.

2. When the grits have about 15 minutes left to cook, get cracking with the shrimp: Heat a large skillet over medium heat and fry the bacon until crispy, 6 to 8 minutes. Using a slotted spoon, transfer the bacon to paper towels, reserving the fat in the pan.

3. Season the shrimp on both sides with a pinch each of salt and pepper. Still over medium heat, add the shrimp to the fat in the pan and cook for 2 minutes. Turn the shrimp over and toss in the bacon, garlic, and scallions. Cook for 2 to 3 minutes more, until the shrimp are pink and cooked through, then remove from the heat.

4. Squeeze in the lemon juice and sprinkle over a hit of cayenne for an extra dose of morning sunshine. Divide the grits into individual serving bowls and top with the bacony shrimp. Garnish with a bit of parsley and serve with lemon wedges.

9

Vegetarian.

NO MEAT? NO WORRIES.

VEGETABLES ARE ROCK STARS. SO FRESH, SO CLEAN, AND ABSOLUTELY SCREAMING WITH FLAVOR.

Eating vegetarian used to be controversial in some circles, but not anymore! Nowadays, even die-hard meat-eaters will gladly sub a vegetarian meal into their weekly meal plans. Growing up under the same roof as an old-school vegetarian, I have an understanding of the struggle for deliciousness that veggie-loving folks have sometimes endured. My mom, a long-time vegetarian, made the conversion to a meat-free diet while pregnant with my baby brother, far before vegetarianism was even remotely hip and before many people knew how to elevate veggie options to next-level meals. The only meat-free dish at most restaurants near us was a timid house salad

with cherry tomatoes, sliced cucumber, and packaged dressing. Not inspiring in the least.

These days, thanks to local restaurants, farmers' markets, passionate chefs, and food bloggers, the options for vegetarians have exploded. We have access to mouth-watering recipes and dishes from folks from all corners of the globe who enjoy a meat-free diet, and grocery stores have finally started properly stocking shelves with products that meet the culinary needs of the many. Exciting times!

This chapter features some of my all-time favorite meat-free recipes. No compromise on flavor, just comforting vegetarian deliciousness.

CRISPY FRIED TOFU RAMEN

MAKES 4 TO 6 SERVINGS • Hi, my name is Dennis, and I adore ramen.
Ramen is a truly magical thing. It's noodle bowl perfection. My first ra-mening occurred during an all-too-stereotypical Vancouver rainstorm, where I sat on the window bench at a downtown noodle shop watching the world go by. I vividly remember the sights and smells of that restaurant: the crispy fried tofu, the loud EDM tunes, and the slurping away of happy noodle-loving West Coasters. Always delicious, ramen is an especially great pick-me-up on a dark and stormy day.

2 tablespoons grapeseed or vegetable oil

2 cups thinly sliced cremini mushrooms

1 tablespoon minced fresh ginger

5 garlic cloves, minced

¼ cup white miso paste

6 cups vegetable stock

7 ounces extra-firm tofu

1 tablespoon toasted sesame oil

5 tablespoons soy sauce

16 ounces ramen noodles

1 tablespoon chile oil

2 teaspoons toasted sesame oil

4 ounces Broccolini, stems trimmed

1 cup snap peas

2 scallions, finely sliced

1 or 2 red chiles, finely sliced

1. In a large stockpot, heat 1 tablespoon of the grapeseed oil over medium heat. Add the mushrooms and sauté until browned, about 5 minutes. Add the ginger and garlic and sauté for 30 seconds.

2. Stir in the miso paste and stock. Increase the heat to medium-high and bring to a boil, then reduce the heat to medium. Let the broth bubble and simmer for 20 minutes.

3. Meanwhile, heat a wok or large skillet over medium-high heat. Cut the tofu into 1-inch cubes and toss them in the sesame oil and remaining 1 tablespoon grapeseed oil. Fry in the hot pan and brown on all sides, about 5 minutes. When the tofu is getting its crispy on, add 1 tablespoon of the soy sauce and give everything a good toss. Transfer to a plate and set aside.

4. Bring a large pot of salted water to a boil and cook the noodles according to the package directions. Drain and set aside.

5. Back to the miso broth! Stir the remaining 4 tablespoons soy sauce, the chile oil, and the toasted sesame oil into the soup, then add the Broccolini and snap peas. Cook for 2 minutes, then remove from the heat.

6. Divide the noodles among individual serving bowls and top each with several ladles of broth and the tofu, scallions, and chiles.

SMASHED SOUTHWESTERN-STYLE BLACK BEAN BURGERS

MAKES 6 SERVINGS • The idea of veggie burgers may conjure up thoughts of bland, cardboard-flavored sandwiches, fit for . . . well, no one. But veggie burgers can be a thing of pure beauty—really! They're heart-healthy and great for the planet, and can even be delicious (or they wouldn't be in this book!). Total win. These black bean burgers are completely filling and have an amazing texture, and not a soul will be wishing they had the "real" thing instead. Get into veggie burgers, my friends.

LIME-SPIKED SOUR CREAM

½ **cup sour cream**

2 **tablespoons fresh lime juice**

½ **teaspoon smoked paprika**

Pinch of sea salt

BLACK BEAN BURGERS

2 **(14.5-ounce) cans black beans, drained and rinsed**

1 **cup bread crumbs (fresh bread crumbs? See opposite, y'all)**

¼ **cup grated onion**

1 **large free-range egg**

2 **tablespoons sour cream**

1 **teaspoon hot sauce**

2 **teaspoons lime zest**

½ **teaspoon chili powder**

¼ **teaspoon ground cumin**

¼ **teaspoon cayenne pepper**

½ **teaspoon sea salt**

¼ **teaspoon freshly cracked black pepper**

1. Make the lime-spiked sour cream: Combine all the sour cream ingredients in a small bowl and stir until smooth. Refrigerate until it's burger-building time.

2. Make the black bean burgers: Pour the beans into a large bowl. Using a fork, mash the life out of the beans, breaking them down almost entirely but keeping a few bean chunks in the mixture for added texture.

3. Add the bread crumbs, onion, egg, sour cream, hot sauce, lime zest, chili powder, cumin, cayenne, salt, and pepper and mix until well combined. Form the mixture into six patties that are slightly larger than the width of the burger buns, about ½ inch thick. Transfer to a plate and chill in the fridge for 30 minutes.

4. In a large nonstick skillet, melt the butter with the olive oil over medium heat. Working in batches as needed, fry the patties for 5 minutes, or until a deep, golden brown crust forms. Flip the burgers and top each one with 2 slices of cheese. Cook the burgers for 4 to 5 minutes more, until the cheese has melted and a dark crust has formed on the bot-

- **1 tablespoon butter**
- **1 tablespoon olive oil**
- **12 slices Monterey Jack cheese**
- **6 brioche burger buns (such as Homemade Brioche Burger Buns, page 76)**
- **1 large tomato, sliced into rounds**
- **½ red onion, sliced into rounds**
- **6 burger-size lettuce leaves**

tom of the patties. Veggies can be tricky little buggers. Be sure to always use a nonstick pan and wait to flip until after a crispy crust forms. This will ensure that the burgers hold together perfectly every single time.

5. Build the burgers on brioche buns with tomato and onion slices, lettuce, and 1 or 2 tablespoons of the lime-spiked sour cream.

Homemade bread crumbs couldn't be easier! Whenever you have stale bread (a day or two old), pop it in a food processor and blitz away until the crumbs reach your desired consistency. I love to flavor them with a little lemon zest, dried oregano, and sea salt. Delicious! All you have is fresh bread? No worries! Dry-toast the bread in a 350°F oven for about 5 minutes. Let cool for a few minutes, then use as directed in the recipe.

VEGETARIAN BIBIMBAP WITH SPICY TOFU

MAKES 4 SERVINGS • Over the past few years, bibimbap has risen to rock-star heights. This super-popular, fun, healthy, and completely gorgeous Korean dish translates to "mixed rice." A rainbow-like assortment of toppings is plated on cooked rice, served in a steaming-hot traditional *dolsot* stone bowl, with a sunny-side-up egg on top. Awesome! You mix and fold the spicy-sweet gochu-jang sauce into the hot rice and veggies, guaranteeing a perfect bite every single time. The whole process is tailor-made for fans of home-plating like a rock star chef.

There are a bajillion variations and methods for preparing this dish, some that take an eternity, others not so much. This recipe comes together really quickly, after overnight marinating in the fridge.

TOFU AND MARINADE

9 ounces extra-firm tofu, cut into 2-inch-long, ½-inch-thick matchsticks

3 tablespoons soy sauce

2 teaspoons pure maple syrup

1 teaspoon gochujang hot pepper paste

1 teaspoon sesame oil

1 tablespoon rice vinegar

1 tablespoon sesame seeds, toasted (see page 193)

SAUCE

⅓ cup gochujang hot pepper paste

2 tablespoons honey

1 tablespoon soy sauce

1 garlic clove, minced

BIBIMBAP

1⅓ cups short-grain rice

1 teaspoon canola oil

12 ounces bean sprouts

(Ingredients continue on page 256.)

1. Make the tofu and marinade: Place the tofu in a sealable freezer bag. Combine the remaining ingredients except the sesame seeds in a small bowl, whisk, and pour the marinade over the tofu, tossing gently to coat. Refrigerate overnight or for at least 1 hour, if you're short on time.

2. Preheat the oven to 350°F and line a baking sheet with parchment paper.

3. Arrange the tofu on the baking sheet in a single layer and pour the marinade on top. Bake for 25 to 30 minutes, turning halfway through, until the tofu is crispy and has developed a deep red color all over. Sprinkle the tofu with the sesame seeds, then tent it with aluminum foil to keep warm. Set aside. Keep the oven on.

4. Make the sauce: In a small dish, whisk together all the sauce ingredients with 2 tablespoons water until smooth. Set aside.

5. Make the bibimbap: Prepare the rice according to the package directions. Cover to keep warm and set aside.

¼ cup almond slivers

Sea salt and freshly cracked black pepper

2 tablespoons sesame oil

3 cups thinly sliced mushrooms (such as shiitake or cremini)

2 tablespoons soy sauce

2 garlic cloves, minced

10 ounces baby spinach

1 tablespoon butter

4 large free-range eggs

2 large carrots, cut into 3-inch segments and spiralized or julienned

2 large zucchini, cut into 3-inch segments and spiralized or julienned

4 scallions, thinly sliced

1 cup baby arugula leaves

6. Reduce the oven temperature to 225°F. Line a large baking sheet with parchment paper and place it in the oven.

7. In a large wok, heat the canola oil over medium heat. When hot, add the bean sprouts and almonds and sauté until the sprouts are softened but crisp, 1 to 2 minutes. Season with a pinch each of salt and pepper and transfer to the baking sheet in the oven to keep warm.

8. Heat 1 tablespoon of the sesame oil in the wok and add the mushrooms. Cook until they are softened and beginning to brown, 4 to 5 minutes, then add the soy sauce. Cook until the soy sauce has evaporated and disappears into the mushrooms, then transfer the mushrooms to the baking sheet.

9. Still in the wok, heat the remaining 1 tablespoon sesame oil over medium heat and add the garlic. Sauté for 20 seconds, then stir in the spinach. Cook, tossing often, until the spinach has wilted, 1 to 2 minutes. Season with a pinch each of salt and pepper and transfer the spinach to the baking sheet.

10. In a large skillet, melt the butter over medium heat. Fry the eggs until the whites are cooked through but the yolks remain runny (for my egg tips, see page 4).

11. Portion the rice into individual bowls. Top each bowl with a fried egg and one-quarter of the cooked vegetables and tofu. Add the carrots, zucchini, scallions, and arugula and serve with the sauce.

12. True to its name, bibimbap requires mixing. So get those chopsticks in there and mix away!

KALE CAESAR FLATBREADS

MAKES 4 SERVINGS • There's little common ground when it comes to kale; folks are either almost evangelical about their love of the little green or dislike it with a burning passion. This delicious little bad boy of a recipe is sure to convert the latter. The crunch factor of the roasted chickpeas paired with a homemade Caesar dressing, piled high on freshly baked flatbread, is serious next-level lunching.

CAESAR DRESSING

1 garlic clove

1 to 2 teaspoons Worcestershire sauce (or 5 anchovies in oil, if you like)

1 teaspoon Dijon mustard

2 large egg yolks

3 tablespoons fresh lemon juice

½ cup extra-virgin olive oil

3 tablespoons grated Parmesan cheese

1 teaspoon freshly cracked black pepper

Sea salt

(Ingredients continue on the next page.)

1. Set a baking stone in the oven and preheat the oven to 400°F.

2. Make the dressing: In a food processor, combine the garlic and Worcestershire sauce and pulse until a paste forms, about 30 seconds. Add the mustard, egg yolks, and lemon juice. With the food processor running on low speed, slowly drizzle in the olive oil, a few drops at a time, until completely incorporated. Transfer the dressing to a dish and fold in the Parmesan and pepper. Season with a pinch of sea salt, cover, and refrigerate until ready to serve.

3. Make the chickpea salad: In a roasting pan, toss the chickpeas, olive oil, paprika, cayenne, and salt. Roast for 20 to 25 minutes, giving the pan a shake halfway through, until golden brown and crispy. Set aside. Keep the oven on. (These little chickpea treasures can be made ahead and stored in an airtight container in the fridge for up to 24 hours. Reheat them in the oven at 400°F for 5 minutes before serving.)

4. Make the flatbread: Increase the oven temperature to 550°F.

5. While the oven is preheating, place the kale leaves in a large bowl, spoon 5 or 6 tablespoons of the dressing over the salad, and massage the leaves well (see page 258). Add the onion and refrigerate while you prepare the flatbread.

CHICKPEA SALAD

1 (19-ounce) can chickpeas, drained and rinsed

1 tablespoon olive oil

1 teaspoon smoked paprika

⅛ teaspoon cayenne pepper

½ teaspoon sea salt

4 cups packed sliced kale leaves

1 small red onion, thinly sliced

FLATBREAD

1 recipe Pizza Dough (page 112)

All-purpose flour, for rolling out the dough

4 teaspoons olive oil

1 garlic clove

Shaved Parmesan cheese, for serving

Massaging kale will help turn down the bitterness level in the greens and turn up the deliciousness. Massage the dressing into the greens using your fingertips. You'll notice that the leaves will darken and shrink and the texture will soften. Take a quick bite and taste the kale. If it's still a tad bitter, massage a little longer. This massaging step will take an extra moment or two, but it's well worth the effort.

6. Divide the dough into four balls. On a floured surface, roll out the dough balls into 10 x 5-inch flatbreads. Brush each flatbread with 1 teaspoon of the olive oil. Working in batches (you should be able to bake two breads at a time if your baking stone is a standard size), use a pizza peel (or two steady and extra-careful hands) to transfer the flatbreads to the oven and bake for 5 to 6 minutes, until puffed and cooked through. Every now and then, flatbreads forget who they are and pretend they're pita breads, puffing up like no-body's business. If necessary, give them a little poke with a sharp knife while baking to deflate them.

7. Rub the flatbreads with the garlic clove and top each with about 1 cup of the kale, some chickpeas, and more shaved Parmesan.

VEGETABLE PANEER JALFREZI

MAKES 4 SERVINGS • Kind of like an Indian stir-fry, *jalfrezi* is perfect served as a main course or as a side dish paired with butter chicken (page 190). When I was first learning to cook, this dish danced its way into the Prescott family recipe box as a curry-night dish for my mom, a longtime vegetarian. She fell head over heels and in no time flat, *jalfrezi* has become one of our favorite dishes, a go-to every time we need to cure our curry cravings.

2 tablespoons vegetable oil

9 ounces paneer (fresh Indian cheese), cut into 1-inch cubes

1 teaspoon cumin seeds

1 large red onion, thinly sliced

2 garlic cloves, minced

1 or 2 green chiles, finely sliced

1 tablespoon minced fresh ginger

¼ teaspoon ground turmeric

1 teaspoon red chile powder

1 teaspoon ground coriander

1 tablespoon dried fenugreek leaves, crushed (seek these out in a specialty grocer)

1 red bell pepper, seeded and sliced

1 large carrot, julienned

1 large tomato, seeded and sliced into wedges

1 cup canned crushed tomatoes

1 cup vegetable stock

½ teaspoon sea salt

2 cups cauliflower florets

½ cup frozen peas

2 tablespoons fresh lime juice, plus 1 lime, cut into wedges, for serving

1 teaspoon garam masala

1 tablespoon minced fresh cilantro, plus sprigs for serving

1. In a large skillet, heat 1 tablespoon of the vegetable oil over medium heat. Add the paneer and brown on all sides, about 5 minutes. Transfer to a plate with a slotted spoon and set aside.

2. With the skillet still over medium heat, heat the remaining 1 tablespoon vegetable oil and the cumin seeds. Toast until the cumin is fragrant and starting to turn a deep golden brown, 1½ to 2 minutes. Add the onion and sauté for 2 minutes. Stir in the garlic, chiles, and ginger and cook for 2 minutes. Stir in the turmeric, chile powder, coriander, and fenugreek, and cook for 30 seconds, keeping the spices moving the entire time. Add the bell pepper, carrot, sliced and crushed tomatoes, stock, and sea salt and bring to a boil.

3. Simmer for 5 minutes, then stir in the paneer, cauliflower, and peas and simmer for 5 minutes. The sauce will have thickened up beautifully at this point. Remove from the heat.

4. Squeeze in the lime juice and stir in the garam masala and cilantro. Serve with fresh cilantro sprigs and the lime wedges. Delicious with basmati rice or naan and a tall glass of your favorite beer.

SWEET POTATO AND TURMERIC BUDDHA BOWLS

MAKES 4 SERVINGS • Despite the potentially overwhelming caloric explosion that you may experience when scrolling through the buttery portal that is the DtheP Instagram account, we eat our fair share of salads, smoothies, and veggies at home, partly because I want to live a long and healthy life, and partly because veggie-based recipes are just screaming with flavor. I love being able to showcase vegetables as the heroes they truly are.

Here's a go-to healthy lunch for us. All the wholesome bits with no compromise on deliciousness.

ROASTED SWEET POTATOES

2 pounds sweet potatoes, unpeeled, cut into 1-inch chunks

2 tablespoons olive oil

¼ teaspoon ground roasted cumin

¼ teaspoon smoked paprika

¼ teaspoon ground coriander

½ teaspoon sea salt

½ teaspoon freshly cracked black pepper

RICE

3 cups vegetable stock

1½ cups short-grain brown rice

1. Make the sweet potatoes: Preheat the oven to 425°F. Line a baking sheet with parchment paper.

2. In a large bowl, toss together all the sweet potato ingredients. Spread on the prepared baking sheet and roast for 40 to 45 minutes, turning the potatoes halfway through, until fork-tender and browned.

3. Meanwhile, make the rice: In a medium saucepan, bring the stock to a boil over medium-high heat. Stir in the rice. Cover and cook according to the package instructions.

4. Make the tahini dressing: In a medium bowl, whisk together all the tahini dressing ingredients until smooth. Set aside.

5. Assemble the bowls: In a large bowl, massage the kale with the olive oil (see page 258).

6. Divide the rice among four large bowls and portion out the sweet potatoes, kale, and carrots. Top with the chickpeas, sprouts, feta, sunflower seeds, and avocado. Spoon the tahini dressing on top and enjoy a happy, healthy bowl of goodness.

TAHINI DRESSING

- ¼ cup tahini
- 3 tablespoons olive oil
- 2 tablespoons fresh lemon juice
- 1 tablespoon pure maple syrup
- ½ teaspoon ground turmeric
- ¼ teaspoon smoked paprika
- ¼ teaspoon cayenne pepper
- ⅛ teaspoon sea salt
- ⅛ teaspoon freshly cracked black pepper

BOWLS

- 3 cups finely sliced kale leaves
- 1½ teaspoons olive oil
- 2 carrots, very finely julienned or grated
- 1 cup canned chickpeas, drained and rinsed
- 1 cup of your favorite sprouts
- ¼ cup crumbled feta cheese
- ¼ cup shelled sunflower seeds
- 1 large ripe avocado, pitted, peeled, and sliced into wedges

HALLOUMI BURGERS

MAKES 6 SERVINGS • Okay. Close your eyes, breathe deep, and imagine a world where the ideal burger exists, forged solely and entirely for legit cheese-lovers. A burger patty that's made almost entirely of cheese. Could something so marvelous exist? Could life be so kind and generous?

Hot damn, this burger is insanely good. I first tried halloumi (a semihard, unripened cheese originally hailing from Cyprus) a few years back in a warm salad and immediately fell in love with the salty flavor and killer texture. It stands up beautifully when fried or grilled, making it perfectly suited for sandwiches, wraps, and salads, or burgerized, as here.

BURGER PATTIES

¼ cup coarsely chopped sun-dried tomatoes

2 tablespoons coarsely chopped fresh flat-leaf parsley leaves

1 garlic clove, coarsely chopped

½ teaspoon dried oregano

¼ teaspoon cayenne pepper

3 Kalamata olives, pitted

1 pound halloumi cheese, grated on the large holes of a box grater

2 large free-range eggs

½ cup bread crumbs (see page 253)

1. Make the burger patties: In a food processor, combine the sun-dried tomatoes, parsley, garlic, oregano, cayenne, olives, and halloumi. Pulse for 1 minute. Add the eggs and bread crumbs and pulse until the mixture comes together.

2. Shape the halloumi mixture into six patties that are ½ inch thick and slightly wider than the burger buns. Transfer to a plate, cover with plastic wrap, and refrigerate for 30 minutes.

3. Make the yogurt spread: In a small bowl, combine all the yogurt spread ingredients and stir until smooth. Cover with plastic wrap and refrigerate until ready to serve.

4. Make the burgers: Heat a large skillet over medium heat. Split and toast the insides of the brioche buns until golden brown, 2 to 3 minutes. Set aside.

5. Working in batches, fry the burgers in the hot, dry pan for 2 to 3 minutes per side, until both sides of the burger patties are browned and crispy.

6. Build the burgers with 2 tablespoons of the yogurt spread, a halloumi patty, 2 tomato slices, ¼ cup of the shaved cucumber, and a small handful of arugula.

LEMON-GARLIC YOGURT SPREAD

½ cup full-fat Greek yogurt

1 garlic clove, minced

2 tablespoons fresh lemon juice

1 tablespoon minced fresh parsley

1 tablespoon finely sliced scallions

½ teaspoon hot sauce

BURGERS

6 brioche burger buns (such as Homemade Brioche Burger Buns, page 76)

1 large tomato, sliced

½ English cucumber, shaved with a vegetable peeler

1 cup baby arugula leaves

CHANA MASALA

MAKES 6 TO 8 SERVINGS • The first time I had a proper chana masala was in London while I was working on a record and developing an appetite for English ale. Our illustrious record producer, Julian Kindred, took us on a quick tour of the southern coast of England, with a stop in the super-fly city of Brighton. I was a newbie to proper vegetarian eating and had no idea that a meat-free dish could be so wonderfully flavorful!

This recipe is a favorite around the Prescott house and has its position on our weekly meal plan permanently on lock. Healthy, easy to throw together, and delicious for days, it's curry night done right!

2 tablespoons sunflower or vegetable oil

1 teaspoon cumin seeds

1 large onion, finely diced

5 garlic cloves, minced

1 tablespoon grated fresh ginger

2 green chiles, finely sliced

1 tablespoon minced fresh cilantro stems

2 tablespoons ground coriander

1 teaspoon chili powder

1½ teaspoons ground turmeric

1 tablespoon tomato puree

1 cup vegetable stock

1 (28-ounce) can diced tomatoes

2 (19-ounce) cans chickpeas, drained and rinsed

1 teaspoon kosher salt

1 teaspoon garam masala

1 tablespoon fresh lemon juice

1 or 2 red chiles, thinly sliced

Handful of fresh cilantro sprigs

1. In a large Dutch oven or heavy-bottomed stockpot, heat 1 tablespoon of the sunflower oil and the cumin seeds over medium heat. When the cumin seeds start to dance, 1½ to 2 minutes, and the smell is intoxicating, add the onion and cook for 5 minutes, until it starts to become translucent.

2. Pour the remaining 1 tablespoon oil into the pan. Add the garlic, ginger, chiles, cilantro stems, coriander, chili powder, turmeric, and tomato puree. Stir to combine and cook for 2 minutes, stirring constantly so it doesn't stick to the bottom of the pot. Add the stock, diced tomatoes, chickpeas, and salt. Bring the curry to a simmer, then reduce the heat to medium-low and simmer for 20 minutes, until the chickpeas have softened and the curry has thickened beautifully.

3. Stir in the garam masala, squeeze in the lemon juice, and top with the chiles and cilantro. For added deliciousness, serve with Chile-Coriander Naan (page 268).

CHILE-CORIANDER NAAN

MAKES 10 TO 12 PIECES • My favorite flatbread on the planet, this is fantastic served alongside Chana Masala (page 267), Butter Chicken (page 190), or Vegetable Paneer Jalfrezi (page 261), or on its own as a late-night snack. Traditionally cooked in a piping-hot tandoor, or oven, naan is crispy, buttery flatbread perfection. This home kitchen–friendly version is easy and all kinds of delicious, with no special equipment required.

1 tablespoon active dry yeast

1 teaspoon honey

2 tablespoons lukewarm water

4 cups all-purpose flour, plus more for dusting

2 teaspoons coriander seeds, lightly crushed

1 teaspoon red pepper flakes

2 garlic cloves, minced

1 teaspoon lemon zest

1½ teaspoons baking soda

1 teaspoon baking powder

½ teaspoon sea salt

1 cup full-fat Greek yogurt

¾ cup whole milk

Olive oil, for the bowl

3 tablespoons butter

1 tablespoon minced fresh cilantro

1. In a medium bowl, combine the yeast, honey, and lukewarm water. Let the yeast come to life, activate, and bubble like crazy, about 10 minutes.

2. In a large bowl, whisk together the flour, coriander, red pepper flakes, garlic, lemon zest, baking soda, baking powder, and salt.

3. Whisk the yogurt and milk into the yeast mixture. Add the yeast mixture to the dry ingredients and stir with a wooden spoon until the dough starts to come together.

4. Turn the dough out onto a lightly floured surface and knead for about 10 minutes, until a soft dough ball starts to form. Transfer the dough ball to a large, lightly oiled bowl and cover with plastic wrap. Give the dough a warm home in the kitchen until doubled in size, about 1½ hours. (If you're a preplanning rock star, you can chill the dough overnight at this point.)

5. Punch the dough down, divide it into ten to twelve equal portions, and shape them into little dough balls. Working on a floured surface, roll the balls into 8 x 4-inch, ¼-inch-thick ovals.

6. Melt the butter in a small saucepan over medium-low heat. Remove from the heat and stir in the cilantro. Set aside.

7. Heat a large skillet with a lid over medium heat. Working one at a time, brush the naan on both sides with the cilantro butter, then transfer them to the hot pan. Cook for 1½ minutes, then flip and cover the skillet. Cook for 1½ minutes more.

8. Transfer the naan to a wire rack as you finish them.

9. These little wonders are best eaten warm, but will keep in an airtight container for up to 2 days. For maximum deliciousness, warm them in the oven for a few minutes to bring them back to life.

DAL MAKHANI

MAKES 4 TO 6 SERVINGS • This superstar of a dish originates from the Punjab region of India and Pakistan. *Dal makhani* is super creamy and totally bursting with flavor, and I would happily enjoy this vegetarian rock star over a meat-laden meal option any day of the week. Lentils are healthy, delicious pulses (see opposite), and there are just about a million ways to cook them. After an easy overnight soak, they're ready to shine. A fantastic staple ingredient to add to every pantry.

1 cup dried black lentils

½ cup dried kidney beans

2 quarts vegetable stock

SPICE MIXTURE

1 teaspoon coriander seeds

½ teaspoon fennel seeds

½ teaspoon ground cardamom

2 whole cloves

¾ teaspoon smoked paprika

¾ teaspoon ground cumin

½ teaspoon cayenne pepper

1½ tablespoons garam masala

MAKHANI

3 tablespoons vegetable oil

2 medium red onions, diced

2 shallots, minced

6 garlic cloves, minced

1 tablespoon minced fresh ginger

1 tablespoon minced cilantro stems

1 (6-ounce) can tomato paste

1 (14-ounce) can crushed tomatoes

1 cinnamon stick

1 bay leaf

1. Put the lentils and kidney beans in a large bowl and cover with cold water. Soak overnight.

2. The next day, drain the lentils and beans and rinse them well. Pour the stock into a large stockpot and add the lentils and beans. Bring to a boil over medium-high heat, then cover and reduce the heat to maintain a simmer. Simmer for 1 hour.

3. Make the spice mixture: Using a mortar and pestle, bash the coriander and fennel seeds together. Transfer to a small bowl along with the rest of the spice mixture ingredients and stir to combine. Set aside.

4. Make the makhani: In a large skillet with a lid, heat the vegetable oil over medium heat. Add the onions and shallots. Cover and let the onions cook and caramelize for about 15 minutes. Keep an eye on the onions (uncover as little as possible) and give the pan a shake every few minutes to keep them from sticking to the bottom.

5. Add the garlic, ginger, and cilantro stems and cook, stirring continuously, for 30 seconds. Stir in the spice mixture and tomato paste and cook for 1 minute, keeping the mixture moving with a wooden spoon.

6. Add the onion mixture, tomatoes, cinnamon stick, bay leaf, salt, and pepper to the pot with the lentils and stir to combine. Bring to a boil over medium-high heat, then reduce

1 teaspoon kosher salt

½ teaspoon freshly cracked black pepper

1 cup heavy cream

4 tablespoons (½ stick) butter, melted

4 scallions, finely sliced, for serving

1 or 2 red chiles, sliced, for serving

Naan (such as Chili-Coriander Naan, page 268) or rice, for serving

the heat to medium-low and gently simmer for 45 minutes to 1 hour, until the lentils and beans are tender. Turn off the heat, pour in the cream, and stir in the butter.

7. Divide among bowls and serve with the scallions, chiles, and naan.

Pulses are a genius little family of ingredients that include dried peas, dried chickpeas, beans, and lentils. Packed to the nines with fiber, protein, and vitamins, they're not only incredibly good for you but also wonderfully sustainable, with a very low carbon footprint. Heart friendly, Earth friendly, farm friendly. So much win.

10

Sidekicks,

SALADS, AND LATE-NIGHT SNACKS

LIKE BONO AND THE EDGE, BATMAN AND ROBIN, AND CHEWIE AND HAN SOLO, EVERY HERO DISH NEEDS AN EQUALLY DELICIOUS, PERFECTLY COMPLEMENTARY SIDEKICK.

Not an afterthought, but a true partner in crime. Starters, sides, salads, and even snacks can be unforgettably tasty and are able to elevate their main-course counterparts to new heights.

From poutine to panzanella, here are some of my favorite sides, salads, and late-night snacks. They're incredible on their own and perfect for pairing with mains to create epic family-style meals.

SUPER-QUICK GARLIC BOK CHOY

MAKES 4 TO 6 SERVINGS • Bok choy is an amazing little green. It's the perfect addition to stir-fries, in soups, and here, served as a side dish. Quick, easy, and delicious. Oh, and it's packed full of nutrients. Sweet bonus!

2 tablespoons toasted sesame oil

10 scallions, trimmed and cut into thirds

5 garlic cloves, minced

1 pound bok choy, ends trimmed and leaves separated

2 tablespoons soy sauce

1 tablespoon sesame seeds, toasted (see page 193)

Heat a wok over medium-high heat and add the sesame oil. When the oil is hot and the smell intoxicating, add the scallions and garlic and stir-fry for 30 seconds, keeping them moving the entire time. Add the bok choy and soy sauce and stir-fry for 2 minutes, then transfer to a serving dish and sprinkle on the toasted sesame seeds. So quick, so delicious.

GARLIC AND ROSEMARY HASSELBACK POTATOES

MAKES 6 TO 8 SERVINGS • Potatoes are a gold-medal sidekick, perfectly matched with almost any main course. This is my all-time, desert island spud recipe. Hasselbacks are really easy to throw together, with just a little extra prep work, and look seriously impressive. The key is a very sharp knife and a slow and steady hand, taking care not to cut entirely through the potato. (If you do, no worries! Your hasselbacks will still taste incredible.)

8 large russet potatoes, scrubbed

¼ cup olive oil

1 teaspoon sea salt

1 teaspoon freshly cracked black pepper

5 garlic cloves, unpeeled

2 fresh rosemary sprigs

4 tablespoons (½ stick) butter, melted

1. Preheat the oven to 425°F.

2. With a sharp knife, cut crosswise parallel slits into the potatoes, about ⅛ inch apart, stopping just before you cut through so that the slices stay connected at the bottom of the potato. Transfer the potatoes to a high-sided roasting pan.

3. Brush the potatoes all over with the olive oil and season with the sea salt and pepper. Scatter the garlic cloves around the pan. Pick the rosemary leaves from the stems and sprinkle them all over the potatoes. Bake for 40 minutes.

4. Brush the potatoes all over with the melted butter and bake for 30 to 40 minutes more, or until the edges of the spuds are crispy and golden brown and you can easily insert a knife into the center of the potato. Serve immediately.

VARIATIONS

This recipe is delicious as is, but mixing up the same old is always fun. Here are a few ways to keep your spuds fresh and exciting:

1. After baking, top with sour cream, bacon bits, and thinly sliced scallion.

2. With about 10 minutes of cooking time remaining, sprinkle the potatoes with Gruyère or aged cheddar cheese, then place back in the oven to melt.

3. After baking, top with chili (page 158), sour cream, sliced avocado, and a pinch of chili powder.

POUTINE, THE KING OF CANADIAN COMFORT

MAKES 4 TO 6 SERVINGS • It was utterly impossible for me not to include my recipe for the King of all Canadian Dishes (and maybe Canada herself), the Almighty Poutine. When you yell comfort food, I scream *poutine*!! Late-night eats at their absolute best. It's the happiest of dishes, covered in a garlicky, thick gravy and squeaky cheese curds. Hold all my calls—you don't interrupt poutine time.

3 pounds russet potatoes, scrubbed

Peanut oil, for frying

⅓ cup butter

¼ cup all-purpose flour

2 garlic cloves, finely minced

3 cups beef stock

2 tablespoons ketchup

1 tablespoon fresh lemon juice

½ teaspoon Worcestershire sauce

1 tablespoon cornstarch

Sea salt and freshly cracked black pepper

2 cups squeaky-fresh cheese curds (check specialty cheese shops)

1. Cut the potatoes into ¼-inch-thick sticks and transfer them to a large bowl filled with cold water. Cover and refrigerate for 1 hour.

2. In a large Dutch oven or stockpot with a kitchen thermometer attached, heat 3 inches of peanut oil over medium heat to 325°F.

3. Drain the potatoes and pat them dry with paper towels. Working in batches, fry the potatoes for 5 minutes, turning every minute or so. The French fries will be lightly colored at this point. Transfer the partially cooked fries to a rack set over a baking sheet lined with paper towels and continue with the rest of the potatoes.

4. In a 3-quart saucepan, melt the butter over medium heat. Whisk the flour into the butter and cook, whisking continuously, for 1 minute. Whisk in the garlic and cook for 30 seconds. In a slow and steady stream, whisk in the stock, then add the ketchup, lemon juice, and Worcestershire. Bring the gravy to a simmer. In a small bowl, stir together the cornstarch and 2 tablespoons water until smooth. Whisk this slurry into the gravy and simmer for 5 minutes, until thickened. Season with a pinch each of salt and pepper. Set aside.

5. Increase the oil temperature to 375°F. Working in batches, fry the fries again for 2 to 4 minutes, until golden brown and super crispy. Drain any excess grease on paper towels and toss with a nice bit of sea salt.

6. Portion the fries into one large or several small serving dishes and top them with the delicious cheese curds. Generously ladle warm gravy on top. Serve and immediately enter Canadian heaven.

SWEET POTATO WEDGES WITH CURRY MAYO DIP

MAKES 3 OR 4 SIDE SERVINGS • Sweet potato wedges are so bomb. The marriage of crispy, sweet, and slightly spicy flavors is to die for. And hey! Sweet potatoes are super healthy, packed with vitamins, and a wonderful alternative to French fries. Sweet indeed! This recipe is fantastic served as a late-night snack on its own or as a side dish served with burgers, steak (à la steak frites), or roast chicken (page 182).

SWEET POTATOES

2 pounds sweet potatoes (about 4 large), scrubbed and dried well

2 tablespoons olive oil

1 teaspoon smoked paprika

½ teaspoon ground coriander

¼ teaspoon cayenne pepper

½ teaspoon sea salt

¼ teaspoon freshly cracked black pepper

CURRY MAYO DIP

¾ cup prepared mayo

2 tablespoons fresh lime juice

1½ teaspoons mild yellow curry powder

¼ teaspoon ground turmeric

¼ teaspoon cayenne pepper

Pinch of sea salt

1. Make the sweet potatoes: Preheat the oven to 400°F. Line a large baking sheet with parchment paper.

2. Halve the potatoes lengthwise, then slice into thick-cut wedges (about 8 total per potato).

3. Transfer the wedges to a large bowl, add the rest of the sweet potato ingredients, and mix well.

4. Arrange the wedges in a single layer on the prepared baking sheet. Bake for 40 to 45 minutes, turning halfway through, until cooked through on the inside and crispy and slightly charred on the outside.

5. Meanwhile, make the curry mayo dip: Combine all the dip ingredients in a small serving dish and mix well. Taste and adjust the seasonings, stir, and refrigerate until ready to serve.

ROASTED CARROTS WITH CARROT TOP–CASHEW PESTO

MAKES 4 TO 6 SERVINGS • Food waste is a major problem plaguing communities around the world. Almost half of all food produced globally is discarded, causing a major strain on both our wallets and the environment. Inspired by the work of the David Suzuki Foundation toward ending food waste, I wanted to create a carrot dish with little to no waste, and that means including the carrot tops. They're chock-full of vitamins, nutrients, and other fabulously health-happy benefits, and there's just no reason at all to chuck them in the bin. If I have extra carrot tops, I'll toss them in a large pot of simmering homemade stock (page 149) or use them in a pesto, as here. Pesto is a fabulous way to incorporate greens into our food that we may sometimes take for granted. Kale, radish leaf, beet greens. Super delicious with little waste = appetite and environment friendly.

These carrots are especially fantastic with roast chicken (page 182) or a juicy seared steak (page 163).

CARROTS

3 pounds carrots, with tops
2 tablespoons olive oil
1 tablespoon pure maple syrup
½ teaspoon sea salt
½ teaspoon freshly cracked black pepper

PESTO

1 garlic clove
3 tablespoons cashews
2 cups carrots tops (reserved from above)
½ cup fresh basil leaves
¼ cup grated Parmesan cheese
½ cup extra-virgin olive oil
Sea salt and freshly cracked black pepper

1. Preheat the oven to 400°F. Line a baking sheet with parchment paper.

2. Remove the carrot tops, leaving about 1½ inches of green remaining on the carrot itself (because it just looks baller). Coarsely chop the carrot tops, then measure out 2 cups for the pesto (save any extra carrot tops for more pesto, homemade stock, or something yet to be imagined). Scrub the carrots (do not peel) and dry them thoroughly. In a large bowl, toss the carrots with the olive oil and maple syrup and season with the salt and pepper. Spread them on the baking sheet and roast for 25 to 30 minutes, or until fork-tender, turning halfway through.

3. While the carrots are roasting, make the pesto: In a food processor, combine the garlic and cashews and pulse until finely chopped. Add the reserved 2 cups carrot tops, the basil, and the cheese and pulse for 1 minute, until finely

chopped. With the food processor running, slowly stream in the olive oil until combined, scraping down the sides of the bowl a few times as you go. When the pesto is smooth, transfer it to a serving dish. Season with a pinch each of salt and pepper.

4. Serve up the sweet roasted carrots and side of pesto with your favorite main course dish.

WICKED STRAWBERRY-PISTACHIO BROCCOLI AND CANDIED MAPLE-BACON SALAD

MAKES 4 TO 6 SERVINGS • The first time I traveled to Paris I lost my food mind. Literally. Like, it might still be there, livin' it up in the French countryside, eating fresh baguettes, Camembert, and a glass (or five) of cabernet. The flavors of that beautiful country forever changed how I understand both food and dining itself, as I was exposed to folks who truly live to eat and invest in taking the time to slow down and savor the joie de vivre that we so desperately need in our daily lives. You're an inspiration, France!

We visited in July, and it seemed as if the combination of strawberries and pistachios had taken over the culinary landscape. While eating an almost rapturous dessert, care of the amazing Pierre Hermé, atop Montmartre at the steps of Sacré-Coeur, I dreamed up this recipe. The views and dessert were some of the most inspiring of my life!

5 thick-cut smoked bacon slices

1½ tablespoons pure maple syrup

LEMON VINAIGRETTE

2 teaspoons Dijon mustard

6 tablespoons fresh lemon juice

3 tablespoons honey

¾ cup extra-virgin olive oil

¼ teaspoon sea salt

¼ teaspoon freshly cracked black pepper

1. Preheat the oven to 350°F. Line a baking sheet with parchment paper.

2. Spread the bacon on the baking sheet and baste each slice with the maple syrup. Bake for 25 to 30 minutes, turning halfway through, or until golden brown and starting to crisp. Transfer the bacon to a rack to cool. Candied bacon is just around the corner.

3. Make the vinaigrette: In a medium bowl, combine the Dijon, lemon juice, and honey. Whisking continuously, slowly drizzle in the olive oil until emulsified and thickened (see opposite). Season with the salt and pepper, and give the vinaigrette a final whisk.

4. Make the salad: In a large bowl, toss the broccoli, onion, strawberries, pistachios, basil, and half the vinaigrette.

5. Cut the candied bacon into ½-inch pieces. Line the bottom of a serving dish with the pea shoots, then top with the bacon and salad. Serve with the remaining vinaigrette.

SALAD

2 broccoli heads, tops cut into florets and stems trimmed (and saved for another recipe, such as a stir-fry or pasta sauce)

¼ cup finely diced red onion

3 cups strawberries, hulled and halved

¼ cup lightly salted pistachios

¼ cup fresh basil leaves, cut into chiffonade

2 cups pea shoots or your favorite sprouts

Emulsifying means binding liquids together that don't usually like to hang out, like oil or eggs with water or broth. This is achieved by adding the oil in a slow and steady stream to the mixture while you whisk continuously. Mustard and eggs function as rock-star natural emulsifiers in dressings and sauces.

SRIRACHA-ROASTED CAULIFLOWER

MAKES 3 TO 4 SIDE SERVINGS • Sriracha lovers, this one's for you. A few years ago I was working for the weekend, cooking at a catering gig just outside of New York City, and decided to add this little cracker of a dish to the menu at the last minute. It's crispy, spicy, and jacked with flavor, and the crowd went totally gangbusters. Sriracha-Roasted Cauliflower very quickly muscled its way onto our weekly meal plan.

This recipe is a fantastic side to any noodle dish, to lettuce wraps, or with banh mi sandwiches (page 60).

3 tablespoons toasted sesame oil

2 tablespoons olive oil

3 tablespoons soy sauce

3 tablespoons sriracha

2 tablespoons fish sauce

2 teaspoons rice vinegar

1 tablespoon fresh lime juice

1 large cauliflower head, cut into medium florets, then halved

1 tablespoon sesame seeds

¼ cup finely sliced scallions

Handful of cilantro

1 lime, cut into wedges, for serving

1. Preheat the oven to 450°F. Line a baking sheet with parchment paper.

2. In a large bowl, lightly whisk the oils, soy sauce, sriracha, fish sauce, vinegar, and lime juice. Toss the cauliflower in the sauce and spread it on the prepared baking sheet.

3. Roast for 25 to 30 minutes, or until tender and nicely charred, turning halfway through. Sprinkle the sesame seeds, scallions, and cilantro and serve with the lime wedges.

ROASTED BUTTERNUT SQUASH SALAD WITH MAPLE-BALSAMIC DRESSING

MAKES 6 TO 8 SERVINGS, AS A STARTER • I first learned of the genius of warm salads thanks to a gorgeous breakfast salad dish in my cookbook bible: *Cook with Jamie,* a book by Jamie Oliver that I borrowed from the Nashville Public Library a few years back. Up to that point, my idea of a salad was a bowl of flavorless iceberg lettuce with a few cherry tomatoes on top, covered in globs of store-bought dressing. Just plain wrong! The beautiful marriage of warm, cooked elements and crisp, cool greens is a game changer. If you have a salad hater in your life, get them started on warm salads. You'll have a convert on your hands in no time flat.

I have mad love for this maple-balsamic dressing. An incredible addition to salads of every stripe, it's on regular rotation in my fridge.

1 small butternut squash (about 2 pounds), peeled, halved, seeded, and cut into 1-inch-thick pieces

1 tablespoon olive oil

½ teaspoon sea salt

½ teaspoon freshly cracked black pepper

2 tablespoons pure maple syrup

¼ teaspoon cayenne pepper

1 cup pecan halves, coarsely chopped

3½ ounces aged speck, thinly sliced

2 ounces aged cheddar cheese, shaved (about ½ cup)

2 cups baby arugula leaves

½ teaspoon flaky sea salt

1. Preheat the oven to 350°F. Line a large baking sheet with parchment paper.

2. Spread the squash in a single layer on the baking sheet, drizzle the olive oil on top, and season with the salt and pepper. Roast for 35 to 40 minutes, or until fork-tender, turning halfway through.

3. While the squash is roasting, combine the maple syrup, cayenne, and 2 tablespoons water in a small dish.

4. Heat a medium skillet over medium heat. Add the pecans and toast for 2 minutes, shaking the pan so they don't burn. Pour the maple syrup mixture over the pecans and toss to combine. Cook for 30 seconds, then transfer the pecans to a plate to cool.

MAPLE-BALSAMIC DRESSING

1 garlic clove, minced

1½ teaspoons whole-grain Dijon mustard

2 tablespoons fresh lemon juice

¼ cup pure maple syrup

¼ cup balsamic vinegar

¾ cup extra-virgin olive oil

⅛ teaspoon sea salt

⅛ teaspoon freshly cracked black pepper

3½ ounces aged speck, thinly sliced

2 ounces aged cheddar cheese, shaved (about ½ cup)

2 cups baby arugula leaves

1 teaspoon flaky sea salt

5. Make the maple-balsamic dressing: In a medium bowl, whisk together the garlic, Dijon, lemon juice, maple syrup, and vinegar. Whisking continuously, slowly stream in the olive oil until the dressing is thick, glossy, and emulsified. Season with the salt and pepper.

6. Drizzle 1 to 2 tablespoons of dressing over each serving plate. Arrange 2 slices of butternut squash in the center of each plate, then add 1 slice of speck, a few cheddar shavings, and a small handful of candied pecans. Top with a small handful of the fresh arugula and a light sprinkle of flaky sea salt.

BACON AND PARMESAN–ROASTED BRUSSELS SPROUTS

MAKES 4 TO 6 SIDE SERVINGS • Brussels sprouts are super delicious but tend to get a bad rap. Often they're overcooked, underseasoned, and underloved. Cooked properly, though, they're a ridiculously awesome main-course side-kick. Roasting transforms these little dudes into perfectly crispy, almost candy-like veggies. Once you pop you seriously can't stop.

This is delicious served with roast chicken (page 182), as a holiday side (see page 178), or as a midnight snack.

2 pounds Brussels sprouts

3 tablespoons olive oil

2 tablespoons pure maple syrup

½ teaspoon kosher salt

½ teaspoon freshly cracked black pepper

6 thick-cut smoked bacon slices

⅓ cup shaved Parmesan cheese

1. Preheat the oven to 400°F. Line a large baking sheet with parchment paper.

2. Give the Brussels sprouts a good rinse under cold running water and dry well with paper towels. Halve the large sprouts, leaving small ones whole, and transfer them to the prepared baking sheet. Drizzle with the olive oil and maple syrup, season with the salt and pepper, and give the lot a mix to coat well. Roast for 25 to 30 minutes, or until the sprouts are tender and crispy, turning halfway through.

3. Meanwhile, heat a skillet over medium heat and fry the bacon until crispy, 6 to 8 minutes. Crumble into bacon bits and set aside.

4. Transfer the cooked Brussels sprouts to a large bowl and toss them with the bacon bits and cheese. Serve immediately.

TUSCAN-STYLE PANZANELLA SALAD

MAKES 6 TO 8 SERVINGS • Panzanella salad is our favorite summertime salad treat, best when tomatoes are perfectly ripe, sunshine is on overdrive, and dining al fresco is a daily happening. It's amazing paired with a glass of chilled rosé and a warm afternoon of doing absolutely nothing.

For best results, use day-old crusty bread and try to incorporate as many kinds of fresh, ripe tomatoes as you can find.

On its own, this vinaigrette is a total knockout, and will keep well in the fridge for several days. Just store it in an airtight jar and give the jar a good shake or two before opening.

SALAD

- **12 ounces ciabatta (or sourdough) bread**
- **2 tablespoons olive oil**
- **1 tablespoon fresh thyme leaves, chopped**
- **2½ pounds mixed fresh tomatoes (heirloom, plum, cherry—the more, the merrier!), halved and quartered if large, halved if smaller**
- **1 large English cucumber, halved lengthwise and sliced into thin half-moons**
- **½ medium red onion, sliced into very thin half-moons**
- **½ teaspoon sea salt**
- **½ cup fresh basil leaves, thinly sliced**

1. Make the salad: Preheat the oven to 350°F.

2. Use a serrated knife to slice the bread into rustic ½-inch cubes (you want about 8 cups), then spread them on a baking sheet. Toss the bread with the olive oil and thyme. Bake for 15 to 20 minutes, until you have golden brown and toasty croutons. Set aside.

3. In a large bowl, combine the tomatoes, cucumber, and onion. Season with the sea salt, add the basil, and give a toss or two to mix.

4. Make the vinaigrette: In a medium bowl, whisk together the vinegar, lemon juice, Dijon, and garlic. Whisking continuously, drizzle in the olive oil until the vinaigrette is thick, smooth, and emulsified. Season with the salt and pepper.

2 tablespoons red wine vinegar

2 tablespoons fresh lemon juice

½ teaspoon Dijon mustard

2 garlic cloves, finely minced

½ cup olive oil

¼ teaspoon sea salt

¼ teaspoon freshly cracked black pepper

5. To the bowl with the chopped goodness, add the croutons and vinaigrette to taste. Toss and serve. (For added deliciousness, let the salad sit for a few minutes before tucking in. This will give the bread a chance to absorb more of that gorgeous dressing. Extra flavor, extra awesome.)

AVOCADO FRIES WITH PICO AND FETA

MAKES 4 APPETIZER SERVINGS • Avocado fries are late-night pub grub done right. A textural dream, they're crispy on the outside and perfectly soft on the inside. Bliss! Top that crispy deliciousness with fresh pico de gallo, chili mayo, and crumbled feta and you're on a rocket ship destined for snack nirvana.

PICO DE GALLO

4 large Roma (plum) tomatoes, diced

3 tablespoons finely diced red onion

2 tablespoons fresh lime juice

1 teaspoon red wine vinegar

1 tablespoon finely chopped fresh cilantro leaves

1 tablespoon fresh basil leaves, cut into chiffonade

¼ teaspoon sea salt

CHILI MAYO

½ cup prepared mayo

1 tablespoon fresh lime juice

1 garlic clove, minced

½ teaspoon chili powder

¼ teaspoon paprika

1. Make the pico de gallo: Combine all the pico ingredients in a large bowl and mix well. Refrigerate until serving time.

2. Make the chili mayo: Combine all the chili mayo ingredients in a dish and stir until smooth. Cover and refrigerate until ready to serve.

3. Make the fried avocados: In a high-sided Dutch oven or heavy-bottomed pot, heat 2 inches of canola oil over medium heat to 375°F. Prepare three separate bowls: one with the panko, salt, and spices; one with the eggs; and one with the flour.

4. Halve, pit, and peel the avocados. Slice each half into 4 thick wedges, 24 in total. Working with one or two at a time, dredge the wedges in the flour, then the egg, then the panko mixture, coating well at each stage. Transfer the breaded wedges to a rack as you finish.

5. Working in batches, fry the avocado wedges for 45 seconds to 1 minute, turning halfway through, until golden brown. Top with the crumbled feta cheese and serve with the pico de gallo, chili mayo, fresh cilantro, and lime wedges.

FRIED AVOCADOS

Canola oil, for frying

1½ cups panko bread crumbs

¼ teaspoon sea salt

½ teaspoon chili powder

⅛ teaspoon cayenne pepper

⅛ teaspoon garlic powder

⅛ teaspoon ground cumin

2 large free-range eggs, beaten

¼ cup all-purpose flour

3 ripe but firm avocados

TO SERVE

¼ cup crumbled feta cheese

Fresh cilantro sprigs and lime wedges

MEXICAN-STYLE GRILLED CORN

MAKES 6 TO 8 SERVINGS FOR CORN-LOVING PEOPLE • Warning: This corn recipe may just blow your mind.

There, I've done my due diligence. For real, though, Mexican-style grilled corn is seriously banging and may just ruin corn prepared any other way for you and your family. Here is my spin on a classic dish, *elotes,* slathered in butter and spicy mayo, then topped with crumbled feta and fresh cilantro. It's almost too delicious! Enter at your own risk.

½ cup prepared mayo

3 tablespoons fresh lime juice

1½ teaspoons ancho chile powder

½ teaspoon smoked paprika

Kosher salt

8 large ears corn

¼ cup (½ stick) butter, melted

¼ cup crumbled feta cheese

¼ cup chopped fresh cilantro

1 lime, cut into wedges

1. In a small bowl, combine the mayo, lime juice, chile powder, smoked paprika, and ¼ teaspoon of salt and give it a good mix. Cover with plastic wrap and refrigerate until ready to serve. (This mayo will keep perfectly for up to 24 hours in the fridge.)

2. Shuck the corn, leaving the end bit to act as a handle (thank you, Mother Nature). Bring a large pot of salted water to a rapid boil over high heat and boil the corn for 3 minutes, working in batches, if necessary. Drain.

3. Heat a grill to medium-high heat (or heat a grill pan over medium-high heat). Grill the corn, turning every minute or so with your trusty kitchen tongs, until nicely charred on all sides, 6 to 8 minutes.

4. Baste the grilled corn with the butter, covering every nook and cranny. Liberally baste the corn a second time with the chile-lime mayo. Go to serious basting town here, kids.

5. Sprinkle the feta cheese on top, garnish with the cilantro, and serve with the lime wedges. Best. Corn. Ever.

LEMON-DILL POTATO SALAD WITH SMOKED SALMON

MAKES 6 TO 8 SIDE SERVINGS • Good night, *this* is potato salad! Crispy roasted spuds tossed in a lemon vinaigrette, then topped with luxurious smoked salmon, sour cream, and fresh dill. Next-level potato deliciousness.

2 pounds fingerling potatoes, scrubbed (do not peel)

2 tablespoons duck fat or olive oil

¾ teaspoon sea salt

2 tablespoons tahini

¼ cup fresh lemon juice

1 tablespoon honey

1 tablespoon Dijon mustard

1 garlic clove, finely minced

¼ cup extra-virgin olive oil

7 ounces smoked salmon

¼ cup sour cream

2 tablespoons fresh dill leaves

Fresh flat-leaf parsley sprigs, for garnish

1. Preheat the oven to 375°F.

2. Put the potatoes in a large pot and cover with cold water. Bring the water to a rapid boil over high heat and cook for 10 minutes, until just fork-tender. Drain.

3. Place a large rimmed baking sheet in the oven to get nice and toasty. After 5 minutes, spoon the duck fat onto the baking sheet and let it melt in the oven. Remove the baking sheet and add the potatoes, giving them a turn to coat in the fat. Season with ½ teaspoon of the sea salt and roast for 40 to 45 minutes, giving the pan a shake halfway through, until the skin is golden and crispy and the flesh is tender.

4. While the potatoes are roasting, in a large bowl, whisk together the tahini, lemon juice, honey, Dijon, garlic, and 3 tablespoons water. Whisking continuously, add the olive oil in a slow and steady stream until the vinaigrette is thick, creamy, and emulsified. Season with the remaining ¼ teaspoon sea salt.

5. Toss the finished roasties in the vinaigrette and set them on a serving platter. Arrange the smoked salmon on top and spoon on the sour cream. Sprinkle the dill over all and garnish with the parsley. Serve warm. (If you don't plan on serving the salad right away, or if you're a fan of cold potato salad, wait to add the smoked salmon, sour cream, and dill until just before serving.)

11

Dessert.

A LITTLE SWEET AFTER YOU EAT.

A FRIEND ONCE ASKED ME, "DENNIS, ARE YOU SWEET OR SAVORY?" UM, BOTH, OF COURSE!!

Dessert is wonderful. A great culinary story needs a fantastic finale, a delicious ending to bid farewell to mealtime with a bang. We tend to think of dessert as an indulgence, but "a little sweet after you eat" can mean anything from a knockout bowl of fresh, in-season berries to a thin slice of homemade double-chocolate cake.

When I was a kid, dessert for me meant a ginormous bowl of ice cream, a slab of chocolate cake, or a handful of chocolate chip cookies. Although those are still favorites, as my palate has expanded, the sweets that I'd run far away from as a kid have become my go-to desserts

of choice. Lemon meringue pie, coconut cream pie, and date squares—my dad's favorites—have become my favorites. Food is community, nostalgia, and good vibes. The classics will always be classics.

This chapter features recipes near and dear to my family's heart, from my mom's Chocolate Chip Cookies to our Grammy Delma's Queen Elizabeth Squares. Some are light and refreshing, others a tad decadent. Whether your vibe is sweet or savory, my hope is that you'll find a new favorite dessert recipe for potlucks, dinner parties, holidays, or anytime you need a little extra joy at mealtime.

MY MOM'S CHOCOLATE CHIP COOKIES

MAKES 12 COOKIES • My mom's chocolate chip cookies are the best chocolate chip cookies on planet Earth. Seriously. They're soft and chewy with a crispy base and filled to the brim with extra mini chocolate chips. In my band days, spent living on the road in a fifteen-passenger van, they were my constant craving, and after much begging, Mom relented and blessed me with her cookie secrets. Truthfully, mine never turn out quite as good as hers, no matter how much I practice. Either she's holding something back, or there's love in those cookies.

½ cup (1 stick) butter, at room temperature

½ cup packed dark brown sugar

¼ cup granulated sugar

1 large free-range egg, at room temperature

½ teaspoon pure vanilla extract

1 cup all-purpose flour

½ teaspoon baking soda

¼ teaspoon sea salt

1 cup semi-sweet chocolate chips

1 cup mini milk chocolate chips

1. Preheat the oven to 375°F with a rack in the center position. Line two baking sheets with parchment paper.

2. In the bowl of a stand mixer fitted with the paddle attachment, combine the butter and sugars and beat on medium speed until smooth, about 1 minute. Turn the speed to low, crack in the egg, and add the vanilla. Beat for 1 minute.

3. Turn off the mixer (to prevent a flour volcano) and add the flour, baking soda, and salt. Turn the mixer back on and beat on low speed until a soft dough forms, scraping down the sides of the bowl as needed. Using a spatula, fold in the chocolate chips, making sure that every inch of the dough is kissed with chocolate goodness.

4. Spoon 2 tablespoon–size dough balls onto the prepared baking sheets, leaving at least 2 inches between each cookie. You should have 12 cookies total. Place the baking sheets in the freezer for 10 minutes. (Chilling the dough prior to baking will help you achieve perfectly chewy cookie happiness.)

5. Working with one baking sheet at a time (leaving the other in the freezer), bake for 12 to 14 minutes, until the bottom of the cookies have browned, but the tops are not quite finished baking—be bold here, fear not! The tops will continue cooking with help from residual heat on the countertop (a must for soft and chewy cookies).

6. Leave the cookies on the baking sheet for 10 minutes, then transfer to a wire rack. Let cool almost entirely, or as long as you can stand the wait.

7. These cookies are best eaten right away, but will keep in an airtight container for a few days. Don't worry, though. They won't last that long.

SMASHED PAVLOVA WITH CITRUS CURD AND BERRIES

MAKES 6 TO 8 SERVINGS • For me this is summertime dessert at its best, when local berries and fruit are in peak form. Not as common in Canada or the United States, pavlova reigns supreme Down Under, and is truly a textural dream come true—crisp on the outside, chewy on the inside. Add homemade citrus curd and berries and you've hit a dessert homerun.

This little cracker is tailor-made for dinner parties, backyard hangouts, or any time you really want to impress the neighbors. The good news? This dessert works perfectly with just about any soft fruit or berry combination under the sun. I love a mix of blackberries, raspberries, and blueberries, but it's really dealer's choice here, friends. Apricot, passion fruit, mango, peaches, pineapple, or sautéed apple—whatever is local and in season where you live will work like a charm!

MERINGUE

- **6 large free-range eggs, at room temperature**
- **1¼ cups superfine sugar (see page 307)**
- **1½ teaspoons unsweetened natural (not Dutch-process) cocoa powder**

CITRUS CURD

- **⅔ cup superfine sugar**
- **½ cup fresh lemon juice (from about 4 lemons)**
- **⅓ cup fresh orange juice (from 1 to 2 oranges)**
- **⅛ teaspoon kosher salt**
- **3 tablespoons butter, melted**

(Ingredients continue on page 307.)

1. Make the meringue: Preheat the oven to 300°F. Line a baking sheet with parchment paper.

2. Separate the eggs, putting the whites in the bowl of a stand mixer fitted with the whisk attachment (or a large bowl) and the yolks in a medium saucepan. Set the saucepan aside.

3. Whisk the egg whites on medium speed until they form stiff peaks. With the mixer running, gradually add the sugar, about 1 tablespoon at a time, until each tablespoon has worked itself into the egg whites. Increase the mixer speed to high and beat for 7 to 8 minutes, until the meringue is super glossy, holds stiff peaks, and the sugar has disappeared (you can check this by pinching a small bit of meringue with your fingers—if you still feel coarse sugar, keep beating away). When the sugar has disappeared into the meringue, you're good to go. Keep a watchful eye and be sure to not

WHIPPED CREAM

½ **cup heavy cream**

½ **tablespoon pure maple
syrup**

½ **teaspoon pure vanilla
extract**

TO SERVE

3 cups mixed berries

¼ **cup fresh mint leaves**

overbeat the meringue, as it will cause it to collapse. No leaving the house to run an errand with the mixer running. Gently fold in the cocoa powder until no streaks remain.

4. Transfer the meringue to the prepared baking sheet and spread it in a single layer that's about 1½ inches thick (the shape doesn't matter). Bake for 1 hour (don't open the oven door). The meringue should be crispy on the outside and perfectly chewy on the inside. When the meringue is done, let it cool on the baking sheet for about 20 minutes.

5. While the meringue is baking, make the citrus curd: Add the sugar, lemon juice, orange juice, and salt to the saucepan with the egg yolks and whisk to combine. Cook over medium heat, whisking continuously as it simmers, until the curd has thickened beautifully, about 5 minutes. Remove from the heat and stir in the butter. Transfer to a sealable container and refrigerate.

6. Meanwhile, make the whipped cream: In the clean bowl of the stand mixer fitted with the whisk attachment, whip the cream until the volume has doubled and stiff peaks form. Fold in the maple syrup and vanilla until no streaks are present.

7. Grab your favorite serving platter. Break the meringue into 2-inch pieces and arrange them in a single layer on the platter. Dollop the citrus curd and whipped cream all on top of the meringue and layer with the fresh berries. Serve with extra citrus curd and garnish with the mint leaves.

If you can't find superfine sugar at the grocery store (or can't be bothered to make a special trip), it's a snap to make at home. Simply pulse an equivalent amount of regular (granulated) sugar, plus 1 or 2 tablespoons extra, in a food processor for about 2 minutes, until the sugar resembles very fine sand. Done!

BLUEBERRY-RHUBARB GALETTE

MAKES 6 TO 8 SERVINGS • Pie is dessert heaven in every form.

Aside from our herb garden, there's one thing that Leanne and I have succeeded in growing: rhubarb.

Stewed, in curd form, or even in a vinaigrette, rhubarb is an incredible vegetable (I know, weird, right?) and a fantastic addition to every backyard garden. It's easy to grow, take my word for it.

As a kid, almost every church potluck or family reunion featured a warm rhubarb pie. Classic as they come, and delicious! This galette-style version features a vodka crust, lemony vanilla rhubarb, and fresh blueberries. Hip, impressive, and easy to prepare.

LEMON-VODKA CRUST

- 1¼ cups all-purpose flour
- 1 tablespoon granulated sugar
- Zest of ½ lemon
- ¼ teaspoon kosher salt
- ½ cup (1 stick) butter, frozen
- 3 to 4 tablespoons chilled vodka

FRUIT FILLING

- 4 or 5 large rhubarb stalks, trimmed and cut into ½-inch pieces (about 4 cups)
- ¼ cup sugar
- Zest of 1 lemon
- 1 teaspoon pure vanilla extract
- 1 large free-range egg, lightly whisked
- 1 teaspoon turbinado sugar
- 1 cup fresh blueberries

1. Make the crust: In a food processor, combine the flour, granulated sugar, lemon zest, and salt and pulse several times to combine. Grate the butter into the food processor using the large holes of a box grater and pulse until the mixture resembles coarse meal. With the processor running on low speed, add 1 tablespoon of the vodka at a time until the dough just comes together, forming itself into a ball. Turn the dough out onto a lightly floured surface and shape it into a flattened disc. Cover the disc tightly with plastic wrap and refrigerate for at least 3 hours, or overnight. (If you're planning ahead, the dough will keep in the fridge for up to 2 days or in the freezer for up to 30 days. If freezing, thaw in the fridge for 24 hours before using.)

2. Preheat the oven to 375°F and line a large baking sheet with parchment paper.

3. Working on a floured surface, roll the dough out into a rustic 12-inch round that's about ⅛ inch thick. Carefully transfer the dough to the prepared baking sheet.

4. Make the fruit filling: In a large bowl, combine the rhubarb, sugar, lemon zest, and vanilla and give everything a good mix.

5. Pile the rhubarb filling into the center of the dough, leaving a 1½-inch border. Gently fold the edges of the dough onto the pastry, pinching it around to create a lovely pleated border. This will help keep the filling from escaping, and it looks awesome. Brush the top of the dough with the whisked egg and generously sprinkle the turbinado sugar on top.

6. Bake for 45 to 50 minutes, until the rhubarb filling is bubbling and softened and the crust is golden brown. Top the galette with the fresh blueberries and serve warm.

MATCHA MINT CHIP ICE CREAM

MAKES ABOUT 2 PINTS • Homemade ice cream is a joy to make and heaps better (and better for you) than store-bought. As a kid, my absolute favorite offering from our local ice cream parlor was mint chip. The combination of chocolate and mint sang an extra-special song to my soul. I couldn't get enough and would ride my bicycle to Four C's Dairy Bar on the daily to get my fix.

This upgraded version of a classic is made with fresh mint and matcha powder—full of flavor, with an extra pinch of nostalgia.

If you feel like going next level, pair this ice cream with homemade chocolate chip cookies (page 303) for the best ice cream sandwiches of your entire life.

2 cups whole milk

2 cups fresh mint leaves

¾ cup pure maple syrup

¼ teaspoon sea salt

6 large free-range egg yolks

2 cups heavy cream

2 tablespoons matcha powder

½ teaspoon pure vanilla extract

3½ ounces dark chocolate (70%)

1. In a 3-quart saucepan, combine the milk, mint leaves, maple syrup, and salt and bring the mixture to a simmer over medium heat. Remove from the heat and let stand for 1 hour, while the milk soaks in all that beautiful mint flavor.

2. Remove the mint with a slotted spoon and transfer to a fine-mesh sieve. Squeeze every drop of liquid from the mint into the milk saucepan. It's an arm workout, but it ends in increased deliciousness. When the mint is dry and has given its all, toss it.

3. Crack the egg yolks into a large bowl set on a damp cloth (this will help keep the bowl from dancing when it's whisking time). Give the yolks a good whisk for about 1 minute, until thickened and pale yellow.

4. Prepare an ice bath.

5. Reheat the milk over medium heat until just before it comes to a simmer, then remove the pan from the heat. Whisking continuously, very slowly pour 1 cup of the hot milk into the yolks, about 1 teaspoon at a time, to temper them. (Take your time with this—scrambled eggs and ice cream are definitely not best friends.) Whisk the remaining milk into the yolks, return the mixture to the saucepan, and whisk in the heavy cream and matcha powder.

6. Place the saucepan over medium heat. While stirring continuously, gently cook the mixture until it's thick enough to coat the back of a wooden spoon, 5 to 7 minutes.

7. Set a bowl in the ice bath and a fine-mesh sieve in the bowl. Pour the mixture through the sieve into the bowl to remove any lumps. Stir in the vanilla. Let the bowl chill in the ice bath for 20 minutes, then cover the bowl with plastic wrap and refrigerate overnight or for at least 3 hours.

8. Run the chilled milk mixture through an ice cream maker according to the manufacturer's instructions. Shave the chocolate into small chunks. When there is about 1 minute of chill time remaining, add the chunks to the ice cream mixture to fold them through.

9. Transfer to an airtight container and freeze for at least 4 hours before serving.

BROWN SUGAR BOURBON AND CANDIED PECAN ICE CREAM

MAKES ABOUT 1½ PINTS • Brown sugar and bourbon are soul mates, divinely orchestrated to be together. This adult-friendly ice cream is a tip of the hat to the South, and my time getting well versed in the Kentucky Bourbon trail.

P.S.! If you're an affogato fan, this is your new favorite ice cream. Make, chill, brew hot coffee, and pour on top. Delicious!

ICE CREAM

¾ cup packed brown sugar

¼ cup bourbon

2 tablespoons butter

6 large free-range egg yolks

1½ cups whole milk

2 cups heavy cream

⅛ teaspoon sea salt

½ teaspoon pure vanilla extract

CANDIED PECANS

1½ cups pecan halves

2 tablespoons pure maple syrup

½ teaspoon pure vanilla extract

1. Make the ice cream: In a small saucepan, heat the brown sugar and bourbon over medium heat. When the sugar has melted and the mixture has come to a boil, remove from the heat and stir in the butter. Set aside as the butter melts. Whisk until smooth.

2. Crack the egg yolks into a large bowl set on a damp cloth (this will help keep the bowl from dancing when it's whisking time). Give the yolks a good whisk for about 1 minute, until thickened and pale yellow.

3. Heat a 3-quart saucepan over medium heat and pour in the milk and cream. Add the sea salt. When the milk mixture is warm and bubbles have started to form around the sides of the pan, remove from the heat.

4. Prepare an ice bath.

5. Whisking continuously, very slowly pour 1 cup of the milk mixture into the yolks, about 1 teaspoon at a time, to temper them. (Take your time with this—scrambled eggs and ice cream are definitely not best friends.) Whisk the remaining milk mixture into the yolks, then whisk the bourbon mixture into the eggy milk. Pour the mixture back into the saucepan and heat again over medium heat. While stirring continuously, gently cook the mixture until it's thick enough to coat the back of a wooden spoon, 5 to 7 minutes.

6. Set a bowl in the ice bath and a fine-mesh sieve in the bowl. Pour the mixture through the sieve into the bowl to remove any lumps. Stir in the vanilla. Let the bowl chill in the ice bath for 20 minutes, then cover the bowl with plastic wrap and refrigerate overnight or for at least 3 hours.

7. Make the candied pecans: Heat a skillet over medium heat. Add the pecans and toast for about 2 minutes, stirring often, until browned and aromatic. Pour in the maple syrup, vanilla, and 2 tablespoons water. Cook, stirring, for 30 seconds, then transfer the pecans to a plate to cool. While the nuts cool, the maple will candy around them. Delish!

8. Run the chilled milk mixture through an ice cream maker according to the manufacturer's instructions. When the ice cream is just about finished chilling, add the pecans to the ice cream to fold through.

9. Transfer to an airtight container and freeze for at least 4 hours before serving.

Tempering is slowly adding a small amount of hot liquid to eggs (or egg yolks), a little bit at a time, to bring them up to temperature. If you add eggs to a hot liquid too quickly, you'll have a bowl of scrambled eggs and a ruined recipe. Total bummer! Patience and a steady whisk are key.

SALTED CARAMEL APPLE PARFAITS

MAKES 8 TO 12 SERVINGS • If you love salted caramel and apples (so, basically everyone), *this* is your dessert. Jacked fall flavors with an extra heaping helping of sticky, salted heaven.

Salted caramel is far easier to prepare than the Interwebs will lead you to believe. Just be extra careful when stirring, as it is hotter than the sun. And best to keep any young ones away from the stove, just in case.

The number of parfaits that this recipe will make will depend on the glass size you use. I prefer smaller glasses or jam jars but have also prepared this recipe using large wineglasses. This is the essence of dinner-party friendly. Mix it up, put your spin on it, have fun, eat dessert. Win/win/win.

SALTED CARAMEL

1 cup sugar

6 tablespoons (¾ stick) unsalted butter

½ cup heavy cream

½ teaspoon pure vanilla extract

1 teaspoon sea salt

MAPLE SAUTÉED APPLES

2 tablespoons butter

1½ pounds Cortland (Honeycrisp or Sweet Tango are also delicious here) apples (4 large), peeled, cored, and cut into ½-inch chunks

½ teaspoon ground cinnamon

2 tablespoons pure maple syrup

(Ingredients continue on page 317.)

1. Make the salted caramel: In a high-sided nonstick pan, heat the sugar over medium heat, stirring continuously. It will turn into strange rock-ish pieces—it's all good, fear not! Slowly but surely, the sugar will melt and turn into a gorgeous amber color. When the sugar has melted entirely and is now golden brown in color, carefully stir in the butter and let it melt. It will bubble like crazy. Stirring continuously, slowly pour the cream into the pan in a slow and steady stream until it has been incorporated into the caramel. Let the mixture bubble away for 1 minute, then remove from the heat. Stir in the vanilla and sea salt and very carefully pour it into a medium heatproof bowl. Set aside.

2. Make the apples: Heat a large skillet over medium heat and melt the butter. Add the apple chunks and cinnamon and cook, stirring often, for about 15 minutes, or until the apples are very soft. Add the maple syrup and give the pan a toss to coat the apples. Cook for 1 minute, then transfer to a bowl and set aside.

QUICK PAN GRANOLA

1½ cups rolled oats

1 cup pecan halves, chopped

1 tablespoon butter

2 tablespoons pure maple syrup

WHIPPED CREAM

1 cup heavy cream

½ teaspoon pure vanilla extract

3. Make the quick pan granola: Heat a large, dry skillet over medium heat and add the oats and pecans. Cook, turning every minute or so, until the oats are fragrant and have started to brown, 3 to 4 minutes. Transfer to a plate.

4. Place the pan back on the burner and melt the butter and maple syrup. When the syrup is simmering, remove from the heat and stir in the oats and pecans. Mix thoroughly to evenly coat the oats, then transfer to a plate and set aside.

5. Make the whipped cream: In the bowl of a stand mixer fitted with the whisk attachment, or armed with a whisk and ambition, whip the cream until thick and glorious and fold in the vanilla.

6. Time to go to parfait town. Build each parfait with 2 tablespoons of the salted caramel, 2 tablespoons of the apples, and 2 tablespoons of the granola. Top with a dollop of whipped cream, then repeat. Finish with a final drizzle of caramel and serve.

DOUBLE-CHOCOLATE SKILLET BROWNIE

MAKES 6 TO 8 SERVINGS • Shareable, family-style, grab-a-fork-and-go dishes are my all-time favorites. Just get stuck in, no fancy plating required! It's the way dining at home was intended. This double-chocolate brownie with crunchy pecans and ice cream is perfect for dinner parties, family gatherings, or any time a hungry crowd wants something sweet and delicious.

BROWNIE

10 ounces bittersweet chocolate, chopped

¾ cup (1½ sticks) butter

1½ cups sugar

4 large free-range eggs

2 tablespoons pure maple syrup

1 teaspoon pure vanilla extract

½ teaspoon kosher salt

½ teaspoon baking powder

¼ cup unsweetened Dutch-process cocoa powder

¾ cup all-purpose flour

½ cup pecan halves, chopped

½ cup milk chocolate chips

TOPPINGS

1 cup vanilla ice cream

2 tablespoons pecan halves, chopped

Fresh mint leaves, for garnish

1. Make the brownie: Preheat the oven to 350°F. Grease a 10-inch cast-iron pan or other oven-safe skillet.

2. Pour 1 inch of water into a saucepan and bring to a simmer. Set a large heatproof bowl on top to create a double boiler (do not let the bottom of the bowl touch the water). Put the bittersweet chocolate and butter in the bowl and gently melt. Stir until smooth.

3. Remove from the heat and whisk in the sugar. Whisk in the eggs, one at a time, until combined and smooth. Carry on whisking in the maple syrup, vanilla, salt, baking powder, and cocoa powder until incorporated. Fold in the flour, pecans, and chocolate chips until the batter is smooth.

4. Pour the batter into the prepared pan and bake for 35 to 40 minutes, or until a toothpick inserted into the center comes out clean. Let the brownie cool slightly in the pan for about 10 minutes, then serve with the ice cream, crushed pecans, and fresh mint. Delicious!

LEMON-RICOTTA MINI DOUGHNUTS WITH CHOCOLATE SAUCE

MAKES 6 TO 8 SERVINGS • When Red Suitcase Doughnuts (see page 15) was alive and kicking, I became ever so slightly obsessed with anything and everything doughnut related. It seems as though almost everywhere you travel on this planet, someone is frying sweet dough to perfection, and folks just can't get enough. Doughnuts are happiness wrapped in pastry and the one food that could help lead us toward world peace.

DOUGHNUTS

Canola oil, for frying

1½ cups all-purpose flour

2 teaspoons baking powder

½ cup granulated sugar

¼ teaspoon sea salt

1 tablespoon lemon zest

3 large free-range eggs

1 teaspoon pure vanilla extract

8 ounces ricotta cheese

CHOCOLATE SAUCE

½ cup unsweetened Dutch-process cocoa powder

½ cup granulated sugar

Pinch of salt

1 teaspoon pure vanilla extract

Confectioners' sugar, for dusting

1. Make the doughnuts: In a Dutch oven, heat 2 inches of canola oil over medium heat to 375°F.

2. In a large bowl, combine the flour, baking powder, sugar, salt, and lemon zest and whisk to combine. In a medium bowl, whisk the eggs, vanilla, and ricotta until smooth. Fold the wet ingredients into the dry ingredients until the batter is smooth.

3. Working in batches, carefully drop 1-tablespoon portions of the batter into the hot oil and fry for 2 minutes, turning halfway through, until golden brown. Open one of the mini doughnuts to ensure they're cooked through. Transfer the cooked doughnuts to a baking sheet lined with paper towels to drain any excess grease, and carry on frying the rest.

4. Make the chocolate sauce: In a small saucepan, combine the cocoa powder, sugar, salt, and 1 cup water and bring to a boil over medium heat. Cook for 1 minute. Remove from the heat and stir in the vanilla.

5. Serve the doughnuts sprinkled with confectioners' sugar and with the chocolate sauce on the side, for your dunking delight.

WATERMELON-LIMONCELLO FRUIT SALAD

MAKES 6 TO 8 SERVINGS • This little adult-friendly dessert recipe is the perfect after-dinner treat for those times when you're jonesing for something sweet after you eat but don't feel like being rolled home in a wheelbarrow. It's light, healthy-ish, a little boozy, and entirely sweet-tooth satisfying—especially delicious served on a hot summer's day.

4 cups ½-inch-cubed watermelon

2 cups strawberries, hulled and quartered

1 cup ½-inch cubed cantaloupe

1 cup blackberries

2 tablespoons finely minced mint leaves, plus whole leaves for garnish

2 teaspoons lemon zest

3 tablespoons limoncello

2 tablespoons pure maple syrup

Combine the fruit, mint, and lemon zest in a large bowl. In a small bowl, stir together the limoncello, maple syrup, and 1 tablespoon water, then drizzle the limoncello mixture over the fruit mixture. Toss to mix, then serve, garnished with the mint leaves. Simple, delicious.

BALSAMIC-ROASTED STRAWBERRY SHORTCAKES

MAKES 10 SERVINGS • Summertime living is full of happiness, with the beach, backyard grilling sessions, and outstanding, in-season fruits and veggies completely rocking the culinary landscape. And the time of year when folks head to local U-Pick farms to collect baskets of fresh, perfectly juicy berries. The king of berries? The almighty strawberry. Delicious! For me, when strawberry season is in high gear, there's really nothing quite like homemade strawberry shortcake. Rich, buttery homemade biscuits and freshly picked strawberries are truly a match made in heaven.

BROWN SUGAR MAPLE-GLAZED BISCUITS

- **5 cups all-purpose flour, plus more for shaping the dough**
- **¼ cup packed dark brown sugar**
- **1 tablespoon kosher salt**
- **1 teaspoon baking soda**
- **1 cup (2 sticks) butter, frozen, plus 2 tablespoons butter**
- **1¾ cups buttermilk**
- **2 tablespoons pure maple syrup**

STRAWBERRIES

- **1½ pints strawberries, hulled and halved**
- **1 tablespoon balsamic vinegar**
- **1 tablespoon pure maple syrup**
- **½ teaspoon pure vanilla extract**

(Ingredients continue on the next page.)

1. Make the biscuits: Preheat the oven to 400°F. Line two baking sheets with parchment paper.

2. Sift together the flour, brown sugar, salt, and baking soda into a large bowl. Using a box grater, grate the frozen butter into the flour. Using the tips of your fingers, gently work the butter into the dough until it resembles coarse crumbs.

3. Add the buttermilk and gently stir to form a soft dough. Turn the dough out onto a floured surface and shape it into an 8 x 12-inch rectangle that's about 1½ inches thick. Using a biscuit cutter (or a drinking glass, in a pinch), cut out as many biscuits as possible. Reshape the dough and repeat, working the dough as little as possible. You should end up with 10 biscuits.

4. Transfer the biscuits to one of the prepared baking sheets and bake for just 20 minutes. Meanwhile, melt the remaining 2 tablespoons butter in a small saucepan and stir in the maple syrup. Liberally brush the biscuit tops with the maple butter and bake for 10 minutes more, or until the tops are golden brown and the biscuits have cooked through. Set the biscuits on a wire rack to cool. Keep the oven on.

WHIPPED CREAM

½ **cup heavy cream**

1 **tablespoon pure maple syrup**

½ **teaspoon pure vanilla extract**

5. Make the strawberries: In a large bowl, toss the berries, vinegar, maple syrup, and vanilla and spread them on the second prepared baking sheet. Roast the strawberries for 20 minutes, or until the berries have softened nicely.

6. Meanwhile, make the whipped cream: In the bowl of a stand mixer fitted with the whisk attachment (or in a large bowl using a hand mixer), whip the cream until thickened. Stir in the maple syrup and vanilla.

7. Split the biscuits horizontally and place a dollop of whipped cream on the bottom half. Spoon on the roasted strawberries and top with the other biscuit half, and some more cream for good measure.

NAKED CHOCOLATE BIRTHDAY CAKE WITH BUTTERCREAM ICING AND SUMMER BERRIES

MAKES ONE 9-INCH TWO-LAYER CAKE • Happy birthday! Let them eat cake!

When the thing you love to do more than anything else in the whole wide world is cooking and photographing your creations, taking the day off, even on your birthday, is sometimes easier said than done. So, a few years ago I quit stressing it and started making my own birthday cake. It's my birthday, and I can cake if I want to.

This gorgeous naked cake easily feeds a crowd, with no fancy icing skills required. Just bake, spread, and decorate the top of the cake to your heart's delight. Perfect for birthdays, special occasions, or any given Wednesday.

CAKE

- **2 cups all-purpose flour**
- **2 cups granulated sugar**
- **¾ cup unsweetened natural (not Dutch-process) cocoa powder**
- **2 teaspoons baking powder**
- **1½ teaspoons baking soda**
- **1 teaspoon kosher salt**
- **1 cup (2 sticks) butter, melted**
- **2 large free-range eggs**
- **2 cups whole milk**
- **½ cup olive oil**
- **2 teaspoons pure vanilla extract**
- **2 tablespoons Irish cream liqueur (such as Baileys)**
- **½ cup boiling water**

(Ingredients continue on the next page.)

1. Make the cake: Preheat the oven to 350°F. Grease two 9-inch cake pans with butter.

2. In the bowl of a stand mixer fitted with the paddle attachment, combine the flour, granulated sugar, cocoa powder, baking powder, baking soda, and salt.

3. In a medium bowl, whisk together the butter, eggs, milk, olive oil, vanilla, and Irish cream. Pour the wet mixture into the dry mixture and beat on medium speed for 2 to 3 minutes, or until the batter is smooth, scraping down the sides of the bowl as needed. Very slowly and carefully pour in the boiling water, then increase the mixer speed to high and beat for 1 minute.

4. Divide the batter evenly between the prepared cake pans and cover with aluminum foil—a little trick that will help give you the most incredibly light, moist cake ever. Bake for 30 to 35 minutes, until a toothpick inserted into the center comes out clean. Let the cake layers cool in the pans for 10 minutes,

BUTTERCREAM

½ cup (1 stick) butter, at room
temperature

2 cups confectioners' sugar

½ teaspoon pure vanilla
extract

3 tablespoons heavy cream

CHOCOLATE GANACHE

4 ounces dark chocolate
(70%), chopped into very
small chunks

⅓ cup heavy cream

Pinch of salt

FRUIT TOPPING

2½ cups fresh strawberries,
hulled and halved

1 cup fresh blackberries

1 cup fresh blueberries

then invert the cake layers onto a wire rack and let cool for
35 to 40 minutes more.

5. Meanwhile, carry on with the buttercream: In the clean
bowl of the stand mixer fitted with the paddle attachment,
beat the butter until creamy, about 1 minute. Add the confectioners' sugar and beat on low speed, then beat in the
vanilla and cream. Increase the speed to medium and beat
until smooth. Set aside.

6. Make the chocolate ganache: Put the chocolate in a medium bowl. Bring the cream to a simmer in a small saucepan
over medium heat. Pour the cream over the chocolate and
set aside for 5 minutes. After about 5 minutes, add the salt
and stir the melted chocolate and cream until smooth.

7. Make the fruit topping: In a medium bowl, combine the
strawberries, blackberries, and blueberries.

8. Place one of the cake layers on a cake stand or serving
tray. Spread the buttercream evenly over the layer. Top with
1 cup of the fruit, pushing down gently into the buttercream.
Place the second cake layer on top and spread the chocolate ganache all over the top, letting a bit of chocolate run
over the edge. Arrange the remaining fruit on top of the cake
like you're a cake boss.

NO-BAKE LEMON MASCARPONE CHEESECAKES

MAKES 6 SERVINGS • When I was in twelfth grade, I traveled with a group of troublemakers, destined for the Big Apple. We spent a week in New York City volunteering at the Bowery Mission—cooking, cleaning, and helping in whatever way possible. One night while on somewhat of a walking tour of the Lower East Side, our group strolled straight into heaven on earth by way of a cheesecake shop, filled with sky-high, beautifully decorated desserts just waiting to be devoured. I was late to the party, but seventeen-year-old Dennis tried his first proper New York—style strawberry cheesecake and almost died. Incredible!

Cheesecake is the embodiment of everything I love about dessert—decadent and entirely soul-satisfying. Sometimes, though, the idea of running a hot oven all afternoon (I'm looking at you, July), is out of the question. This no-bake version is just as delicious, but with no baking and very little assembly required.

STRAWBERRY DELICIOUSNESS

2 cups strawberries, hulled and cut into small chunks
¼ cup sugar
1 tablespoon cornstarch

GRAHAM CRACKER CRUST

¾ cup graham cracker crumbs
2 tablespoons butter, melted

CHEESECAKE FILLING

8 ounces cream cheese, at room temperature
½ cup sugar
1 teaspoon pure vanilla extract
2 teaspoons lemon zest
1 cup mascarpone cheese
½ cup heavy cream

TO SERVE

Strawberries, cherries, and blueberries
Fresh mint

1. Make the strawberry deliciousness: In a medium saucepan, combine the strawberries, sugar, cornstarch, and ¾ cup water and whisk until smooth. Bring to a simmer over medium heat and cook, stirring often, until thickened and glossy, 6 to 8 minutes. Puree directly in the pot with an immersion blender until smooth and set aside to cool completely.

2. Make the crust: In a medium bowl, mix the graham crumbs and butter until well combined. Spoon 2 tablespoons into the bottom of each of six small drinking glasses or jam jars.

3. In the bowl of a stand mixer fitted with the paddle attachment (or in a large bowl using a handheld mixer), beat the cream cheese and sugar until smooth. Add the vanilla, lemon zest, mascarpone, and salt and beat until smooth. Fold in the cream until combined. Evenly divide the cream cheese mixture among the prepared glasses. Top each glass with strawberry puree and refrigerate for 1 hour or up to overnight.

4. Just before you serve these desserts, top with fresh fruit and mint leaves.

DELMA'S QUEEN ELIZABETH SQUARES

MAKES 16 SQUARES • During the writing and testing of this cookbook we lost a truly amazing lady, my honorary grandmother, Delma. Like her dessert's namesake, Delma Shorey was the closest thing that our family had to royalty. She was always dressed to the nines, hands down the best comedian in the room, and infinitely more concerned with the well-being of others than her own. Delma was my biggest fan, and I've since learned that she loved to share stories of my journey with visitors who paid her a visit at the hospital, even into her final days.

These are Delma's squares, a dessert that she made for every special holiday for friends and family. I hope that they bring your family as much joy as they will continue to bring ours.

1 cup dates, finely diced

1 cup boiling water

1 teaspoon baking soda

1 cup sugar

½ cup (1 stick) plus 3 tablespoons butter, at room temperature

1 large free-range egg, beaten

1 teaspoon pure vanilla extract

1½ cups all-purpose flour

1 teaspoon baking powder

¼ teaspoon kosher salt

1 cup packed dark brown sugar

3 tablespoons whole milk

½ cup sweetened shredded coconut

1. Place the dates in a small bowl and cover with the boiling water. Stir and set aside to cool completely, 30 minutes. Stir in the baking soda.

2. Preheat the oven to 350°F. Lightly grease an 8-inch square baking pan with butter and set aside.

3. In a large bowl, using a handheld mixer (or in the bowl of a stand mixer fitted with the paddle attachment), cream the sugar and ½ cup of the butter. Add the egg and beat until smooth. Add the date mixture and vanilla. Sift in the flour, baking powder, and salt and mix until the batter is smooth.

4. Pour the batter into the pan and bake for 35 minutes.

5. Meanwhile, in a medium bowl, combine the brown sugar, remaining 3 tablespoons butter, the milk, and the coconut and mix well. Spread the topping over the cake and bake for 5 minutes more.

6. Let the cake cool in the pan for about 20 minutes, then cut into small squares.

7. Serve just like Delma would, on fine china with a hot cup of orange pekoe tea and lots of laughter.

Thank You. You're Awesome.

Thank you. Thank you. Thank you.

I never imagined in my wildest dreams that I would/should/could ever write a book, let alone a cookbook. My unwavering (and slightly obsessive) passion for all things delicious has led me to this unbelievable point, and I'm beyond thankful. More than a year of recipe testing, writing, photographing, eating, and dreaming would not be have been possible without the team of rock stars in my life. Thank you.

Sarah Passick, Celeste Fine, and my Sterling Lord Literistic family—you championed this project and believed in me even before I believed in myself. Best literary agents in the business. Period.

My editors in the United States and Canada, Cassie Jones, Kate Cassaday, Brad Wilson, and Kara Zauberman—you are so next-level, it's insane. This book would not exist without you. Best editors on the planet, no contest. The highest of fives all around! As if the opportunity to write a book isn't enough, the privilege to work with both William Morrow and HarperCollins Canada is like hitting the literary jackpot. Thank you for fostering creativity and allowing *Eat Delicious* to have its own unique voice.

The rock-star team at William Morrow: Cassie Jones, Kara Zauberman, Liate Stehlik, Lynn Grady, Tavia Kowalchuk, Anwesha Basu, Rachel Meyers, Ploy Siripant, Renata De Oliveira, and Anna Brower. Thank you!

The heroes at HarperCollins Canada: Kate Cassaday, Brad Wilson, Michael Guy-Haddock, Sandra Leef, Catherine Knowles, Cory Beatty, and Mike Millar. Thank you!

I have the best family a dude could ever ask for.

Leanne, my best friend/my heart. You are everything. Thank you for the joy of living life together. If our sixteen-year-old selves could only see us now!

Mom and Dad—thank you for lovingly supporting me through every against-the-grain decision I've made in my life. You're amazing. I love you.

Josh, Katie, Ella, Emerson, Lennon, and Maisie. Red Suitcase represent! Mad love for my incredible brother, wonderful sister, and the best nieces and nephews ever. Serious squad goals. I love you all.

Aubrey and Debbie—whether in music, in food, or as a son-in-law, you've been my superfans since day one. I have four of the best parents a kid could ask for.

Eldon and Delma. Thank you for adopting a guitar-playing kid with tattoos as an honorary grandson so many years ago, for the stories, life lessons, and so much laughter. Delma, you're without question my number-one fan. I look forward to eating fancy desserts, drinking tea, and laughing our faces off again one day.

I have the best friends a dude could ever ask for.

In no particular order (and all equally awesome)—Marc and Esther Jolicoeur, Jay and Barb Muir, Dave and Lori Loveless, Thomas and Trish Endres, Nick and Ashley Ross, Jeff and Andrea Somers, Matt Sutherland and Becky Molloy, Blake and Jessica Easter, Curt and Monica Gibbs, AJ VanBoxel and Jennifer Wren, Tony and Sue McKee, Luke and Breanne Anderson, Christopher Le, Ben and Angela Treimer, Justin and Jennifer MacRae, the Miethe Clan, Roxanne Morrell, Shawn and Cheryl Hawley.

The *Food & Wine* / FWx crew. Alex Vallis, you believed in a Canadian kid armed with an iPhone and "Stacked" recipes.

Hunger Free and World Vision—thank you for your passion to see folks everywhere not just survive, but thrive.

To all the folks who've supported me and continue to inspire me on the daily: Dana Cowin, Aimée Wimbush-Bourque (Simple Bites), the *Globe and Mail,* Farrah Shaikh (*Food & Wine* / FWx), Noah Kaufman (*Food & Wine* / FWx), Paul Newnham, Daniel Krieger, Justin Chapple, Food Bloggers of Canada, the Infatuation, Gaby Dalkin (What's Gaby Cooking), Nashville!, Rob Glenen (world's best art teacher), Joe Were, CBC's *Maritime Noon,* the feedfeed, Beautiful Cuisines, Joel MacCharles and Dana Harrison (Well Preserved), Mary Mar Keenan Ceramics (MMclay), Jon Morrison, Tony Cooper, Jesse Vergen, Max Moser, Jillian Zieske, Luc Doucet and Jessie Richard (Barolo & Co), Jonna Brewer and the crew at

CBC Moncton, Charlie and Susan Somers, Lynn and Lester Morrell, Red Lama Media (Mark Moore, Trevor Jones, and Adams Townsend), Voula Halliday, the *Times & Transcript,* Wawira Njiru (Food for Education), David Loftus (oodles of inspiration), Julian Kindred, Andris Lagsdin (Baking Steel), Jessica Emin, Stephanie Le (i am a food blog), Lisa Q. Fetterman (Nomiku), Monica Lo, Patrick Wong, Sigma, Hasselblad, Nikon, Hatchery, Frigidaire Professional, Nik Sharma (A Brown Table), Mayor Dawn Arnold, Zane Kelsall and Dean Petty at Anchored Coffee, Melody Hillman Ceramics, Lynn and Katherine Nichols, Damann Nichols and Matthew Taylor, Thug Kitchen, Clerkenwell Boy, Radiohead, Terroir Symposium, Hedley and Bennett, Judy Kim (The Judy Lab), Tilit Chef Goods, Instagram, Taste of Nova Scotia, Bouffe Média, Maxime Daigle (BeauSoleil Oysters), World Wine Expo, Pierre Richard and the crew at Little Louis' Oyster Bar, Doug Townsend and Renée Lavallée (The Canteen), Georgina Hayden, Les Brumes du Coude, Matthew Jennings (Townsman), Jessica Murnane (One Part Podcast), Lia Rinaldo and Devour! Fest, BroadFork Farm, the Pump House Brewery, Courtney Langford, the Farmer's Truck, the Moncton Fish Market, the Moncton Farmers Market, Marché Dieppe, Danielle LeBlanc and the Frye Festival, the City of Moncton. Big love, y'all.

And Mr. Jamie Oliver. Seriously, dude. Thank you for inspiring a broke musician living on the dollar menu that he could create delicious, crowd-pleasing, beautiful meals.

Cooking Meat & Poultry

Touch, smell, taste, and sight will always reign supreme in the kitchen. Cooking is a full contact sport—zero spectators or armchair critics allowed. Kneading dough by hand. Smelling the aroma of butter and garlic gently bubbling away in a pan. Tasting soup throughout the cooking process to ensure that your seasoning is on point. Watching a steak deeply caramelize in a cast-iron pan.

With most foods, your God-given senses (and a little practice) will get the job done nicely. When cooking meat, however, a little extra technology helps to guarantee that a recipe is cooked exactly to your liking, each and every time. Develop a habit of using an instant-read thermometer for a quick and sure-fire way to hit those temperatures goals, from rare to well done. Here are some guidelines to help you on your path toward doneness perfection.

This chart offers similar guidelines to those used by professional kitchens in preparing your favorite cuts of meat for juicy, cooked-to-perfection deliciousness. The temperatures listed may not correspond precisely to USDA guidelines.

BEEF

Rare—120° to 125°F

Medium-rare—130° to 135°F

Medium—135° to 140°F

Medium-well—140° to 150°F

Well done—155° to 160°F

Ground beef (hamburgers)—160°F

CHICKEN AND TURKEY

Every which way but ground—165°F

Ground—170°F

PORK

Medium-rare—145°F

Medium—150°F

Well done—160°F

Ground—160°F

LAMB

Rare—120° to 125°F

Medium-rare—130° to 135°F

Medium—135° to 140°F

Medium-well—140° to 150°F

Well done—155° to 160°F

Ground—160°F

Universal Conversion Chart

OVEN TEMPERATURE EQUIVALENTS

250°F = 120°C

275°F = 135°C

300°F = 150°C

325°F = 160°C

350°F = 180°C

375°F = 190°C

400°F = 200°C

425°F = 220°C

450°F = 230°C

475°F = 240°C

500°F = 260°C

MEASUREMENT EQUIVALENTS

Measurements should always be level unless directed otherwise.

⅛ teaspoon = 0.5 mL

¼ teaspoon = 1 mL

½ teaspoon = 2 mL

1 teaspoon = 5 mL

1 tablespoon = 3 teaspoons = ½ fluid ounce = 15 mL

2 tablespoons = ⅛ cup = 1 fluid ounce = 30 mL

4 tablespoons = ¼ cup = 2 fluid ounces = 60 mL

5⅓ tablespoons = ⅓ cup = 3 fluid ounces = 80 mL

8 tablespoons = ½ cup = 4 fluid ounces = 120 mL

10⅔ tablespoons = ⅔ cup = 5 fluid ounces = 160 mL

12 tablespoons = ¾ cup = 6 fluid ounces = 180 mL

16 tablespoons = 1 cup = 8 fluid ounces = 240 mL

Index

Note: Page references in *italics* indicate photographs.